DATE DUE			

POLITICS AND PUBLIC POLICY SERIES

Advisory Editor

Robert L. Peabody

Johns Hopkins University

*Financing Politics: Money, Elections
and Political Reform*
Herbert E. Alexander

*Interest Groups, Lobbying and
Policymaking*
**Norman J. Ornstein
Shirley Elder**

Congressional Procedures and the Policy Process

WALTER J. OLESZEK

Congressional Quarterly Press

A DIVISION OF CONGRESSIONAL QUARTERLY INC.
1414 22nd Street, N.W., Washington, D.C. 20037

Fourth Printing

Library of Congress Cataloging in Publication Data

Oleszek, Walter J.
    Congressional procedures and the policy process.

    Bibliography: p.
    Includes index.
    1. United States.   Congress.   I. Title.
 JK1096.043   328.73   78-17373
 ISBN 0-87187-153-1

For
My Mother and Father

Contents

Illustrations

Foreword

Most Americans have a rather limited knowledge about the workings of their national government. Fewer than half can identify their representative, and fewer than 60 percent can name one of their state's two senators. Even to well-informed citizens, details of congressional procedure and terms such as "the five-minute rule" or "unanimous consent agreement" or "cloture" might seem to fall into the category of trivia, like baseball or movie esoterica.

Walter J. Oleszek, author of *Congressional Procedures and the Policy Process*, believes in broadening the base of understanding. His basic assumptions are "that Congress matters and that its rules and procedures are important," and he shows, through description and example, just how rules affect the course and content of legislation.

This is the first book in more than a decade to focus upon the organization, rules, and procedures of the Senate and the House of Representatives. Oleszek's contributions are especially timely, given the major preoccupation in both houses of Congress with reform in the 1970s.

Walter Oleszek has been both a participant in and a close observer of the congressional scene for more than ten years. After receiving his Ph.D. from the State University of New York at Albany in 1968, he joined the staff of the Congressional Research Service of the Library of Congress. He participated as a staff member on the House Select Committee on Committees, chaired by Representative Richard Bolling, and the Senate select committee on the committee system, chaired by Senator Adlai E. Stevenson III. He has taught at Colgate University, the University of Maryland, The American University, and in the State University of New York Washington Semester program.

In *Congressional Procedures and the Policy Process,* Oleszek begins by setting Congress in its constitutional context and traces the path of legislation through the labyrinth that is Congress. In a series of chapters, rich in depth and detail, he explains where legislation comes from, how it moves through committees to the floor, and what happens when it reaches the chambers. Throughout the discussion, he concentrates on the strategic use of rules and procedures to affect legislation and on the consequences of changes in the rules.

The end result is a book with many virtues. Its presentation is clear and concise. It is a book from which a citizen can readily learn in an interesting way how floor debate is managed in the House and how filibusters inhibiting the flow of legislation in the Senate can be controlled. Short enough to be suitable for adoption as a supplementary text in an introductory American government course, the book will be most valuable in more advanced courses on the legislative process and public policy formation.

Congressional rules and procedures are seldom neutral in their impact. Their prime purpose is to allow majorities to work their will while, at the same time, protecting the rights of minorities. And, as Thomas Jefferson pointed out in a manual that is still incorporated as part of the rules of the House, "it is much more material that there should be a rule to go by than what that rule is." *Congressional Procedures and the Policy Process* sets forth both what those rules are and what they do.

Robert L. Peabody

Preface

It has been more than ten years since Lewis A. Froman, Jr., wrote *The Congressional Process*. The numerous procedural changes in Congress since then have made it in many ways a different body from what it was in the mid-1960s. A new study of lawmaking, then, is appropriate.

My objective in this book is to examine how the contemporary Congress makes laws and how its rules and procedures shape public policy. Although the legislative branch has always been a source of interest to scholars and journalists, the interplay of rules, precedents, pressures, and strategies has received less attention. This book describes, from introduction to final passage and presidential action, the procedural route taken by most major legislation. In chapters 1 and 2 I also look at the constitutional role assigned to Congress and at the key actors and pressures surrounding congressional decisionmaking. Chapter 9 surveys Congress' efforts to oversee the implementation of its laws. The emphasis throughout is on the use of the rules for strategic purposes — to expedite or delay legislation, to secure passage or bring about defeat of bills.

The major theme of the book is that rules and procedures are important; they can significantly shape domestic and foreign policy, and they are the object of continuous scrutiny by members of Congress and interested outsiders. I have included numerous examples of this interaction between rules and policymaking. These examples will, I hope, convey some sense of the congressional atmosphere.

Finally, this book implicitly addresses the question of why Congress is not the efficient, streamlined, disciplined body some people want it to be. Congress' procedural rules encourage deliberation, collegial decisionmaking, dissent, openness, participation, and accessibility. These qualities lead to the need for coalition politics at every stage of the process and they underscore the importance of bargaining and accommodation. They are not, however, qualities that encourage quick decisions or tidy organizational patterns.

In the book I emphasize the rules and procedures most significant to congressional decisionmaking; I do not attempt to survey every detail of the parliamentary procedures used by Congress.

I am grateful to the numerous individuals who contributed to this book by offering constructive criticisms and suggestions at every stage of preparation. I am deeply indebted to my editors at Congressional Quarterly Press, my colleagues at the Congressional Research Service, and scores of congressmen, legislative staff aides, scholars, and political commentators for their insights on Congress. All the faults and shortcomings of this book are mine, however.

Several individuals read the entire manuscript with great care and deserve my special thanks. These include my editors at Congressional Quarterly, Robert A. Diamond and Jean L. Woy, who merit particular acknowledgement for the clarity of their suggestions and ideas. I am under heavy obligation to them for their help in shaping this book. I would also like to extend thanks to Robert Cuthriell for his advice during the formative stages of this project and to Richard C. Schroeder for his contributions. My deep appreciation goes to Robert L. Peabody, advisory editor of this series, for his insightful suggestions.

Whatever understanding of the legislative process I might have comes in no small part from my colleagues at the Congressional Research Service of the Library of Congress. That institution, I should note, bears no responsibility whatsoever for the views or interpretations expressed in this book. Several CRS colleagues offered valuable insights on drafts of the book or on questions I had about congressional procedure. In particular, I am indebted to Louis Fisher, Fred Pauls, Clark Norton, Walter Kravitz, Robert Keith, and Jim Saylor. I also gladly acknowledge the contributions of Arthur Stevens, Ronald Moe, Stanley Bach, Paul Rundquist, Fred Kaiser, Judith Parris, and Marc Yacker.

There are several others who offered valuable assistance. These include Roger H. Davidson, my collaborator on *Congress against Itself,* Matt Pinkus, and several anonymous scholars. Each read preliminary chapters of the book and offered constructive comments on them.

Finally, I want to thank my wife, Janet, and my son, Mark, for their good humor and patience during the writing of this book. My special appreciation for so many reasons goes to my parents, Nellie Elizabeth and Walter George, to whom this book is dedicated.

Walter J. Oleszek

1

Congress and Lawmaking

"In republican government," wrote James Madison, "the legislative authority necessarily predominates."[1] And Madison, among others, tried to ensure that in the new United States government, Congress *would* emerge as the central policymaking authority.

Lawmaking is Congress' most basic response to the entire range of national concerns, from agriculture to housing, environment to national defense, health to the economy. The process by which Congress transforms an idea into national policy is the subject of this book. This process is complicated and variable, but it is governed by rules, procedures, precedents, and customs, and is open to the use of some generally predictable strategies and tactics.

Members of Congress have major responsibilities other than lawmaking — to represent their constituents and to review the implementation of laws. All these functions are integral parts of the congressional process.

This first chapter examines the constitutional foundation of congressional policymaking, the functions of rules and procedures in organizations, the interaction of rules (formal and informal) and policymaking in the congressional context, and the important features of congressional decisionmaking.

THE CONSTITUTIONAL CONTEXT

Congress' central role in policymaking can be traced to the writers of the Constitution. Madison, Hamilton, and the others developed a political system that established Congress as the lawmaking body and set out its relationship with the other branches of government and with the people. Several familiar basic principles underlie the specific provisions of the Constitution. These include limited government, separation of powers, checks and balances, and federalism. Each principle continues to shape lawmaking today despite the enormous changes that have transformed and enlarged the role of government in American society.

Limited Government

The framers of the Constitution wanted a strong and effective national government, but at the same time, they wanted to avoid concentrating too much power in the central government lest it threaten personal and property rights. Limitation of government, the framers believed, could be achieved by dividing power among three branches of national government and between the nation and states. The division of power ensured both policy conflicts and cooperation because it made officials in the several branches responsive to different constituencies, responsibilities, and perceptions of the public welfare.

The framers believed that the "accumulation of all powers, legislative, executive, and judiciary, in the same hands may justly be pronounced the very definition of tyranny."[2] As men of practical political experience, they had witnessed firsthand the abuses of King George III and his royal governors. They also wanted to avoid the possible "elective despotism" of their own state legislatures.[3] Wary of excessive authority in either an executive or legislative body, the framers were also familiar with the works of influential political theorists, particularly Locke and Montesquieu, who stressed such concepts as the separation of powers, checks and balances, and popular control of government.

Separation of Powers

The framers combined their practical experience with their theoretical outlook and established three independent branches of national government with none having a monopoly of governing power. Their objective was twofold. First, separation of powers was designed to restrain the power of any one branch. Second, it was meant to ensure that cooperation would be necessary for effective government.

The framers held a strong bias in favor of lawmaking by representative assemblies, and so viewed Congress as the prime national policymaker. The Constitution names Congress the first branch of government, assigns it "all legislative power," and grants it explicit and implied responsibilities. Almost half the words of the Constitution — Article I — are devoted to the legislative branch, enumerating the many specific powers of Congress.

In sharp contrast, Articles II and III, creating the executive and judicial branches, describe only briefly the framework and duties of these governmental units. Although separation of powers implies that Congress "enacts" the laws, the president "executes" them, and the Supreme Court "interprets" them, such a rigid division of labor was not intended by the framers. They did grant certain unique responsibilities to each branch, and ensured their separateness by, for example, prohibiting any officer from serving in more than one branch simultaneously. They linked the branches through a system of checks and balances.

Checks and Balances

An essential corollary of separation of powers is checks and balances. The framers of the Constitution realized that individuals in each branch might seek to aggrandize power at the expense of the other branches. Inevitably, conflicts would develop. In particular, the Constitution is often an open invitation to struggles for power by Congress and the president.

To restrain each branch, the framers devised a system of checks and balances. Congress' own legislative power was effectively "checked" by establishing a bicameral body consisting of the House of Representatives and the Senate. The laws Congress passes may be vetoed by the president. Treaties and high presidential appointments require the approval of the Senate. And many decisions of Congress and the president are subject to review by the federal judiciary.

Checks and balances have a dual effect; they encourage cooperation and accommodation among the branches — particularly the popularly elected Congress and the president — and they introduce the potential for conflict. And since 1789, Congress and the president have indeed both cooperated and protected their own powers. Moreover, each branch depends in various ways on the other. When conflicts occur, they are most frequently resolved by negotiation, bargaining, and compromise.

Federalism

Just as the three branches check each other, the state and federal governments are also countervailing forces. This division of power is another way to curb and control governing power. While the term "federalism" (like separation of powers or checks and balances) is not mentioned in the Constitution, the framers understood that federalism was a plan of government acceptable to the 13 states. The "supremacy" clause of the Constitution ensured that the states would not pass unconstitutional laws; however, powers not granted to Congress remained with the states.

Federalism has infused "localism" into congressional proceedings. As a representative institution, Congress and its members respond to the needs and interests of states and congressional districts. The nation's diversity is given ample expression in Congress by legislators whose tenure rests on the continued support of their constituents.

Thus, the Constitution outlines a complicated system. Power is divided among the branches and between levels of government, and popular opinion is reflected differently in each. Congress and the president, for example, each with different constituencies, terms of office, and times of election, can both claim to represent majority sentiment on national issues. Given each branch's independence, formidable powers, different perspectives on many issues, and intricate mix of formal and informal relationships, it is apparent that important national policies reflect the judgment of both the legislative and executive branches, as well as the views of pressure groups and influential individuals.

CONGRESS: AN INDEPENDENT POLICYMAKER

Much has been written about the growth of executive power in the twentieth century and the diminished role of Congress, but in fact there has been a dynamic, not static, pattern of activity between the branches. First one and then the other may be perceived as the predominant branch, and various periods are characterized as times of "congressional government" or "presidential government."[4] Such descriptions often underestimate the other branch's strategic importance, however. President John F. Kennedy, who served during a period regarded by some observers as one of presidential resurgence, observed that Congress "looks more powerful sitting here than it did when I was there." From his position in the White House, he looked at the collective power of Congress and found it "substantial."[5] In short, the American political system is largely congressional *and* presidential government.

The strength and independence of Congress contrast sharply with the position of legislatures in other democratic countries. In most, policymaking is concentrated in the hands of a prime minister and cabinet who are normally elected members of the legislature and are leaders of the majority party. As a result, the policy of the prime minister and the cabinet is normally approved by the legislature, with voting divided strictly along party lines. Conversely, if a prime minister falls out of favor with the majority party, a new election will usually be held.

The U.S. Congress, by contrast, is elected separately from the president and has independent policymaking authority. As a result, a study of policymaking in the United States requires a separate examination of the congressional process.

FUNCTIONS OF RULES AND PROCEDURES

Any decisionmaking body, Congress included, needs a set of rules, procedures, and conventions, formal and informal, in order to function. In the case of Congress, the Constitution authorizes the House and Senate to formulate their

5

own rules of procedure. Thomas Jefferson, who, as vice president, compiled the first parliamentary manual for the United States Senate, emphasized the importance of rules to any legislative body.

> It is much more material that there should be a rule to go by, than what the rule is; that there may be uniformity of proceeding in business not subject to the caprice of the Speaker or captiousness of the members. It is very material that order, decency, and regularity be preserved in a dignified public body.[6]

Rules and procedures in an organization serve many functions. Among them are to provide stability, legitimize decisions, divide responsibilities, reduce conflict, and distribute power. Each of these functions will be illustrated both by examples drawn from a college or university setting and by parallel functions in Congress.

Stability

Rules provide stability and predictability in personal and organizational affairs. Individuals and institutions can conduct their day-to-day business without having to debate procedure. Universities, for example, have specific requirements for bachelors, masters, and doctorate degrees. Students know that if they are to progress from one degree to the next they must comply with rules and requirements. Daily or weekly changes in those requirements would cause chaos on any campus. Similarly, legislators need not decide each day who can speak on the floor, offer amendments, or close debate. Such matters are governed by regularized procedures that continue from one Congress to the next and afford similar rights and privileges to every member.

Legitimacy

Students typically receive final course grades that are based on their classroom performance, examinations, and term papers. They accept the professors' evaluations if they believe in their fairness and legitimacy. If professors suddenly decided to use students' political opinions as the basis for final grades, there would be a storm of protest against such arbitrary procedures. In a similar fashion, members of Congress and citizens accept legislative decisions when they believe the decisions were approved according to orderly and fair procedure.

Division of Labor

Any university requires a division of labor if it is to carry out its tasks effectively and responsibly, and rules establish the various jurisdictions. Hence there are history, chemistry, and art departments; admissions officers and bursars; and food service and physical plant managers, all with specialized assignments. For Congress, committees are the heart of its legislative process. They provide the division of labor and specialization that Congress needs in order to handle the more than 20,000 measures introduced biennially, and to review the administration of scores of federal programs. Like specialized bodies in many organizations, committees do not make final policy decisions but propose recommendations to their respective chambers.

Conflict Resolution

Rules reduce conflicts among members and units of organizations by distinguishing appropriate actions and behavior from the inappropriate. For example, universities have procedures by which students may drop or add classes. There are discussions with faculty advisors, completion of appropriate paperwork, and the approval of a dean. Students who informally attempt to drop or add classes may encounter conflicts with their professors as well as sanctions from the dean's office. Most of the conflicts can be avoided by observance of established procedures. Similarly, congressional rules reduce conflict by, for example, establishing procedures to fill vacancies on committees when several members are competing for the same position.

Distribution of Power

A major consequence of rules is that they generally distribute power in any organization. As a result, rules are often a source of conflict themselves. During the 1960s, for example, many campuses witnessed struggles among students, faculty, and administrators involving the curriculum. The charge of irrelevance in course work was a frequent criticism of many students. As a result, the "rules of the game" for curriculum development were changed on many campuses. Students, junior faculty, and even community groups became involved in reshaping the structure and content of the educational program.

Like universities, Congress distributes power according to its rules and customs. Informal party rules, for example, establish a hierarchy of leadership positions in both chambers. And House and Senate rules accord prerogatives to congressional committee chairmen that are unavailable to noncommittee leaders. Rules are, therefore, not neutral devices. They help to shore up the more powerful members as well as protect the rights of the minority. Thus, efforts to change the rules are almost invariably efforts to redistribute power.

RULES AND POLICYMAKING IN
THE CONGRESSIONAL CONTEXT

Rules play similar, but not identical, roles in most complex organizations. Congress has its own characteristics that affect the functions of the rules. First, members of Congress owe their positions to the electorate, not to their congressional peers or to influential congressional leaders. No one in Congress has authority over the other members comparable to that of university presidents and tenured faculty over junior faculty or to that of a corporation president over lower level executives. Members cannot be fired except by their constituency. And each member has equal voting power in committees and on the floor of the House or Senate.

Congress' rules, unlike those of many organizations, are especially sensitive to the rights of *minorities*, including the minority party, ideological minorities, and individual members. Skillful use of the rules enables the minority to check majority action by delaying, defeating, or reshaping legislation. Intensity often counts as much as numbers — an apathetic majority may find it difficult to prevail over a well-organized minority. Except in the few instances when extraordinary majorities are needed, such as overriding presidential vetoes (two-thirds), Senate ratification of treaties (two-thirds), and the decision to stop extended debate in the Senate (three-fifths), the rules of the House and Senate require a simple majority to decide public policies.

Congress is also different from other organizations in its degree of responsiveness to external groups and pressures. The legislative branch is not as self-contained an institution as a university or a corporation. Congress is involved with every significant national and international issue. Its agenda compels members to respond to changing constituent interests and needs. Congress is also subject to numerous other influences, such as the president, pressure groups, political parties, and state and local officials.

Finally, Congress is a collegial and not a hierarchical body. Power does not flow from the top down, as in a corporation, but in practically every direction. There is only minimal centralized authority at the top; congressional policies are not "announced" but are "made" by shifting coalitions that vary from issue to issue. Congress' deliberations are also more accessible and public than those of perhaps any other kind of organization. These are some of the characteristics that set Congress apart from other organizations; inevitably these differences affect the decisionmaking process.

Procedure and Policy

Legislative procedures and policymaking are inextricably linked in at least four ways. First, procedures affect policy outcomes. Congress processes legislation by complex rules and procedures that permeate the institution and touch every public policy. Some matters are only gently brushed by the rules, while others become locked in their grip. Major civil rights legislation, for example, failed for decades to pass Congress because southern senators used their chamber's rules and procedures to kill or modify such measures.

A second point is that very often policy decisions are expressed as procedural moves. Representatives and senators, on various occasions, prefer not to make clear-cut decisions on certain complex and far-reaching public issues. Should a major weapons system be continued or curtailed? Should the nation's energy production needs take precedence over environmental concerns? Should financial assistance for the elderly be reduced and priority be given to aiding disadvantaged children? On questions like these, members may be "cross-pressured" (the president might be exerting influence one way while constituent interests dictate the opposite). Legislators may lack adequate information to make informed judgments. They may be reluctant to oppose powerful pressure groups. Or the issue, they believe, does not lend itself to a simple "yes" or "no" vote.

As a result, legislators employ various procedural devices to handle knotty problems. A matter may be postponed on the ground of insufficient committee hearings. Congress may direct an agency to prepare a detailed report before an issue is considered. Or a measure may be "tabled" by the House or Senate, a procedural vote that effectively defeats a proposal without rendering a judgment on its substance. When the 95th Congress convened, for example, the Senate debated a proposal that would put it on record against blanket amnesty for Vietnam draft evaders. The controversial measure was tabled on a 48 to 46 vote leaving the whole matter to the president.

Third, the nature of the policy can determine the use of certain procedures. The House and Senate generally consider noncontroversial measures under expeditious procedures whereas controversial proposals normally involve lengthy deliberation. Extraordinary circumstances might prompt Congress to invoke rarely-used practices to enact legislation with dispatch. For example, because of the severe winter of 1977, President Carter urged Congress to approve quickly a law granting him authority to order transfers of natural gas to states hard hit by gas shortages. On January 26, 1977, the measure was introduced in the Senate. To speed the bill's passage, the Senate employed a rarely-used procedure that brought the measure immediately to the floor for debate, bypassing the usual committee stage entirely.[7] Moreover, under pressure from its leadership, the Senate rejected all substantive amendments and passed the measure 91 to 2 after two days of debate. As national issues change, moreover, some procedures become nearly extinct, while others are used more and more frequently to meet new needs.

Finally, policy outcomes are more likely to be influenced by members with procedural expertise. Members who are skilled parliamentarians are better prepared to gain approval of their proposals than those who are only vaguely familiar with the rules. Just as carpenters and lawyers must learn their trade, members of Congress need to understand the rules if they expect to perform effectively. And congressional procedures are confusing to newcomers. "To table, to refer to committee, to amend — so many things come up," declared freshman Senator S. I. Hayakawa, R-Calif., "you don't know whether you are coming or going."[8] Former Speaker of the House John McCormack once advised freshmen House members:

> Learn the rules and understand the precedents and procedures of the House. The congressman who knows how the House operates will soon be recognized for his parliamentary skills — and his prestige will rise among his colleagues, no matter what his party.[9]

Members who know the rules well always have the potential to shape legislation to their ends. Those who do not reduce their proficiency and influence as legislators.

Precedents and Folkways

Congress is regulated not only by formal rules, but by informal ones that influence legislative procedure and member behavior.[10] Two types of informal rules are precedents and "folkways." Precedents, the accumulated past decisions on matters of procedure, represent a blend of the formal and informal. They are the "common law" of Congress and govern many procedures not explicitly covered in the formal rules. For example, formal rules prescribe the order of business in the House and Senate, but precedents permit variations through the unanimous consent of the members. The rulings of the Speaker of the House and presiding officer of the Senate form a large body of precedents. They are given formal status by the parliamentarians in each chamber and distributed to representatives and senators.[11]

Folkways, on the other hand, are unwritten norms of behavior that members are expected to observe. "Without these folkways," concluded Donald Matthews, "the Senate could hardly operate with its present organization and rules."[12] Several of the more important are "legislative work" (members should concentrate on congressional duties and not be publicity seekers), "courtesy" (members should be solicitous toward their colleagues and avoid personal attacks on them), and "specialization" (members should master a few policy areas and not try to be a "jack of all trades"). Those who abide by these and other norms are often rewarded with increased influence in the policy process, for example, by being appointed to prestigious committees. Conversely, legislators who persistently violate Congress' informal customs are apt to see legislation they support blocked in committee or on the floor. Congressional decisionmaking, then, is shaped by each chamber's formal and informal structure of rules, precedents, and traditions.

CONGRESSIONAL DECISIONMAKING

The congressional decisionmaking process is constantly evolving, but there are certain enduring features of it that affect consideration of all legislation. The first is the decentralized power structure of Congress, characterized by the numerous specialized committees and a weak central party leadership. A second feature is the existence of multiple decision points for every piece of legislation. The many decision points mean that at each step of a bill's progress, a majority coalition must be formed to move the measure past the decision point. This leads to the third important feature of the process, the frequent need for bargaining and compromise at every juncture in order to form the coalition. And finally, each Congress has only a two-year life cycle in which to pass legislation introduced; the pressure of time is an ever-present force underlying the process.

Decentralized Power Structure

Congress' decentralized character reflects both political and structural realities. Politically, legislators owe their re-election to voters in widely differing states and localities; structurally, the legislative branch has an elaborate division of labor to help it manage its immense workload. Responsibility for specific subject areas is dispersed among numerous committees and subcommittees (more than 300 in the two chambers).

Structural decentralization means that policymaking is subject to various disintegrative processes. Broad issues are divided into smaller subissues for consideration by the committees. Overlapping and fragmentation of committee responsibilities can impede the development of comprehensive and coordinated national policies. More than a dozen House committees, for example, consider some aspect of the energy issue. Jurisdictional controversies occur as committees fight to protect their "turf." Finally, committees develop special relationships with pressure groups and executive agencies. These alliances, often called "subgovernments," dominate numerous policy areas. Committees, then, become advocates of policies and not simply impartial instruments of the House or Senate.[13]

In theory, political parties could provide the cohesive force to balance the centrifugal influences of a fragmented committee system. For the most part, the reality is much different. Parties serve to organize their members and elect the formal leaders. From time to time, congressional Democrats and Republicans meet in policy committees and caucuses to discuss policy issues. Neither party, however, commands the consistent support of all its members. Too many countervailing pressures (constituency, individual conscience, career considerations, or committee loyalty) influence the actions of representatives and senators. As a result, public policies usually are enacted because diverse elements of both parties temporarily coalesce to achieve common goals.

The absence of disciplined parties, in or out of Congress, underscores the difficult and delicate role of congressional party leaders. They cannot dictate policy because they lack the means to force agreement among competing party factions or autonomous committees and subcommittees. A number of legislators are not particularly dependent on their state or local parties for reelection. This means that party leaders cannot count on automatic party support but rely heavily on their skills as bargainers and negotiators to influence legislative decisions. In addition, the power and style of any party leader depend on several factors, some outside of the leader's control. Among them are personality, intellectual and political talent, the leader's view of the job, the size of the majority or minority party, whether the White House is controlled by the opposition party, the expectations of colleagues, and the institutional complexion of the House or Senate during a particular historical era.

Multiple Decision Points

Although Congress can on occasion act quickly, normally legislation must pass successfully through multiple decision points. One congressional report identified more than 100 specific steps that might mark a "bill's progress through the Congress, from introduction to possible enactment into law."[14] After a bill is introduced, it is referred to committee and then frequently to a subcommittee. The views of executive departments and agencies are often solicited. Hearings are held and reports on the bill are issued by the subcommittee and full committee. The bill is then "reported out" and scheduled for consideration by all the members. After floor debate and final action in one chamber, the same steps are generally repeated in the other house. At any point in this sequential process, the bill is subject to delay, defeat, or modification. "It is very easy to defeat a bill in Congress," noted former President Kennedy. "It is much more difficult to pass one."[15]

The diagram on page 15 outlines the major procedural steps in how a bill becomes law. First, congressional procedures require bills to overcome numerous hurdles before they can become law. At each stage, measures and procedures must receive majority approval. All along the procedural route, therefore, strategically located committees, groups, or

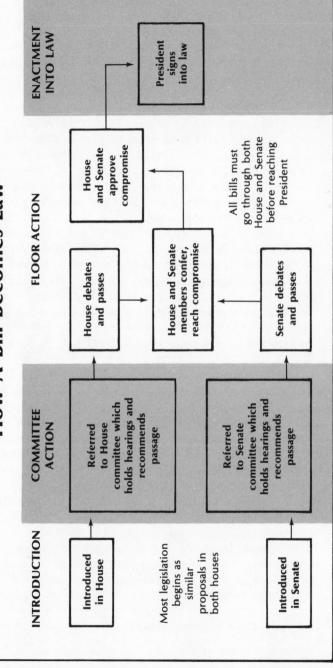

How A Bill Becomes Law

INTRODUCTION

COMMITTEE ACTION

FLOOR ACTION

ENACTMENT INTO LAW

Introduced in House

Introduced in Senate

Most legislation begins as similar proposals in both houses

Referred to House committee which holds hearings and recommends passage

Referred to Senate committee which holds hearings and recommends passage

House debates and passes

Senate debates and passes

House and Senate members confer, reach compromise

All bills must go through both House and Senate before reaching President

House and Senate approve compromise

President signs into law

individuals can delay, block, or change proposals if they can form majority coalitions. Bargaining may be necessary at each juncture in order to build the majority coalition that advances the bill to the next step in the legislative process.

Bargaining and Coalition Building

There are three principal forms of bargaining used to build majority coalitions — logrolling, compromise, and non-legislative favors. Logrolling is an exchange of voting support on different bills by different members of Congress. It is an effective means of coalition building because members are rarely equally concerned about all the measures before Congress. For example, representatives A, B, and C strongly support a bill that increases government aid to farmers. A, B, and C are indifferent toward a second bill that increases the minimum wage and is strongly supported by representatives D, E, and F. Because D, E, and F do not have strong feelings about the farm bill, a bargain is struck: A, B, and C agree to vote for the minimum wage bill; and D, E, and F agree to vote for the farm bill. Both bills are thereby helped on their way past the key decision points at which A, B, C, D, E, and F have influence.

Logrolling may either be explicit or implicit. A, B, and C may have negotiated directly with D, E, and F. Alternatively, A, B, and C may have voted for the minimum wage bill — letting it be known through the press or in other informal ways that they anticipate similar treatment on the farm bill from D, E, and F. The expectation is that D, E, and F will honor the tacit agreement — since at a later date, they may again need the support of A, B, and C.

Compromise, unlike logrolling, builds coalitions through negotiation over the *content* of legislation. Each side agrees to modify policy goals on a given bill in a way that is generally acceptable to the other. A middle ground is often found — particularly with bills involving money. A, B, and C, for example, support a $50 million education bill; D, E, and F want to increase the funding to $100 million. The six meet and compromise on a $75 million bill they all can support.

Note the distinction between logrolling and compromise.

In the logrolling example, the participants did not modify their objectives on the bills that mattered to them; each side traded voting support on a bill which meant little in return for support on a bill in which they were keenly interested. Under compromise, both sides modified their positions.

Nonlegislative favors are useful because policy goals are only one of the many objectives of members of Congress. Other objectives include assignment to a prestigious committee, getting reelected, running for higher office, obtaining larger office space and staff, or even being selected for a conference abroad. The wide variety of these non-policy objectives creates numerous bargaining opportunities — particularly for party leaders, who can dispense many favors — from which coalitions may be built. As Senate majority leader, Lyndon Johnson was known for his skill in using his powers to satisfy the personal needs of senators in order to build support for legislation Johnson wanted.

> For Johnson, each one of these assignments contained a potential opportunity for bargaining, for creating obligations, provided that he knew his fellow senators well enough to determine which invitations would matter the most to whom. If he knew that the wife of the senator from Idaho had been dreaming of a trip to Paris for ten years, or that the advisers to another senator had warned him about his slipping popularity with Italian voters, Johnson could increase the potential usefulness of assignments to the Parliamentary Conference in Paris or to the dedication of the cemeteries in Italy.[16]

In this way, Johnson made his colleagues understand that there was a debt to be repaid.

The Congressional Cycle

Every bill introduced in Congress faces the two-year deadline of the congressional term. (The term of the 95th Congress, elected in November 1976, began at noon on January 4, 1977, and expires at noon on January 3, 1979.) Each bill introduced must pass both the House and the Senate in identical form within the two-year term in order to become law. In fact, because Congress normally adjourns prior to the end of the two-year term, bills usually have less than two years to become law. Bills that have not completed the required procedural journey prior to final adjournment of a Congress automatically die and must be reintroduced in the new Congress. Inaction or postponement at any stage of the process can ultimately mean the defeat of a bill. This book repeatedly focuses on the various delaying and expediting tactics available to members during the legislative process.

Many measures considered by Congress come up in cycles. Much of Congress' annual agenda is filled with legislation required each year to finance the activities of federal agencies and programs. Generally, this kind of legislation appears regularly on the congressional agenda at the same time each year. Other legislation comes up for renewal every few years.

There are emergencies that demand immediate attention. Other issues become timely because public interest has focused on them; consumer product safety, environmental protection, and the energy shortage are examples of such issues.

Complex legislation is often introduced early because it takes longer to process than a simple bill. A disproportionately large number of major bills are enacted during the last few weeks of a Congress. Compromises that were not possible in July can be made in December. By this time — with the two-year term about to expire — the pressures on members of the House and Senate are intense.

Finally, many ideas require years or even decades of germination before they are enacted into law. Controversial proposals — reintroduced in successive Congresses — may need a four, six, or eight-year period before enactment. Many of the 1960s policies of Presidents Kennedy and Johnson, for example, were first considered during the Congresses of the 1950s.

SUMMARY

Rules and procedures affect what Congress does and how it does it. They define the steps by which bills become law, decentralize authority among numerous specialized committees, distribute power among members, and permit orderly consideration of policies. Above all, the rules and organization of Congress create numerous decision points through which legislation must pass in order to become law. As a result, congressional decisionmaking presents many opportunities for members opposed to a given bill to defeat it. Proponents, by contrast, must win at every step of the way. At each procedural stage, they must assemble a majority coalition. Throughout the legislative process, time is a critical factor as members maneuver to enact or defeat legislation.

In chapter 1, an overall view of the congressional *process* has been presented. In chapter 2, the focus shifts to the organizational and environmental *setting* of Congress to examine differences between the House and the Senate; the leadership structure in Congress; pressures exerted on Congress by the executive branch, interest groups, and public opinion; and the extensive overhaul of congressional procedures which has occurred in the 1970s.

Chapter 3 turns to the initial steps of the legislative process — the introduction and referral of bills to House and Senate committees, and committee action on bills. Chapter 4 explains how legislation that has emerged from committee is scheduled for floor action in the House. Chapter 5 then examines floor action in the House. In chapter 6, the spotlight is put on the Senate with a discussion of how legislation is scheduled in that chamber. Senate floor action is the subject of chapter 7. Chapter 8 describes how House-Senate differences are reconciled when each chamber passes a different version of the same bill. Chapter 9, "Legislative Oversight," discusses how Congress monitors the implementation of the laws it has passed. The final chapter re-examines the legislative process, pulling together the major themes of this book.

NOTES

1. Benjamin Fletcher Wright, ed., *The Federalist By Alexander Hamilton, James Madison, and John Jay* (Cambridge, Mass.: The Belknap Press of Harvard University Press, 1961), p. 356 (Federalist No. 51).
2. Paul L. Ford, ed., *The Federalist, A Commentary on the Constitution of the United States by Alexander Hamilton, James*

Madison, and John Jay (New York: Henry Holt and Co., 1898), p. 319 (Federalist No. 47). James Madison wrote this commentary on "Separation of the Departments of Power."

3. Thomas Jefferson, "Notes on Virginia" in *Free Government in the Making,* ed., Alpheus Thomas Mason (New York: Oxford University Press, 1965), p. 164.

4. Woodrow Wilson, *Congressional Government* (Boston: Chapman Publishers, 1885) and James MacGregor Burns, *Presidential Government* (Boston: Houghton Mifflin Co., 1966).

5. Donald Bruce Johnson and Jack L. Walker, eds., "President John Kennedy Discusses the Presidency," in *The Dynamics of the American Presidency* (New York: John Wiley and Sons, 1964), p. 144.

6. *Constitution, Jefferson's Manual, and Rules of the House of Representatives,* 94th Congress, 2nd Session, House Document No. 94-663, pp. 121-122.

7. U.S. Congress, Senate, *Congressional Record,* January 26, 1977, 123, S 1538-S 1541. Majority Leader Robert C. Byrd requested and received the unanimous consent of the Senate to bypass the committee stage and place the measure directly on the calendar for immediate floor consideration. For important bills, this in an unusual procedure.

8. *Los Angeles Times,* February 7, 1977, p. 5.

9. U.S. Congress, House, *Congressional Record,* March 9, 1976, 122, H1779.

10. The formal rules of the House are contained in *Constitution, Jefferson's Manual, and Rules of the House of Representatives,* 94th Congress, 2nd Sess, House Document No. 94-663. The Senate's formal rules are in *Senate Manual,* 95th Congress, 1st Session, Senate Document No. 95-1.

11. Lewis Deschler, *Deschler's Procedure, A Summary of the Modern Precedents and Practices of the U.S. House of Representatives, 86th-94th Congress* (Washington, D.C.: Government Printing Office, 1974) and Floyd M. Riddick, *Senate Procedure, Precedents and Practices* (Washington, D.C.: Government Printing Office, 1974).

12. Donald Matthews, *U.S. Senators and Their World* (Chapel Hill, N.C.: University of North Carolina Press, 1960), Chapter 5. Several of the folkways described by Matthews have undergone considerable change. For example, the norm of "apprenticeship," specifying that new members should be seen and not heard, has all but disappeared in both chambers.

13. Roger H. Davidson and Walter J. Oleszek, *Congress against Itself* (Bloomington, Ind.: Indiana University Press, 1977) and Roger H. Davidson, "Breaking Up Those 'Cozy Triangles': An Impossible Dream?" in *Legislative Reform and Public Policy,*

ed. Susan Welch and John G. Peters (New York: Praeger Publishers, 1977), pp. 30-53.

14. *The Bill Status System for the United States House of Representatives.* Committee on House Administration, July 1, 1975, p. 19.
15. "President John Kennedy Discusses the Presidency," *The Dynamics of the American Presidency,* p. 144.
16. Doris Kearns, *Lyndon Johnson and the American Dream* (New York: Harper & Row, 1976), p. 119.

2

The Congressional Environment

Congress is an independent policymaker. This does not mean that it is impermeable to influences from outside it, nor does it mean that each member operates independently of every other member. Rather, there is a tangled, multifaceted relationship between Congress and the other governmental and nongovernmental forces. Similarly, there are complicated internal hierarchies and networks that affect the way Congress goes about its business. This chapter will focus on some of the conditions that form the congressional environment, including the bicameral nature of Congress, the key actors in the congressional leadership, the pressures from outside Congress, and the procedural changes that swept through the House and Senate in the 1970s.

THE HOUSE AND SENATE COMPARED

The "House and Senate are naturally unlike," observed Woodrow Wilson.[1] Each chamber has its own rules, precedents, and customs; different terms of office; varying constitutional responsibilities; and differing constituencies. "We are constituted differently, we serve different purposes in the representative system, we operate differently, why should [the House and Senate] not have different rules," commented former Oregon Senator Wayne Morse.[2] Table 2-1 summarizes the major differences between the chambers.

Table 2-1 Major Differences Between the House and Senate

House	*Senate*
Larger (435)	Smaller (100)
Shorter term of office (2 years)	Longer term of office (6 years)
Less flexible rules	More flexible rules
Narrower constituency	Broader, more varied, constituency
Policy specialists	Policy generalists
Less press and media coverage	More press and media coverage
Power less evenly distributed	Power more evenly distributed
Less prestige	More prestige
More expeditious in floor debate	Less expeditious in floor debate
Less reliance on staff	More reliance on staff

Probably the three most important differences between the two chambers are that the House is more than four times the size of the Senate, that senators represent a broader constituency than do representatives, and that senators serve longer terms of office. These differences affect the way the two houses operate in a number of ways.

Complexity of Rules

Certainly the factor of size explains much about why the two chambers differ. Because it is larger, the House is a more structured body than the Senate. The restraints imposed on representatives by rules and precedents are far more severe than those affecting senators. House rules for the 95th Congress are described in more than 300 pages and its precedents from 1789 to 1936 are contained in 11 huge volumes.[3] In contrast, the Senate's rules are contained in 109 pages and its precedents in one volume.[4] Where Senate rules maximize freedom of expression, House rules "show a constant subordination of the individual to the necessities of the whole House as the voice of the national will."[5]

The Senate, as a result, is a more personal and individualistic institution than is the House. It functions to a large extent by unanimous consent, in effect adjusting or disregarding its rules as it goes along. It is not uncommon for votes to be rescheduled or delayed until an interested senator can be present. Senate party leaders are careful to consult all senators who have expressed an interest in the legislation; in the House, the leadership can only consult key members, usually committee leaders, about floor activities. Where procedure is "king" in the House, it is equivalent to a distant "royal cousin" in the Senate.

Policy "Incubation"

Incubation entails "keeping a proposal alive, while it picks up support, or waits for a better climate, or while the problem to which it is addressed grow."[6] Both houses fulfill this role, but it is promoted in the Senate because of that body's flexible rules, more varied constituent pressures on senators, and greater press and media coverage. As the chamber of greater prestige, lesser complexity, longer term of office, and smaller size, the Senate is simply easier for the media to cover than the House.[7] As a result, the Senate is comparatively less concerned with the technical perfection of legislation and more involved with cultivating national constituencies, formulating questions for national debate, and gaining general public support for policy proposals. The policy-generating role is particularly characteristic of senators with presidential ambitions, who need to capture both headlines and national constituencies.

Specialists *vs.* Generalists

Another difference between the chambers is that representatives tend to be known as subject matter "specialists" while senators tend to be "generalists." "If the Senate has been the nation's great forum," a representative said, then the "House has been its workshop."[8] Indeed its greater work force and division of labor facilitates policy specialization in the House. "Senators do not specialize as intensively or as exclusively in their committee work as House members do," because senators must spread their "efforts over a greater span of subjects than the average representative."[9] During the 95th Congress (1977-78), for example, the average senator served on 11 committees and subcommittees compared to six for the average representative.

One reason for the specialist-generalist distinction is that senators represent a broader constituency than House members. This compels the former to generalize as they attempt to be conversant on numerous national and international issues that affect their state. With their six-year term, senators are less vulnerable to immediate constituency pressures; therefore, they can afford to be more cosmopolitan in their viewpoints than House members. Journalists, too, expect senators, more than representatives, to have an informed opinion on almost every important public issue.

A result of the generalist role is greater reliance by senators on knowledgeable personal and committee staff aides for advice in decisionmaking. A House member, on the other hand, is more likely to be an expert on particular policy issues. If not, he often relies on informed colleagues rather than staff aides for advice on legislation. "House members rely most heavily upon their colleagues for all information," one study concluded. "Senators, in contrast, will often turn to other sources, especially their own staffs, for their immediate information needs."[10] Consequently, Senate staff aides generally have more influence over the laws and programs of the nation than do their counterparts in the House.

Distribution of Power

Another difference between the two chambers is that power to influence policy is more evenly distributed in the Senate than it is in the House. This is highlighted by comparing opportunities for assuming leadership positions on committees. Freshman Senator John Culver, D-Iowa, (a former five-term House member) put it this way, "I'm chairman of one [Senate] subcommittee and on a two-man task force studying tank procurement in another committee. In the House, that used to take eight to ten years."[11] House reforms in the 1970s have created additional committee leadership opportunities for junior representatives, but it still is easier for junior senators to exert influence over significant policy matters. "All of a sudden I'm making a difference," declared first-term senator John Heinz, R-Pa., who spent five years in the House. "You have more say, more of an input. You're more intimately involved with the executive branch. Your vote, you feel, counts for much more."[12] Unlike the average representative, senators find it easier to exercise initiative in legislation and oversight, to have their floor amendments adopted to legislation reported from committees on which they are not members, to influence the scheduling of measures, and, in general, to participate more widely and equally in all Senate and party activities.

Similarities

There are many similarities between the House and Senate. Both chambers are essentially equal in power and share similar responsibilities in lawmaking, oversight, and representation. They both have heavy workloads, decentralized committee and party structures, and somewhat parallel committees. The roles and responsibilities of one chamber interact with those of the other. House and Senate party leaders often cooperate closely to coordinate action on legislation. Cooperation is made easier when both houses are controlled by the same party. Senate Majority Leader Robert C. Byrd, for example, informed his colleagues that he had "talked with the Speaker of the House" about the 1977 Emergency Natural Gas Act. "He hopes that the Senate will act today and get the measure over to the House without amendments," Senator Byrd said, so the bill can be enacted quickly under expeditious House procedures.[13] The Speaker's hope was realized by the Senate.

LEADERSHIP IN THE HOUSE AND SENATE

In both the House and the Senate, the party leadership is crucial to the smooth functioning of the legislative process. Leaders help to organize orderly consideration of legislative proposals, try to line up party support for or against measures, attempt to reconcile differences that threaten to disrupt the chambers, and plan strategy on important bills. The chart on the next page depicts the leadership structure of Congress.

In the House, the formal leadership consists of the Speaker, who is both the chamber's presiding officer and the majority party's overall leader; the majority and minority leaders; whips from each party; assistants to the whips; and various committees to assist with party strategy, legislative scheduling, and the assignment of party members to committees.

In the Senate, there is no party official comparable to the Speaker. The vice president is the constitutional president of the Senate, and in his absence the president pro tempore or (more commonly) a temporary presiding officer presides, but none of these individuals has political power comparable to that of the Speaker. The Senate has majority and minority leaders, whips, assistant whips, and party committees. The leadership structures in both houses have great influence over the course a bill might take; few important bills become law without the support of the majority leadership.

The significance of leadership pressures on members of Congress was summed up succinctly years ago by Speaker of the House Sam Rayburn of Texas, who advised members that "to get along, you have to go along."[14] Speaker Rayburn's advice is no longer as relevant as it once was, but rules and customs of both houses of Congress still place significant resources in the hands of the leaders to help them work their will.

Party leaders in both houses use these various resources to achieve their objectives. Leaders may offer tangible incentives to influence the course of legislation. These include influencing committee assignments, allocating public works projects, awarding campaign funds from the congressional and senatorial campaign committees, helping to obtain outside campaign contributions, and endorsing members for reelection.

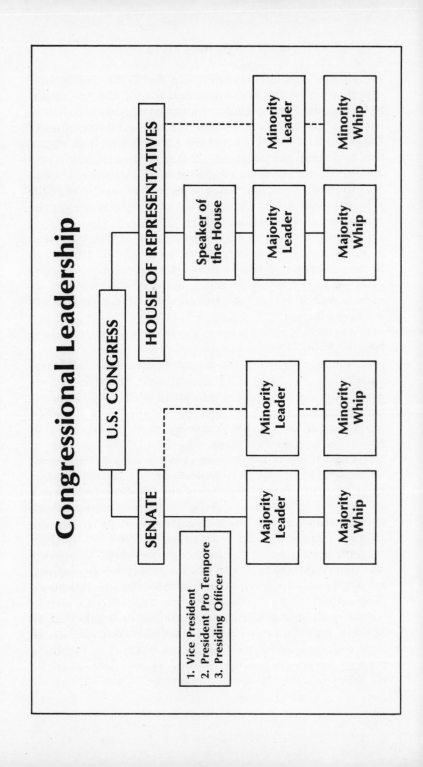

Congressional Leadership

U.S. CONGRESS

SENATE

1. Vice President
2. President Pro Tempore
3. Presiding Officer

Majority Leader

Majority Whip

Minority Leader

Minority Whip

HOUSE OF REPRESENTATIVES

Speaker of the House

Majority Leader

Majority Whip

Minority Leader

Minority Whip

A less tangible resource has been the leadership's expression of approval and personal friendliness toward the party faithful, and coolness toward party defectors. House party leaders, for example, "are in good position to influence the attitude of the House toward a member early in his career by telling other members what they think of him. There are also visible ways, such as the Speaker's selection of members to preside over the House or over the Committee of the Whole, by which party leaders indicate the younger members whom they regard highly."[15]

Most party leaders have been eager to dispense favors to members both of their own and of the opposition party so as to create a stack of IOUs to call upon in the event of close votes on important measures. Leaders usually rely on tact and persuasion rather than threats or harsh criticism to win members' support.

Speaker of the House

Former Speaker of the House Thomas Reed of Maine once called that office "the embodiment of the House, its power and dignity," and it is treated as such by the members.[16] Associated with the prestige and dignity of the office are numerous powers that enable Speakers to play a central role in the legislative process.

The position of the Speaker is established by the Constitution, but until the early nineteenth century the Speaker had little real power. The power of the office reached its peak in the early 1900s, under a series of Speakers who extended and sometimes abused the prerogatives of the office. Drastic reform of the rules came about as a result of the 1910 "revolt" against Speaker Joseph Cannon, when the Speaker was stripped of the authority to sit on the House Rules Committee, to appoint committee members, and to control all floor action.

Modern Speakers achieve their influence largely through personal prestige, mastery of the art of persuasion, legislative expertise, and the support of the members. The Speaker's primary powers are presiding over the House; deciding points of order; referring bills and resolutions to the appropriate

House committees; scheduling legislation for floor action; and appointing members to joint and conference committees. The Speaker may participate in debate and may vote, like any other member, although most recent Speakers have voted only to break a tie.

Although the Constitution does not specify that the Speaker must be a member of the House, no nonmember has ever been elected to the post. It has become common practice to elect the majority leader as Speaker when an opening occurs. Since the Civil War, neither party has ousted a sitting Speaker as long as the party remained in the majority. As Randall Ripley has observed, "In general, the Speaker retains leadership status in his party as long as he remains in the House."[17]

Majority and Minority Leaders

Both the majority and minority parties of the House and Senate appoint officials to shape and direct party strategy on the floor. These officials, elected by their respective party caucuses, try to hold together the loose alliances that compose their parties in hopes of shaping them into voting majorities to pass or defeat bills. Majority leaders have considerable influence over the scheduling of debate. The majority leader in the House ranks just below the Speaker in importance. In the Senate, the majority leader is the most influential officer, because neither the vice president nor the president pro tem holds substantive powers over the chamber's proceedings.

Duties of the House majority and minority leaders are not spelled out in the standing rules of the House, nor is official provision made for the offices (except through appropriations specifically made for their offices). In practice, the majority leader's job has been to formulate the party's legislative program in cooperation with the Speaker and other party leaders, steer the program through the House, ensure that committee chairmen report bills deemed of importance to the party, and help to establish the legislative schedule.

Everyday duties for the minority leader correspond to those of the majority leader, except that the minority leader has no authority over scheduling. The minority leader speaks for his party and acts as field general on the floor. It is the minority leader's duty to consult ranking minority members of House committees and encourage them to follow adopted party positions. If the minority party occupies the White House, its leader will probably be the president's spokesman in the House.

The functions of the Senate majority leader are similar to those of his counterpart in the House. The leader can nominate members to party committees, influence the election of party officers, affect the assignment of members to committees, or appoint *ad hoc* task forces to study and recommend substantive or procedural reforms. Traditionally, the "primary role of the majority leader remains similar to that at its inception, namely, to program and to expedite the flow of his party's legislation."[18] Not only is his party's legislation involved, but all the Senate's floor business is essentially scheduled by the majority leader in consultation with the minority leadership. Scheduling, perhaps, is the bedrock on which the majority leader's fundamental authority rests.

If used aggressively by the majority leader, scheduling, discussed in chapter 6, can be transformed from a largely procedural responsibility to one with significant programmatic and political overtones. Legislation can be scheduled to suit party or White House interests; to facilitate comprehensive policymaking through the sequential consideration of related topics; to expedite policies supported by the central leadership; or to coordinate House-Senate decisionmaking.

With the aid of the majority whip, the majority leader is also responsible for securing the attendance of party colleagues during floor sessions and ascertaining in advance how senators might vote on issues. Measures may be scheduled to maximize the attendance of a bill's supporters and to minimize attendance by its opponents. The leadership expends great effort to insure that senators favorable to a measure's passage are on the floor for any important vote.

Occupying center stage in the Senate, the majority leader is best positioned institutionally to know the status of legislation, when it might be scheduled, how intensely committed are its supporters and opponents, what strategies are being formulated to pass or defeat it, and under what conditions the president will intervene to help secure the measure's enactment. A knowledgeable majority leader is in a good position to guide colleagues and advise them.

The minority leader in the Senate has important responsibilities. These include summarizing minority criticism of the majority party's legislation, mobilizing support for minority party positions, and acting as Senate spokesman for the president if both are of the same party.

Whips

Each party in both chambers appoints a whip and a number of assistant whips to assist the floor leader in execution of the party's legislative program. The main job of the whips is to canvass party members on a pending issue and give the floor leader an accurate picture of the support or opposition expected for the measure. Whips also are responsible for making sure that party members are on hand to vote.

Party Caucuses

Over the years, both parties have relied periodically on caucuses of party members (called "conferences" by Republicans in both houses and by Senate Democrats) to adopt party positions on legislation, elect party leaders, approve committee assignments, and, on rare occasions, discipline party members. After decades of relative inactivity during much of the twentieth century, party caucuses emerged in the late 1960s as important bodies. Modern caucuses meet regularly to debate substantive and procedural issues.

Party Committees

Both parties maintain informal party committees in each chamber to assist the party leadership and deal with other party business. Steering committees recommend the order in which measures should be taken up and help with floor tactics, while policy committees research proposed legislation and recommend party positions. The two functions may be combined in a single committee, as happened in 1973, when the House Democratic Caucus voted to create a new 23-member Democratic Steering and Policy Committee to give added coherence to the party's legislative strategy. In 1974 the committee was given responsibility for assigning Democrats to committees.

The Leadership and the White House

For the most part, congressional leaders have sought to cooperate with a president of their own political party and to defeat or amend programs put forth by a president belonging to the opposite party. Over the years, however, there have been several important instances in which congressional leaders have resisted the program of a same-party president or have developed their own legislative program and imposed it on the White House. Cases in which a party's congressional leadership has cooperated in a substantial way with an opposing party's president are less frequent and have been limited mainly to national defense and foreign policy issues. One notable exception occurred during the later years of the Eisenhower administration. President Eisenhower said, in describing his relationship with Democratic Senate Majority Leader Lyndon Johnson, "We had our differences . . . yet when put in perspective, he was far more often helpful than obstructive. . . ."[19]

Other Groups

In addition to the party leadership, there are numerous informal groupings of senators and representatives that play a significant role in the legislative process. By definition, the groups operate outside the regular procedures of Congress, and their impact on regular congressional procedures is frequently hard to discern. Underlying all of these groups are the bonds of mutual interests and personal friendship that play such a large part in the functioning of Congress. Many of these groups were formed to represent specific interests, such as the Rural Caucus and the Congressional Black Caucus. Other informal groups, such as the House Democratic Study Group and House Republican Wednesday group, focus in part on procedural issues. Still other groups are formed of members who have similar outlooks on certain issues, such as the Members of Congress for Peace through Law.

PRESSURES ON CONGRESS

In making their legislative decisions, members of Congress are influenced by numerous pressures — from their constituents, the White House, the news media, lobbyists and organized interest groups, and their own party leadership and colleagues on Capitol Hill. These pressures are a central feature of the congressional environment; they affect the formal procedures and rules of Congress. All of these pressures are present in varying degrees in every step of the legislative process; the interests and influence of groups and individuals outside Congress have a considerable impact on the fate of a bill on Capitol Hill. This section highlights some major influences on the members.

The Executive Branch

The executive branch constitutes one of the most important sources of external pressure exerted on Congress. As mentioned in chapter 1, there is an ongoing institutional struggle between the executive and legislative branches. Sometimes the rivalry is seen as no more than a means by which members of Congress develop public stature by demonstrating their ability to thwart the president's objectives. British political scientist Harold Laski subscribed to such a view when he wrote, "There can be no doubt that in its own eyes, Congress establishes its prestige when it either refuses to let the president have his own way, or compels him to compromise with it."[20]

Many of the president's legislative functions and activities are not mentioned in the Constitution. For example, the president is able to influence congressional action through the manipulation of patronage, the allocation of federal funds and projects that may be vital to the reelection of a member of Congress, and the handling of constituents' cases in which senators and representatives are interested. As leader of the Democratic or Republican Party, the president is the party's chief election campaigner. As the leading political figure, the president occupies a strategic position for promoting broad coalitions of social groups and interests. The president also has ready access to the news media for promoting administration policy and commanding headlines.

The president's role as legislative leader, however, derives from the Constitution. While the Constitution vests "all legislative powers" in Congress, it also directs the president to "give to the Congress information of the state of the union and recommend to their consideration such measures as he shall judge necessary and expedient." This function has been broadened; the president presents to Congress each year, in addition to his State of the Union message, two other general statements of presidential aims — an economic report including proposals directed to the maintenance of maximum employment, and a budget message outlining appropriations proposals. And during a typical session, the president transmits to Congress scores of other legislative proposals, some on his own initiative or that of his Cabinet officials, and others in conformity with various statutes.

Another legislative vehicle for presidential leadership in Congress is the constitutional power to veto acts it passes, or to threaten to veto them. Presidents also find their office a "bully pulpit," as President Theodore Roosevelt said, from which to make direct appeals to public opinion through television, radio, and the press. Even in the early days of the Republic, presidents reached out to the people, often successfully, to build support for their legislative programs.

To enhance the prospects for securing a good working relationship with Congress, presidents in recent years have established congressional liaison offices in the White House to keep tabs on legislative activities on Capitol Hill and to lobby on behalf of administration policies. In addition, all federal departments now have their own congressional liaison forces. Although the White House liaison team in 1978 consisted of fewer than a dozen professionals, it was the tip of the sizable pyramid of executive branch officials charged with handling the administration's relations with Congress.

The Press

Of all the pressures on Congress, none is such a two-way proposition as the relationship between members and the press.

While senators and representatives must contend with the peculiarities of the news-gathering business, such as deadlines and limited space or time to describe events, and with constant press scrutiny of their actions, they also must rely on news organizations to inform the public of their legislative interests and accomplishments. At the same time, reporters must depend to some extent on "inside" information from members, a condition that makes many of them reluctant to displease their sources lest the pipeline of information be shut off.

But Congress basically is an open organization. Information flows freely on Capitol Hill and secrets rarely remain secret for long. It has always been true that an enterprising reporter can usually learn what is necessary to write newsworthy copy. But in the 1970s, rules and procedural changes opened to the public and press more activities of Congress than ever before.

This new openness has created pressures on members that, although present before, were less intense. Members' actions are subject to closer scrutiny by the press and by constituents — as well as by political opponents.

Congress has more journalists assigned to it than any other branch of the federal government. In 1976, the House and Senate press galleries had a membership of approximately 2,700 accredited reporters (including newspaper, periodical, radio and television reporters and photographers) — several times the size of the White House Correspondents Association.

At least a few reporters now cover every floor session of both chambers and every committee proceeding of any importance except those closed to the public. Reporters often outnumber the members on hand for a committee hearing and sometimes even outnumber the legislators present on the House or Senate floor. As former California representative Clem Miller wrote: "If the press did not report Congress, Congress could hardly function. If the sound of congressional voices carried no farther than the bare walls of the Chambers, Congress could disband."[21]

Most members of the House and Senate are skilled in public relations and realize that almost every Capitol Hill reporter must file one or more stories each day. That the legislators seek to benefit from this situation is indicated by the stacks of press releases and background statements that almost always inundate both the House and Senate press galleries. A study of Congress and the press concluded: "Regardless of the occasional hostility and suspicion between them, the working relationship of newsmen and legislators is fundamental to the democratic process; to be a congressman is to work with the press."[22]

Constituent Pressures

There are many external pressures competing against those of constituents, but it is still constituents, and not the president or the party or the congressional leadership, who grant and can take away a member's job.[23] A member who is popular back home can defy all three in a way unthinkable in a country such as Great Britain, where the leadership of the legislature, the executive, and the party are the same.

The extent to which a member of Congress seeks to follow the wishes of the constituents is determined to a considerable extent by the issue at stake. Few members would actively oppose construction in their district of a dam or post office wanted by most constituents. Few, if any, would follow locally popular policies that they were convinced would seriously endanger the nation. Between these extremes lies a full spectrum of different blends of pressure from constituents and from conscience. It is in this grey area that members must make most of their decisions.

Constituent opinion may set clear limits beyond which the member is unlikely to trespass. A representative from a farm district who seeks reelection is not likely to push policies designed to lower the price of foods grown by those who elect him. But on most questions the member has great leeway. The character of a particular constituency may have more effect on the kinds of questions the member takes up than on the member's voting record. Thus a representative from a district with a large ethnic minority might become a champion of immigration reform, and a senator from a western state might concentrate on natural resources policies. The committees on which the senator or representative seeks membership also are often determined by the type of constituency served.

Washington Lobbyists

Of all the pressures on Congress, none has received such widespread publicity and yet is so dimly understood as the role of Washington-based lobbyists and the groups they represent. The popular image of an agent for special interests who buys members' votes is a vast oversimplification.

Lobbyists and lobby groups have played an increasingly active part in the modern legislative process. The corps of Washington lobbyists has grown markedly since the 1930s, in line with the expansion of federal authority into new areas and with the huge increase in federal spending. The federal government has become a tremendous force in the life of the nation, and the number of fields in which changes in federal policy may spell success or failure for special interest groups has been greatly enlarged. Thus commercial and industrial interests, labor unions, ethnic and racial groups, professional organizations, citizen groups and representatives of foreign interests — all from time to time and some continuously — have sought by one method or another to exert pressure on Congress to attain their legislative goals.

Pressure groups, whether operating at the grass-roots level to influence public opinion or through direct contacts with members of Congress, perform some important and indispensable functions. Such functions include helping to inform both Congress and the public about problems and issues, stimulating public debate, opening a path to Congress for the wronged and needy, and making known to Congress the practical aspects of proposed legislation — whom it would help, whom it would hurt, who is for it and who is against it. The spin-off from this process is considerable technical information produced by research on legislative proposals.

Many critics point out, however, that interest groups may, in pursuing their own objectives, lead Congress into decisions that benefit the pressure group but do not necessarily serve other parts of the public. A group's power to influence legislation often is based less on its arguments than on the size of its membership, the amount of financial and manpower resources it can commit to a legislative pressure campaign, and the astuteness of its representatives.

CONGRESS IN FLUX

The Congress of the 1970s is markedly different from that of a decade earlier. These sweeping changes have influenced the lawmaking process and the distribution of power in many ways. They have also affected Congress' responsiveness to national problems and its policymaking capabilities.

The first steps toward a revitalized Congress came in the late 1960s and early 1970s, induced by external events and internal institutional pressures. Of fundamental importance were the two overriding issues of the period: the Vietnam War and the Watergate scandal. Both forced Congress to examine itself and reflect on whether it had the tools, and the will, to handle those crises and others that could arise in the future. Meanwhile, House and Senate membership was changing drastically: roughly two-thirds of the House and more than half the Senate changed hands from the 1964 elections on. Many of those new members came to Congress determined to revitalize the institution and restore it to an equal position with the presidency. Rules were revised and procedures rewritten as Congress prepared to exert more influence in governing the nation.

The first major reform in this period occurred with passage of the Legislative Reorganization Act of 1970 (PL 91-

510). Under that law, much of the secrecy surrounding the actions of members and their positions on various issues, particularly in the House, was peeled off. All roll-call votes taken in committees — where the vast majority of legislation is formulated — were to be made public. For the first time, House members' positions on floor amendments were to be individually recorded and printed in the *Congressional Record* in the same manner as senators' on roll-call votes (previously members had voted in virtual anonymity by non-recorded teller votes, and often many did not vote at all).[24]

The 1970 act was the precursor of further reforms to make Congress a more open institution. The House in 1973 and the Senate in 1975 decided to hold most of their committee bill-drafting sessions, called markups, in the public view. In addition, the House-Senate conference committees that iron out differences in bills passed by the two chambers and that traditionally met behind closed doors, were formally opened to the public in 1975.

Indeed, by the end of that year, both chambers had stripped away most vestiges of secrecy that had cloaked their committee proceedings. Both chambers also took steps to permit radio or television coverage of floor proceedings. These actions meant that the press, and therefore average citizens, had access to information about the actions of individual members of Congress that was difficult to obtain before. Special interest organizations, from labor unions to corporations, generally had had easy access to such information in the past through their continual contacts with legislators, and the pressures on members of Congress were accordingly one-sided. The new work-in-the-open requirements were designed to give citizens and less powerful organizations additional influence in legislative proceedings.

In addition to opening up its operations to more public scrutiny, Congress in the 1970s made fundamental changes in its power structure. One of these changes involved seniority — status based on length of service. Until the 1970s there had been few concerted or successful attacks on a system that tended to reward members' electoral longevity with favorable committee assignments and powerful committee chairmanships. Beginning around 1970, however, newly elected and liberal members of both houses, aided by outside pressure groups, started to chip away at the system. They revived long-dormant party units, such as caucuses, to bring about numerous procedural changes. By 1975, both chambers had instituted reforms whereby all committee chairmen had to stand for election by their party colleagues; and indeed in that year House Democrats voted to unseat three incumbent committee chairmen.

At the same time, new positions of responsibility were opened to junior members whose energies had been lost in the past. In 1973, the House Democratic Caucus drew up a subcommittee "bill of rights" that curbed chairmen's powers, assured that subcommittees would have defined jurisdictions, guaranteed each committee an adequate budget, and required chairmen to refer most measures to subcommittees within two weeks. The changes affecting House and Senate committee chairmen are considered more fully in chapter 3.

Paradoxically, House and Senate party leaders and caucuses gained new authority despite the general trend toward further decentralization. The Speaker, for example, became chairman of the Democratic committee that assigns party members to standing committees.

The problem of concentrated power was somewhat different in the Senate, whose relatively smaller size allowed more members to have responsible committee jobs. As part of the 1970 Legislative Reorganization Act, newly elected senators were restricted as to the number of committees on which they could serve.

The unique problem faced by the Senate was the filibuster under which bills could be talked to death, and the cloture rule which required a two-thirds majority of senators voting to end debate. This stiff requirement gave considerable power to a minority of senators — one-third plus one — who could prevent the majority from even bringing a bill to an up or down vote. The Senate in 1975 restricted the filibuster as a major method to obstruct legislation by lowering the number of votes needed for cloture to a "constitutional majority" of three-fifths of the full Senate — or 60 votes if there are no vacancies.

Institutionally, one of the basic changes the 94th Congress made was to establish a new congressional budget control system, designed to bring order out of the prevailing chaos of the legislative appropriations process. The new law, the 1974 Congressional Budget and Impoundment Control Act, was intended to give Congress far more influence in deciding the fundamental governmental issue of who gets how much money and for what purpose. And just as important, it would allow Congress to make spending decisions in a rational framework that related income to expenditures — something that Congress had never really done before. *(Box, p. 44-45)*

These are the highlights of several important changes Congress made in its power structure and procedures in the 1970s, and there have been numerous explanations for them. Certainly the perceived erosion of Congress' power relative to the White House, a process that had occurred over several decades, stimulated legislative reorganization. The loss of congressional control over the power of the purse and warmaking authority, particularly under Presidents Lyndon Johnson and Richard Nixon, provoked the national legislature to strengthen itself in both areas by passing the 1974 budget act and the 1973 War Powers Resolution.

Another factor was public disenchantment with Congress. Many members believed it imperative for Congress to "put its house in order" if public confidence in the legislative branch was to be restored. Both the House and Senate enacted in 1977 strong codes of ethics in response to public distrust of legislators.

The large influx of new members during the late 1960s and 1970s also contributed to the legislative resurgence. By the start of the 96th Congress in 1979, almost half the House will have begun their service in 1975 or since. With little stake in the status quo, new members supported institutional changes that would enhance their power.

Finally, there were members and groups within Congress who worked with outside interests, such as Common Cause

Passage of the landmark Congressional Budget and Impoundment Control Act of 1974 had a major institutional and procedural impact on the legislative branch. Institutionally, Congress created three new entities: the House Budget Committee, the Senate Budget Committee and the Congressional Budget Office (CBO), which provide committees and members with independent budget estimates and information to evaluate the president's budgetary proposals.

Procedurally, the 1974 act established a rigorous timetable for Congress and its committees to act on spending bills. The timetable permits Congress to review the federal budget as a whole, relating tax and spending decisions and determining budgetary priorities among competing national programs.

Congress' new budget process adds another element to the traditional two-step procedure of authorization and appropriation. Authorizations establish the policies for federal agencies, recommend the moneys for them, and are submitted to the president for signature or veto. Congress must then enact an appropriations law before any federal agency receives money from the treasury.

Background to Budget Act

Prior to 1974, Congress had made appropriations for individual federal programs with little effort to add up the overall cost or determine priorities among them. Congress lacked a mechanism that would permit it to calculate the overall effect of individual spending decisions on the national economy or to relate income to expenditures. In short, Congress clearly needed a central focal point for budget preparation and an annual plan relating how much taxes needed to be raised to meet suggested expenditures.

Challenges from the White House, rising deficits and members' dissatisfaction with Congress' fragmented approach to budget-making contributed to the enactment of the 1974 budget act. The new law required Congress

IMPOUNDMENT CONTROL ACT OF 1974

before acting on appropriations and spending measures to adopt a budget resolution setting targets for total appropriations, total spending and appropriate tax and debt levels.

Congressional Budget Timetable

On or before:	*Action to be completed:*
November 10	President submits current services budget.
15th day after Congress meets	President submits budget to Congress.
March 15	Committees submit reports to budget committees.
April 1	Congressional Budget Office submits report to budget committees.
April 15	Budget committees report first concurrent resolution on the budget to their houses.
May 15	Committees report bills authorizing new budget authority.
May 15	Congress adopts first concurrent resolution on the budget.
7th day after Labor Day	Congress completes action on bills providing budget authority and spending authority.
September 15	Congress completes actions on second required concurrent resolution on the budget.
September 25	Congress completes reconciliation process implementing second concurrent resolution.
October 1	Fiscal year begins.

and other public interest lobbying groups, to modernize Congress' organization and procedures. In the House, for example, the Democratic Study Group, the largest informal group of representatives, provided much of the organization, ideas and votes needed to bring about numerous procedural changes.

A principal result of the 1970s changes has been to reinforce the decentralized tendencies of Congress. Power has been dispersed further throughout Congress' components — committees, subcommittees, caucuses, party committees, the leadership, and informal groups — rather than concentrated in a few individuals such as committee chairmen and party leaders. This development affects legislative-executive relations as well. "The [old] seniority system is gone," declared a representative. "Before, the president had a chain of command to work with and through, but it has disappeared. Now, no one can deliver the votes."[25] In short, the 1970s changes have greatly increased the need for bargaining and coalition building.

SUMMARY

This chapter has discussed the general environment in which members of Congress operate, the many influences, both internal and external, on congressional procedures and decisionmaking, including: the party leadership; outside pressures from the executive branch, constituents, news media, and lobbying groups; and procedural and structural reforms undertaken by Congress itself in the 1970s. Also highlighted have been some of the general differences and similarities in the character of the House and Senate that affect their operations. This chapter completes a preliminary overview of Congress.

Chapter 3 turns to the initial steps of the legislative process — the introduction and referral of bills to House and Senate committees and committee action on bills. The executive branch and pressure groups are usually given most of the credit for initiating ideas that Congress eventually enacts. The legislative branch, however, also initiates numerous proposals. And frequently, ideas for legislation have been discussed for years in Congress, academic circles, private associations, executive agencies, federal advisory committees, national commissions, citizen and pressure groups, professional societies and by knowledgeable individuals.

In essence, legislation "is an aggregate, not a simple production," Woodrow Wilson wrote. "It is impossible to tell how many persons, opinions and influences have entered into its composition."[26]

NOTES

1. Woodrow Wilson, *Constitutional Government in the United States* (New York: Columbia University Press, 1911), p. 87.
2. U.S. Congress, 90th Cong., 1st sess., *Congressional Record,* February 7, 1967, 112, 2838.
3. *Constitution, Jefferson's Manual, and Rules of the House of Representatives,* House Document No. 94-663, 95th Congress. *Hinds' and Cannon's Precedents of the House of Representatives,* Volume I-XI (Washington: Government Printing Office, 1907, 1941); and *Deschler's Procedure in the U.S. House of Representatives* (Washington: Government Printing Office, 1974). The latter volume is a condensed version of up-to-date precedents. Precedents from 1936 through 1973 have been compiled for publication. The first volume is *Deschler's Precedents of the United States House of Representatives,* House Document No. 94-661, 94th Congress, 2d session.
4. *Senate Manual,* Senate Document No. 95-1, 95th Congress, 1st session (1977), pp. 1-109. Like the House, the Senate is also governed by numerous public laws, orders, and resolutions. Floyd M. Riddick, *Senate Procedure, Precedents, and Practices,* Senate Document No. 93-21, 93rd Congress, 1st session (1974).
5. Asher C. Hinds, *Hinds' Precedents of the House of Representatives,* Vol. I, p. v.
6. Nelson W. Polsby, "Policy Analysis and Congress," *Public Policy* (Fall 1969), p. 67.
7. Michael Green, "Obstacles to Reform: Nobody Covers the House," *The Washington Monthly* (June 1970), pp. 62-70.
8. Quoted in Charles Clapp, *The Congressman* (Garden City, N.Y.: Doubleday, 1963), p. 39.
9. Richard F. Fenno, *Congressmen in Committees* (Boston: Little, Brown, 1973), p. 172.
10. Norman J. Ornstein, "Legislative Behavior and Legislative Structure: A Comparative Look at House and Senate Resource

Utilization," in *Legislative Staffing,* ed. James J. Heaphey and Alan P. Balutis (New York: John Wiley and Sons, 1975), p. 175.

11. *Wall Street Journal,* May 8, 1975, p. 12.

12. *New York Times,* March 8, 1977, p. 16.

13. U.S. Congress, Senate, 95th Cong., 1st sess., *Congressional Record,* January 31, 1977, 123, S 1676.

14. Quoted in Richard Bolling, *House Out of Order* (E. P. Dutton, 1965), p. 48.

15. Randall B. Ripley, *Party Leaders in the House of Representatives,* (Washington: The Brookings Institution, 1967), p. 7.

16. U.S. Congress, 52d Cong., 2d sess. *Congressional Record,* March 3, 1893, 24, 2614.

17. Ripley, *Party Leaders in the House,* p. 13.

18. Robert L. Peabody, *Leadership in Congress* (Boston: Little Brown, 1976), p. 336.

19. Dwight D. Eisenhower, *Waging the Peace, 1956-1961* (Garden City, N.Y.: Doubleday, 1965), p. 593.

20. Harold J. Laski, *The American Presidency: An Interpretation* (New York: Harper & Bros., 1940), p. 116.

21. Clem Miller, *Member of the House: Letters of a Congressman* (New York: Scribner's, 1962), p. 60.

22. Delmar D. Dunn, "Symbiosis: Congress and the Press," in *To Be A Congressman: The Promise and the Power* (Washington: Acropolis Books, 1973), p. 50.

23. For a valuable discussion of constituent pressures, see David Mayhew, *The Electoral Connection* (New Haven: Yale University Press, 1974).

24. The *Congressional Record* is issued each day that Congress is in session. It contains, according to law, "substantially a verbatim report of proceedings." Members may edit a transcript of their remarks or may, with permission, "revise and extend" them. Until March 1, 1978, members could insert speeches into the *Record* as if they had been delivered on the floor. A rule now requires a "bullet" (a black dot) to precede and follow any material added, so that it may be distinguished from what was actually said on the floor. Page citations to the *Congressional Record* that contain a page number preceded by "H" or "S" refer to the daily edition, not the bound volumes.

25. Dom Bonafede, "Carter and Congress — It Seems that If Something Can Go Wrong, It Will,' " *National Journal,* Nov. 12, 1977, p. 1759.

26. Woodrow Wilson, *Congressional Government* (Boston: Houghton Mifflin, 1885), p. 320.

3

Preliminary Action
In the House and Senate

Introduction of a bill in the House or Senate is a simple procedure. In the House, members just drop their bills into the "hopper," a mahogany box near the clerk's desk at the front of the chamber. In the Senate, members usually submit their proposals and accompanying statements to clerks in the Senate chamber, or they may introduce their bills from the floor. House and Senate bills are printed and are made available to all members.

The simple act of introducing a bill sets off a complex and variable chain of events that may or may not result in the final passage of a bill by Congress. Most bills follow a path in which the steps are fairly predictable, governed by rules and convention, but where the outcome is not certain. This chapter considers some of the factors that affect the probable route a bill might take and focuses on the early stages in the life of a bill — its referral to committee and, most importantly, its consideration in committee.

Although thousands of pieces of legislation are introduced in every Congress, only a relatively small number become law. Table 3-1 shows that of the more than 20,000 bills and resolutions introduced in *each* Congress since 1965, fewer than 5,000 emerged from committee, and of the bills emerging from committee, fewer than 1,000 became law. Committees are clearly the primary graveyard for most bills that die in Congress. Stated positively, committees select from the

Table 3-1 Bills and Public Laws

Congress	Measures Introduced	Reported from Committee	Public Laws
89th (1965-67)	26,566	4,200	810
90th (1967-69)	29,133	3,657	640
91st (1969-71)	29,041	3,250	695
92nd (1971-73)	25,354	2,703	607
93rd (1973-75)	26,222	2,787	649
94th (1975-77)	24,283	2,870	588

SOURCE: Final Daily Digest of the appropriate *Congressional Record*. Refers to all public bills and resolutions introduced each Congress.

vast number of bills introduced those that merit further consideration.

The winnowing process that occurs in committee suggests that the thousands of bills introduced in each Congress may be broken down roughly into three categories — bills having so little support that they are ignored and die in committee, uncontroversial bills that are expedited through Congress, and finally, major bills that are generally so controversial that they occupy the major portion of Congress' time.

Bills having little support are usually introduced with no expectation that they will be enacted into law. Members introduce such bills for a variety of reasons — to go on record in support of a given proposal, to satisfy individual constituents or interest groups from the member's district or state, to publicize an issue, to attract media attention, or to fend off criticism during political campaigns. Once a member has introduced a bill, he or she can report "action" and can blame the committee to which the bill has been referred for its failure to proceed. These bills make up a majority of the large number introduced in each Congress.

Uncontroversial bills make up another large group of the measures introduced. Examples of such legislation are bills that authorize construction of statues of public figures, establish university programs in the memory of a senator, rename a national park, or provide staff assistance for the chief justice of the United States Supreme Court. Committees in both chambers have developed rapid procedures for dealing with such measures; and, as we will see in chapters five and seven, these bills generally are passed on the floor without debate in a matter of moments.

MAJOR LEGISLATION

Bills taking up the largest percentage of committee time have some or all of the following characteristics: They are prepared and drafted by executive agencies or by major pressure groups; they are introduced by committee chairmen or other influential members of Congress; they are supported by the majority party leadership; or they deal with issues on which a significant segment of public opinion and the membership of Congress believe that some sort of legislation is required. Bills having these characteristics do not necessarily become law, nor is there any assurance that they will become law in the form in which they were originally introduced. Indeed, opinion over them may be so sharply divided that they do not even emerge from committee. Nevertheless, these are the major bills before Congress each year — bills that affect the wage earner's paycheck (taxes and Social Security) and the consumer's pocketbook (health insurance and natural gas deregulation), bills that are repeatedly brought up at presidential news conferences and covered in the electronic and print media; bills to which Congress, therefore, devotes the largest proportion of its committee and floor time. These bills account for perhaps only a hundred or so of the more than 20,000 introduced in each Congress.

Executive Branch Bills

The president's leadership in the initial stages of the legislative process is pronounced. The administration's legislative proposals are outlined in the president's annual State of the Union address, delivered before a joint session of Congress. In the weeks and months following the address, the president sends to Congress special messages detailing pro-

proposals in specific areas of legislation, such as energy, welfare, and health. Bills containing the administration's programs are drafted in the executive agencies; and members of Congress, usually committee chairmen, are asked to introduce them simultaneously as "companion" bills in both chambers. The Carter administration's 1977 energy proposals were an example of complicated executive proposals that required extended committee consideration, lengthy floor action in the House and the Senate, and protracted negotiation in conference committee.

Bills Introduced by Influential Members

Bills supported by influential members of Congress stand a good chance of receiving attention in committee. In 1977 and 1978, a controversial bill to revise the federal criminal code was the subject of extensive Senate hearings and debate before it finally passed that chamber in January 1978. Its passage can be attributed in large part to the skill and high committee rank of Senator Edward M. Kennedy, D-Mass., and the late Senator John L. McClellan, D-Ark. Both ranked among the top three majority members of the Judiciary Committee, which had jurisdiction over the bill, and Senator McClellan chaired the Judiciary subcommittee that developed the criminal code measure. Both senators worked diligently to develop trade-offs and compromises among liberal and conservative senators that eventually resulted in a winning coalition for the measure.

"Must" Legislation

As legislators, members of Congress may not want to deal with controversial "no-win" public issues such as abortion or gun control. As politicians answering constituent mail, responding to inquiring journalists, and of course, facing reelection, they may not ignore them. Hence, it frequently occurs that members widely agree that legislation must be enacted to deal with a given problem, but are in sharp disagreement over the solution to the problem. Under these circumstances, members work hard to compromise their differences because they believe that some sort of legislation is desirable or unavoidable.

Thus, many of the factors determining the probable route a bill will take are apparent when it is introduced. Bills having little support will be buried in committee. Uncontroversial legislation will move quickly through Congress. Major bills may or may not become law, but command the greatest portion of Congress' time.

REFERRAL OF LEGISLATION

Once a bill is introduced it receives an identifying number. Measures introduced in the House are identified by the letters "H.R." and an accompanying number; Senate bills by the letter "S" and a number. Usually, bills are assigned numbers according to the sequence in which they are introduced. Occasionally, however, members will request the bill clerk to reserve a particular number. During consideration of statehood for Alaska and Hawaii, various bills were introduced as S. 49 or H.R. 50, representing the new states. Some measures are assigned the same number for several Congresses. This is done to avoid confusion among legislators and the public who have grown accustomed to referring to a proposal by its bill number. Informally, bills also come to be known by the names of their sponsors, such as the Humphrey-Hawkins bill.

Bills, with few exceptions, are referred to appropriate committees.[1] The job of referral is formally assigned to the Speaker of the House and the presiding officer of the Senate,[2] but the job is done most of the time on their behalf by the parliamentarians of the House and Senate.[3] Precedent, public laws, and the jurisdictional mandates of the committees as set forth in the rules of the House and Senate determine which committees receive what kinds of bills. Table 3-2, for example, shows the jurisdiction of the House Committee on Education and Labor. The vast majority of referrals are routine. Bills dealing with farm crops are sent to the House Agriculture Committee and the Senate Agriculture, Nutrition and Forestry Committee; tax bills are sent to

Table 3-2 Jurisdiction of House Committee on Education and Labor

1. Measures relating to education and labor generally.
2. Child labor.
3. Columbia Institution for the Deaf, Dumb, and Blind; Howard University; Freedmen's Hospital [Institutions in the District of Columbia].
4. Convict labor and the entry of goods made by convicts into interstate commerce.
5. Labor standards.
6. Labor statistics.
7. Mediation and arbitration of labor disputes.
8. Regulation or prevention of importation of foreign laborers under contract.
9. Food programs for children in schools.
10. United States Employees' Compensation Commission.
11. Vocational rehabilitation.
12. Wages and hours of labor.
13. Welfare of miners.
14. Work incentive programs.

SOURCE: *Constitution, Jefferson's Manual and Rules of the House of Representatives,* H. Doc. No. 94-663, 95th Congress, 1st Session, pp. 362-363.

the House Ways and Means Committee and the Senate Finance Committee; and bills dealing with veterans' benefits are sent to the Veterans' Affairs Committees of each chamber.[4] Thus, most referrals are generally cut-and-dried decisions. The standing committees of both houses are listed on page 56. In the House, members are not permitted to appeal referral decisions to the floor except in the rare instances of erroneous referral; in the Senate, the rules do permit an appeal to the floor for a majority vote, but in fact such appeals do not take place. Differences over referral in the Senate are resolved informally through negotiation prior to introduction of the legislation.

Legislative Drafting and Referral Strategy

Occasionally, opportunities are present to draft a bill in such a fashion that it will be referred to a committee that is likely to act favorably on it. One technique is to draft a bill ambiguously enough so that it could legitimately fall within the jurisdiction of more than one committee — thus presenting the Speaker or the presiding officer with some options in determining referral. The classic example of this occurred with the 1963 civil rights bill, which was drafted somewhat differently for each chamber so that it could be referred to the Judiciary Committee in the House and the Commerce Committee in the Senate. The two committees were chaired respectively by Emanuel Celler, D-N.Y., and Warren Magnuson, D-Wash., strong proponents of the legislation. Opposed to the legislation were Oren Harris, D-Ark., and James O. Eastland, D-Miss., chairmen of the House Interstate and Foreign Commerce Committee and the Senate Judiciary Committee. Careful drafting, therefore, coupled with favorable referral decisions in the House and Senate, prevented the bill from being bogged down in hostile committees.

A more recent example occurred in 1977. Senator Pete V. Domenici, R-N.M., sought legislation imposing fees on barge operators who ship freight on the nation's canals and rivers. These operators had never before paid any waterway charges for using the national network of federally built and maintained locks, dams, and channels. Traditionally, proposals similar to Domenici's had been designated "taxes" and were referred to the Senate Finance Committee, which has jurisdiction over tax legislation, and had killed such measures in the past. In an effort to bypass the Finance Committee, Domenici designated his proposal an "inland waterways charge"; as a result, the bill was referred jointly to the Public Works and Commerce Committees.[5] Senator Domenici, a member of the Public Works subcommittee that began hearings on the waterways bill (the Commerce Committee deferred to the Public Works panel), won Senate passage of the measure in June 1977.

Other examples of successful drafting resulting in a favorable referral could be cited; nevertheless, it is important to understand that these are the exceptions and not the rule. Committees guard their jurisdictional turfs closely, and the parliamentarians know and follow the precedents. It is only

STANDING COMMITTEES

Standing Committees of the Senate

Agriculture, Nutrition and Forestry
Appropriations
Armed Services
Banking, Housing and Urban Affairs
Budget
Commerce, Science and Transportation
Energy and Natural Resources
Environment and Public Works
Finance
Foreign Relations
Governmental Affairs
Human Resources
Judiciary
Rules and Administration
Veterans' Affairs

Standing Committees of the House

Agriculture
Appropriations
Armed Services
Banking, Finance and Urban Affairs
Budget
District of Columbia
Education and Labor
Government Operations
House Administration
Interior and Insular Affairs
International Relations
Interstate and Foreign Commerce
Judiciary
Merchant Marine and Fisheries
Post Office and Civil Service
Public Works and Transportation
Rules
Science and Technology
Small Business
Standards of Official Conduct
Veterans' Affairs
Ways and Means

the rare case of genuine jurisdictional ambiguity that provides an opportunity for the draftsman and referral options for the Speaker and presiding officer of the Senate to bypass one committee in favor of another.

Referral of Legislation to Several Committees

Many bills obviously cut across the jurisdiction of several committees so that it is often difficult for the Speaker or presiding officer to decide where to refer a bill. There are often particular portions of a bill that fall outside the main jurisdiction. And committees will sometimes assert their jurisdiction over bills, refusing to be bypassed on referrals. For example, in 1977 the House Post Office and Civil Service Committee chairman, Robert N. C. Nix, D-Pa., successfully claimed joint jurisdiction of bills dealing with Defense Department and State Department personnel. Both classes of employees were formerly under the almost exclusive control of the Armed Services and International Relations Committees, respectively.

To respond to this complexity, the Senate has long permitted the practice of multiple referral, referring legislation to two or more committees. There are three types of multiple referral: joint referral of a bill concurrently to two or more committees; sequential referral of a bill successively to one committee, then a second, and so on; and split referral of parts of a bill to several committees for consideration of each part. In 1977 more than 90 Senate bills and resolutions were multiply referred.

The Federal Election Campaign Act of 1971, for example, was referred to three Senate committees — Commerce, Finance, and Rules and Administration. A part of the bill dealing with communications went to the Commerce Committee; a second part concerning campaign finance regulation went to the Rules and Administration Committee; the third part, dealing with the Internal Revenue Code, went to the Finance Committee. As agreed by these three committees, after the first committee reported the bill, the other two had 45 days to submit reports on it.

In the Senate, multiple referral is implemented by unanimous consent agreements. In 1977, the Senate authorized multiple referrals upon joint motion of the majority leader and minority leader. That is, when introducing a bill, a senator wishing multiple referral will rise and say: "I ask unanimous consent that my bill be referred to . . . (committee names)." The request is normally granted by the Senate because the senator has generally worked out an agreement previously with all interested parties — committee chairmen, party leaders, and other members concerned about the bill. Thus by the time the bill is introduced, the appropriate bases have been touched and no member is likely to object to the multiple referral.

In the House, until 1975 the precedents dictated that the Speaker could refer a bill to only one committee. Flexibility was injected into the House referral process in 1975 by two changes in the rules. First, the Speaker was permitted to refer a bill to more than one committee through joint, sequential, or split referral. As a consequence, more than 1,000 bills and resolutions were multiply referred in 1977. Second, the Speaker, subject to the approval of the House, was permitted to create ad hoc committees to consider bills that overlap the authority of several committees. Speaker Thomas P. O'Neill, D-Mass., exercised this option in 1977 by creating an Ad Hoc Energy Committee to expedite action on the Carter administration's complex energy proposals. The ad hoc committee was composed of members selected from the five committees — Interstate and Foreign Commerce; Ways and Means; Banking, Finance and Urban Affairs; Government Operations; and Public Works and Transportation — to which separate parts of the energy proposal had been referred. In the Senate, the administration's 1977 energy proposals were referred to the Finance Committee and the Energy and Natural Resources Committee. There is no Senate provision for the creation of ad hoc committees by party leaders.

Several observations may be made about multiple referral. First, because contemporary problems tend to have repercussions in many areas, more and more of the major bills coming before Congress — particularly those in new problem areas — will be candidates for multiple referral. Second, to the extent that multiple referral is chosen as an option, the decentralized nature of congressional decisionmaking is reinforced. Third, every time an additional committee is added to the legislative process, there is one more hurdle for a bill to overcome and additional opportunities for delay, negotiation, compromise, and bargaining. Creative use of ad hoc committees in the House may expedite consideration of important legislation, however.

CONSIDERATION IN COMMITTEE:
AN OVERVIEW

Once a bill has been referred to committee, the committee has several options. It may consider and report the bill, with or without amendments, to the House or Senate. It may rewrite the bill entirely, reject it, or simply refuse to consider it. Failure of a committee to act on a bill is usually equivalent to killing it. The House and Senate rarely reexamine a committee decision to kill a bill. And where a committee does report a bill, the House and Senate generally accept the main thrust of the bill even when they amend the bill on the floor.

There are several reasons for this deference to the decisions of the committee, a practice which one scholar has referred to as the "sanctity of committee decisions."[6] Committee members and their staffs have a high degree of expertise on the subjects within their jurisdiction, and it is at the committee stage that a bill comes under its sharpest congressional scrutiny. It is understandable, therefore, that a bill that has passed the scrutiny of the experts will be given serious consideration by the generalists on the floor of the House and Senate. It is equally true that a committee's decision not to report a bill will generally be respected by the chamber as a whole. After all, if the experts have not chosen to report a bill, why should their decision be second-guessed? Furthermore, since all members of Congress are members of committees and do not wish the decisions of their own committees to be overturned, they will normally reciprocate by not questioning the decisions of other committees. Finally, the general impact of the rules in both chambers (particularly the House) is to "protect the power and prerogatives of the . . . committees . . . by making it very difficult for a bill that does not have committee approval to come to the floor."[7] There

HOUSE INTERSTATE AND
FOREIGN COMMERCE COMMITTEE

Subcommittees:

Communications
Consumer Protection and Finance
Energy and Power
Health and the Environment
Oversight and Investigations
Transportation and Commerce

are procedures, to be examined in chapters four and seven, for overturning committee decisions or even for bypassing committees, but these procedures are rarely employed.

When a committee decides to take up a major bill, its normal procedure is as follows. The bill may be considered by the full committee, but more often the committee chairman assigns the bill to a subcommittee for study and hearings. Subcommittees of one committee, the House Interstate and Foreign Commerce Committee, are listed above.

The subcommittee usually schedules public hearings on the bill, inviting testimony from interested public and private witnesses. After the hearings have ended, the subcommittee meets to "mark up" the bill — that is, to consider line by line and section by section the specific language of the legislation for recommendation to the full committee. The subcommittee may approve the bill unaltered, amend it, rewrite it — or block it altogether. It then reports its recommendations to the full committee. When the full committee receives the bill, it may repeat the subcommittee's procedures, all or in part, or it may simply ratify the action of the subcommittee. If the committee decides to send the bill to the House or Senate, it justifies its actions in a written statement called a *report*, which must accompany the bill.

On a major legislative proposal the entire committee process may stretch over several Congresses, and a new bill (with similar provisions) is introduced at the beginning of each Congress. For example, action on the criminal code revision occurred during three recent Congresses, starting in 1971. Finally, on November 15, 1977, the Senate Judiciary Committee reported the federal Criminal Code Reform Act of 1977. The committee's explanatory report on the bill was more than 1,400 pages, clear testimony to the measure's complexity. On January 30, 1978, the Senate passed the 682-page bill.

On the other hand, the process can be compressed into a very short period of time. For example, the House acted with uncharacteristic speed in 1978 when considering "emergency" legislation to grant federal aid to the states for repair of potholes caused by the harsh winter weather. The bill was introduced in the House February 14. On February 16 a subcommittee of the House Public Works and Transportation Committee held hearings, amended the bill and approved it for full committee action. The full committee approved it that same day, and the House passed it February 21 by a vote of 274-137.

The remainder of this chapter will focus on the key steps in committee consideration of a major bill — hearings, the markup and the report. To simplify analysis, assume — as sometimes happens — that the committee chairman is also the chairman of the subcommittee to which the bill is referred and assume further that the full committee ratifies the subcommittee decision. Because the committee chairman is a central figure in the legislative process, it is first necessary to focus on the chairman's role.

THE ROLE OF THE COMMITTEE CHAIRMAN

To a large extent, the options available to a committee in dealing with a bill are exercised by the chairman, who has wide discretion in establishing the legislative priorities of the committee. The sources of the chairman's authority are many; a brief listing includes control of the committee's legislative agenda, referral of legislation to subcommittees, management of committee funds, and control of the committee staff. The chairman usually has long service on the committee and is likely to be better informed than most other members on issues coming before the committee. Chairmen can use these and other resources to delay, expedite, or modify legislation.

A chairman who opposes a bill can simply refuse to schedule hearings on it until it is too late for final congressional action on the bill. The same result can be achieved by allowing the hearings to drag on interminably. A chairman having strong negative feelings about a bill can instruct the committee staff to "stack" the witnesses testifying on it, asking witnesses holding opposing views to submit statements rather than appear in person.[8] Committee members who will raise dilatory questions or employ obstructive tactics can be recognized before others. And through control of committee funds and the power to hire and fire most committee staffers, the chairman can effectively block action on a bill by directing the staff to disregard it.[9]

A chairman who favors a bill can give it top priority by mobilizing staff resources, compressing the time for hearings and markups, and, in general, encouraging expeditious action by committee members.

Restraints on the Chairman: Reforms of the 1970s

The general picture of the chairman as an almost omnipotent figure has been undergoing modification in the 1970s. Until this decade, the chairman was *the* central figure, holding power equalled only by a few party leaders of great influence such as longtime House Speaker Sam Rayburn (D-Texas 1913-61, Speaker 1940-47, 1949-53, 1955-61) or Senate Majority Leader Lyndon Johnson (D-Texas 1937-61, Majority Leader 1955-61). Since 1970, however, the powers of the chairman have been trimmed under pressure from an increasing number of new members elected to Congress and more senior members who wanted to equalize the distribution of power. Congress approved numerous and fundamental changes that have ended the nearly absolute authority enjoyed by committee chairmen.

In 1970, a change in the House rules limited the authority of a chairman to block legislative action by simply refusing to call a committee meeting. The new rule permitted three committee members to request a meeting in writing. If the chairman refuses, then within seven days of the request, a majority of members can call the meeting. Former Rules Committee Chairman Howard W. Smith, D-Va. (1955-67), had effectively blocked action on the 1957 civil rights bill by leaving Washington reportedly to inspect a "burned barn" on his Virginia farm. Hearing of the incident, Speaker Rayburn said, "I knew Howard Smith would do most anything to block a civil rights bill, but I never suspected he would resort to arson."[10]

The most significant change in the position of the chairman came when both parties modified the long-standing seniority system, the practice of automatically selecting as committee chairman the member of the majority party with the longest continuous service on the committee. Seniority meant that chairmen normally came from safe congressional districts, were repeatedly reelected, and served until their retirement or death. Because many safe districts during the 1950s and 1960s were in the conservative Democratic South, chairmen were often sharply at odds with Democratic presidents, party leaders, and northern Democrats in Congress. Nevertheless, the chairmen could not be removed and used their entrenched positions to block civil rights and social welfare legislation proposed by Democratic administrations.

House Reforms. In 1971, the minority party in the House, the Republicans, made the first assault on seniority when they adopted a policy declaration stating that seniority need not be followed in making committee assignments and required a secret ballot on electing the ranking minority member of the committee. (The ranking member is the most influential member of the minority party in a Senate or House committee. This member's powers include appointment of minority members to subcommittees and control of minority funds and staff. Generally, through seniority, the ranking minority member became committee chairman when there was a shift in party control of a chamber.)

Democrats in 1971 also established the policy that seniority need not be followed in naming committee chairmen and permitted party members to challenge any nominee for chairman through a separate ballot of their party caucus (an organization of House Democrats). The actions emphasized the responsibility of the chairmen to the caucus. Democrats further adopted party rules that said no member could chair more than one subcommittee and that committee chairmen could head no more than one subcommittee within their own committees. Both provisions were designed to create additional committee leadership opportunities for relatively junior members.

House Democrats adopted a subcommittee "bill of rights" in 1973. Powers that had been exercised exclusively by committee chairman were assigned to all Democrats on committees. Thus the Democrats on a committee were given power to select subcommittee chairmen, determine subcommittee jurisdictions, ensure that each subcommittee had an adequate budget, and guarantee each Democrat at least one major subcommittee assignment. Chairmen were also to be required to refer legislation to subcommittees within two weeks of receiving it unless the full committee determined otherwise.

In 1975, Democrats in the House strengthened their procedures for approving committee chairmen. They required all committee chairmen, and even the subcommittee chairmen of the powerful Appropriations Committee, to be elected by secret ballot. In a dramatic move, the Democrats deposed three incumbent committee chairmen. This act demonstrated that chairmen who lost the support of their party colleagues risked losing their coveted posts. Two years later, Democrats voted to oust the incumbent chairman of the Military Construction Appropriations Subcommittee.

Senate Reforms. Reforms since 1970 have also reduced the authority of committee chairmen in the Senate. While there was no dramatic removal of sitting Democratic chairmen, both parties dropped seniority as a basis for automatically determining who would become chairman. In 1975, the Democrats (the majority party) adopted a rule (effective in 1977) requiring a secret ballot on any nominee for committee chairman if one-fifth of the party members in the Senate requested it. In 1973, the Republicans (the minority party) adopted a rule authorizing Republican members of each committee to elect their "ranking member" subject to ratification by all Senate Republicans.

In other important changes since 1970, the Senate has generally restricted the opportunities for senior members to monopolize key positions. In 1970, members were restricted to service on only one of the four "elite" committees: Appropriations, Armed Services, Finance, and Foreign Relations. In 1971, the Republicans adopted a rule permitting a party member to be a ranking minority member of only one committee. And in 1977, the Senate adopted a rule, effective in 1979, prohibiting a committee chairman from serving as chairman of more than two subcommittees.

The Senate reforms have been designed to allow junior members to obtain leadership positions on important subcommittees. These changes reinforce a characteristic of the Senate that was stressed in chapter 1: power has always been more evenly distributed in the Senate than in the House. The trend of the 1970s is a further diffusion of power from committee chairmen to subcommittees and to individual members of the Senate.

The Chairman in Perspective

Changes in the power structure of congressional committees in the 1970s have clearly chipped away at the power of House and Senate committee chairmen. By and large, one-person rule is being replaced increasingly by bargaining and negotiation between committee chairmen and committee members, particularly chairmen of subcommittees. Some observers contend that Congress is no longer "committee government" but subcommittee government.

Nevertheless, the committee chairman remains a crucial figure in the legislative process. Congressional decisionmaking may be becoming increasingly decentralized within the committee; but as long as Congress functions primarily through its committees, the person who heads one has considerable influence over the advancement or the defeat of legislation. "There is no doubt he runs that committee," commented a Finance Committee member about his chairman, Senator Russell B. Long, D-La.[11]

HEARINGS

Purpose of Hearings

Ostensibly, hearings are primarily important as fact-finding instruments. Witnesses from the executive branch, interested members of Congress, interest group representatives, academic experts, and interested citizens appear before the committee to inform it of the merits or pitfalls of a given piece of legislation. From this encounter the committee members gather the information needed to act as informed lawmakers. The box on page 67 lists Senate committee witnesses testifying on regulation of air transport in 1977.

Much of this information, however, is available to committee members long before the hearings take place. Major bills have been the subject of public debate and coverage in the media. The positions of the administration and the pressure groups are well known, and, in all likelihood, executive branch officials and pressure group lobbyists have already presented their views to committee members well in advance of the hearings. The members themselves often have strong partisan positions on the legislation and thus may have little interest in whatever additional information emerges from the hearings.[12]

Hearings can become perfunctory, particularly where similar legislation has been before the committee for several years in succession. Witnesses usually read from prepared texts while the committee members present often feign interest or simply look bored until the statement has been read. Once the testimony has been read, each committee member, usually in order of seniority, will ask the witness questions. House rules allot at least five minutes per member to question witnesses. Senate rules have no such provision. Instead, each committee establishes its own rules governing internal procedures. For example, the rules of the Senate Energy and Natural Resources Committee limit members to five minutes in the questioning of witnesses until all members have had an opportunity to ask questions.

COMMITTEE WITNESSES

The following list was selected from a roster of more than 40 witnesses who testified during hearings on regulatory reform of air transport held by the Aviation Subcommittee of the Senate Commerce, Science and Transportation Committee in March 1977:

W. Michael Blumenthal, secretary of the treasury
Frank Borman, president, Eastern Airlines
Raul H. Castro, governor of Arizona
Mimi Cutler, director, Aviation Consumer Action Project
Edward J. Driscoll, president, National Air Carrier Assn.
Edward M. Kennedy, Senator, D-Mass.
James A. Miller, president, American Society of Travel Agents
James C. Miller III, Center for the Study of Government Regulation, American Enterprise Institute for Public Policy Research
Ralph Nader, consumer advocate
John E. Robson, chairman, Civil Aeronautics Board
Charles L. Schultze, chairman, Council of Economic Advisers
William T. Seawell, chairman, Pan American World Airways
Frederick J. Stephenson, assistant professor of transportation and business logistics, Northwestern University
Norman Weintraub, research director, International Brotherhood of Teamsters

The traditional format for questioning witnesses in the House and Senate does not lend itself to opportunities for extended exchanges between members and witnesses, analysis of different points of view, or in-depth probing of one witness's views by another. However, this is changing as numerous committees today structure their hearings to ensure that conflicting viewpoints are heard. Committees often hold panel sessions where members and witnesses of different persuasions sit in roundtable fashion to discuss the merits of public policies.

Despite their limitations, hearings remain an integral part of the legislative process. They provide a permanent public record of the positions of the various groups on a legislative proposal, and preparation of congressional testimony is regarded as an important function by executive agencies and interest groups. Above all, hearings are important because members of Congress believe them to be important. The decision to hold hearings is a critical point in the life of a bill. Seldom is a measure considered on the floor without first being the subject of hearings. The sanctity of the committee decision is based on the assumption that the experts in committee have carefully scrutinized a proposal. Hearings provide a demonstrable record of that scrutiny.

"Hearings can really count," declared Representative John Brademas, D-Ind.[13] They are part of any overall strategy to get bills enacted into law. Committee members and staff typically plan with care who should testify, when, and on what issues. Ralph Nader's testimony before several congressional committees on his 1965 best-selling book, *Unsafe at Any Speed*, led to passage of the Traffic Safety Act of 1966. More recently, the Carter administration's top economic experts testified before six House and Senate committees during a nine-day period in 1977 urging passage of a $31 billion economic stimulus program. Their "road show" helped to enact economic legislation.

Hearings serve other functions as well: They may be used to generate public support or opposition to a bill, to assess the capabilities of an executive agency official, to publicize the role of politically ambitious committee chairmen and members, to allow citizens to express their views to their representatives, and to investigate problems and issues.

Investigation is a key power of the Congress. Investigative hearings serve several purposes. They promote efficient program administration, secure information needed to legislate, and inform public opinion. Practically every American household watched on television the unfolding drama of the 1954 Army-McCarthy hearings, the 1957 hearings into corruption of the Teamsters union, the Senate Foreign Relations Committee's hearings during the 1960s on the Vietnam War, and the Watergate hearings of the 1970s. These investigative hearings often prompted the introduction of bills to deal with the problems uncovered and led to subsequent legislative hearings on those measures. On occasion, individual members conduct ad hoc or "informal" investigative hearings of their own.

Strategic Timing

The chairman's control over the timing and duration of hearings is an important resource in determining the fate of a bill. Postponing or dragging out hearings is an obvious ploy if the chairman is opposed to a bill or wants it extensively modified. There are times, however, when a delay in hearings will help the bill survive. This might be true if sentiment in favor of the bill is much stronger in the other chamber than in the chairman's. For example, the House Judiciary Committee waited for the Senate to act first on the Criminal Code Reform Act. Senator Edward M. Kennedy, D-Mass., said he "hoped the lopsided Senate vote (72 to 15) would boost the bill's chances in the House," where its fate was uncertain.[14]

Another possibility is that both House *and* Senate chairmen supporting a bill may want to expedite hearings because of time pressures. For example, House Education Subcommittee Chairman John Brademas, D-Ind., moved quickly in 1970 to hold hearings on an environmental education measure. Hearings began in March and were completed by the end of May. However, that left only six months to pass the bill in the House, get it through the Senate, into conference, back to each chamber for final approval, and to the president for his signature, all in a busy election year.

Representative Brademas' key supporter in the Senate was Senator Gaylord Nelson, D-Wis., who sponsored the bill there and conducted hearings on it. Their strategy "called for a maximum of cooperation between [them] and their staffs to allow them to take advantage of all the opportunities that might become available to speed the passage of the bill."[15] For example, Representative Brademas held 13 days of hearings on the measure and developed an extensive public record. There was no need to duplicate these hearings in the Senate. Senator Nelson conducted only two days of hearings. The result of this cooperative effort by the two chairmen was passage of the Environmental Education Act of 1970 one month before the November elections.

In short, committee chairmen take into account a variety of factors when scheduling hearings. Among the more important are the positions of the White House, pressure groups, executive agencies, the other chamber, and key legislators; the climate of public opinion; the intensity of feeling of principal participants; and the mix of witnesses that can create momentum and support for legislation.

THE MARKUP

Purposes of the Markup

At the conclusion of the hearings, the committee or subcommittee meets to "mark up" the bill. The chairman's task is to keep the committee moving, getting unanimous agreement on some sections of the bill, trying to resolve differences through compromise, and sensing when to delay or expedite matters. Because the chairman will likely be responsible for the bill on the floor and direct the debate, he or she will try throughout the markup to gather as much support within the committee as possible. A sharp split among the committee members of the same party will seriously damage the chances for the bill on the floor. A graphic description of the markup process was given in 1962 by Representative Clem W. Miller, D-Calif. (1959-62):

> The committee staff has a proprietary interest in our bill. The bill we went to hearing with was probably its creature to begin with. Its details were worked out in conferences with the executive department "downtown." The staff knows every byway in the bill, has hedged against every technical problem. . . .
>
> What we are seeking is maximum majority support at markup time. The hostility of the [subcommittee] chairman is almost fatal and division between the Majority members almost equally so. . . .
>
> After hearings, to be sure of some unity, the subcommittee chairman calls a meeting of Majority members to look over some possible changes in the bill. The Chairman insists on informality. It is a "discussion." Nothing is to be "final." Your "ideas" are sought. One member wants a much tougher section in one part of the bill. There is a chance of agreement. The staff had anticipated this with some appropriate language. Another member, not primed by a staff man, throws out an innocent suggestion which it turns out the Chairman is most opposed to. The "suggestion" is permanently shelved.

Quickly the friction points are reviewed, and assent is secured for our Majority position. We are now ready for the executive session of the full subcommittee, the marking up with a united front. . . .[16]

The Minority function at the subcommittee markup is to test every major segment of the bill, looking for weakness. One member leads off with a challenge to the whole bill. He has a substitute which is disposed of in a second. Then the bill is read, line by line. At the appropriate places, the Majority amendments are offered. There is some discussion. Staff members hover behind members, counseling in whispers. A vote is taken and the clerk reads on.

At step after step the Minority amendments are offered. The attitude is off-hand and perfunctory. If a glimmer of interest or a shade of response is elicited from the Majority side, the proposal is pressed. One amendment does seem reasonable. A word or two is said in its behalf. The chairman stirs about unhappily, seeing an opening wedge in Majority unity. It is disposed of, but the restlessness is noted for future exploitation by the Minority in full committee and on the Floor. Finally, the bill has been read. The disagreements — first among Democrats, then between Democrats and Republicans — have resulted in much new language, changing the shape of the bill, accommodating to our needs.[17]

The markup, then, is where committee members redraft portions of the bill, attempt to insert new provisions and delete others, bargain over final language, and, in general, determine the final committee product. If committees significantly revise legislation, they may report a "clean bill" with a new bill number.

Strategies During the Markup

Members use various strategies during the markup. One ploy, sometimes used by opponents of a bill, is to add amendments to *strengthen* the bill. During markup of a gun control measure by the House Judiciary Committee in 1976, the National Rifle Association, the major lobbying group opposing gun control, told its supporters in Congress that it would be easier to defeat a strong firearms proposal. "The way we look at it," said an NRA lobbyist, "the stronger the bill that comes out of committee, the less chance it has of passing on the floor."[18] Conversely, proponents of a strong bill might try to *weaken* it in committee so that it stands a better chance of passing on the floor. Supporters can then try to persuade the other chamber or the conference committee to strengthen the measure.

Another approach used by a bill's opponent is to offer a flurry of amendments to make a bill complicated, confusing and unworkable for the executive branch agencies that will have responsibility for administering the law. "We've passed so many amendments," declared a member during the 1976 gun control markup, that "we don't know what's in the bill, and nobody else does either."[19]

In Senate committees, the well-known floor tactic of unlimited debate (the filibuster) can be applied during a markup. In 1977, a filibuster in the Senate Judiciary Committee blocked action for seven weeks on a proposal by Senator Birch Bayh, D-Ind., to abolish the electoral college and replace it with direct presidential election. Opponents of Bayh's proposal finally agreed to permit the committee to vote to report the proposal in return for concessions by Bayh to hold additional hearings on the subject.

Another factor affecting markup strategies in the Senate is that Senate rules permit the consideration of legislation on the floor that has been blocked in committee. In the example above, Bayh could have offered his proposal on the floor as an amendment to almost *any* bill and threatened to do so. The opportunity to offer such *nongermane* amendments on the Senate floor indicates a significant difference between House and Senate committees: Efforts to block legislation in committee are less successful in the Senate than the House. Senate floor procedures provide various ways (examined in chapter seven) to bypass committees if they refuse to report measures. Nevertheless, bypassing a Senate committee occurs infrequently; all senators have an interest in seeing that the prerogatives of their own committees are respected. Thus they will make every effort — as did Bayh and the opponents of his proposal — to resolve their differences within the committee.

Compromise during the markup — and indeed, at any stage of the legislative process — is more likely when the

Table 3-3 Major House-Senate Differences on Introduction, Referral, and Committee Action

House	*Senate*
Bills are dropped in the "hopper."	Bills may be introduced from the floor.
No effective way to challenge the Speaker's (parliamentarian's) referral decisions.	Referrals are subject to appeals from the floor.
The Speaker is granted authority by House rule to refer bills to more than one committee.	Multiple referrals occur by unanimous consent, although the majority leader and minority leader can jointly offer a motion to that effect.
The Speaker is authorized, subject to House approval, to create ad hoc panels to consider legislation.	Neither the majority leader nor presiding officer has authority to create ad hoc panels to process legislation.
Difficult to bypass committee consideration of measures.	Bypassing committee consideration of measures occurs more easily.
Floor is less important for policymaking than committees.	Floor is as important as committees in decisionmaking.

members recognize that some sort of legislation is necessary. Strip mining proposals had been defeated five times prior to 1977 — twice by presidential veto. By 1977, however, it was clear to everyone — members, environmental and energy lobbyists, and the administration — that some kind of strip mining bill had to be enacted. As a result, markup was expedited. "Now industry has recognized that there is going to be a bill," said Morris K. Udall, D-Ariz., chairman of the House Interior and Insular Affairs Committee. "They'll have to live with it, so they're trying to make it a workable bill."[20]

Table 3-3 summarizes several major House-Senate differences on introduction, referral, and committee action.

THE REPORT

Assuming that major differences have been ironed out in the markup, the committee meets to vote the bill out of committee. The chairman then instructs the staff to prepare a report describing the purposes and scope of the bill. The report explains committee action, notes proposed changes in existing law, and usually includes the views of executive branch agencies consulted. Committee members opposing the bill will often submit dissenting minority views. Any committee member may file minority, supplemental, or additional views, which are printed in a back section of the committee report. On a major bill, a report can be more than 1,000 pages long, as noted earlier on the Criminal Code Reform Act.

Reports are directed primarily at members of the House and Senate and seek to persuade the membership to endorse the committee decision when it comes up for a vote on the floor.[21] For many members, or their staff aides, the report is the only document they read before deciding how to vote on an issue. The report is thus the principal formal means of communicating a committee decision to the entire chamber.

Bills voted out of committee unanimously stand a good chance on the floor. A sharply divided committee vote combined with dissenting minority views usually presages an equally sharp dispute on the floor. In 1977, the House Interstate and Foreign Commerce Committee voted 30 to 12 to report a bill requiring tighter tailpipe emission standards on automobiles; the committee had previously rejected a rival proposal on a 21-to-21 tie vote — a proposal fails if it receives a tie vote. This was followed by a heated debate in the House and a close 190-to-202 vote against the committee's position on auto emission standards. The House then adopted an amendment that weakened the car exhaust standards recommended by the committee.

Reports are numbered, by Congress and chamber, in the order in which they are filed with the appropriate clerks of the House and Senate (H Rept 95-1, S Rept 95-1, etc.) Both the reported bill and its accompanying report are then as-

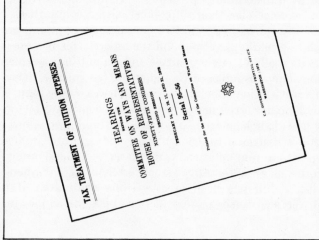

The bill (center), hearings testimony (l), and committee report (r) for a tuition tax credit measure

signed to the appropriate House and Senate calendars to await scheduling for floor action. Chapters four and six discuss the House and Senate calendars and scheduling floor action in each chamber.

SUMMARY

Of the thousands of bills introduced in each Congress, the vast majority have little support and provoke little controversy. Congress appropriately either ignores these measures or rushes them through the legislative process, reserving the bulk of its time for the relatively small number of bills dealing with the nation's major problems and programs.

Once a bill is introduced, it is usually referred to a single committee having jurisdiction over its subject area. In cases of overlapping jurisdiction, a bill may be referred to several committees.

In committee, the critical decision is made to ignore, expedite, or carefully examine a legislative proposal. Since committee members and their staffs have more expertise on matters within their jurisdiction than members of Congress as a whole, the "sanctity of the committee decision" will generally be accepted. The rules and precedents of both chambers reinforce committee prerogatives. Exceptions to these rules exist, but members of Congress are generally reluctant to see the committee system weakened by frequent recourse to extraordinary procedures. Hence, members are encouraged to resolve their differences within committees.

The key stages in committee consideration of a bill are hearings, the markup, voting, and the report. This process is controlled largely by subcommittee and committee chairmen who have many resources at their disposal to expedite, delay, or modify legislation. Chairmen choose tactics on the basis of their assessment of the many political and legislative factors in play and their long-range objectives for the bill. Opportunities for a chairman to act arbitrarily have been trimmed somewhat by recent reforms, particularly the abandonment of seniority as an automatic system for choosing chairmen.

When a bill has been reported from committee, it is ready to be scheduled for floor action. Like the winnowing process that occurs in committee, scheduling involves the budgeting of congressional time. Important political choices are made in determining in which order bills should be taken up on the floor, how much time should be devoted to each measure, and to what extent the full chamber will be permitted to reexamine a committee decision. We take up House scheduling in the next chapter and Senate scheduling in chapter six.

NOTES

1. On rare occasions a member introducing a bill may ask unanimous consent that it be passed. Unanimous consent is more likely to be granted in the Senate and only on a noncontroversial measure.
2. Article I, Section 3 of the Constitution provides that the vice president is president of the Senate, but he infrequently presides over that body. The Constitution also provides for a president pro tempore, a largely honorary position elected by the majority party; the position is usually held by the most senior member of the majority party. Usually, however, junior members of the Senate, designated by the majority leader, preside over the daily sessions of the Senate.
3. Each chamber has a parliamentarian, who is an expert on rules of procedure. The parliamentarians, or one of their assistants, are always present to advise the chair on all points of order and parliamentary inquiries. They also provide technical assistance to members in drafting bills or motions.
4. Committee structure and jurisdiction are not identical in the House and Senate. There are 22 standing committees in the House and 15 in the Senate.
5. *The Washington Post*, March 31, 1977, p. A-1.
6. Randall B. Ripley, *Congress: Process and Policy* (New York: W.W. Norton & Co., 1975), p. 75.
7. *Ibid.*
8. "Stacking" was modified somewhat by the Legislative Reorganization Act of 1970, which permits the minority party on a committee at least one day in which to call witnesses. However, on issues where the two parties share similar views, the opportunities for witnesses who oppose both parties' views to appear is limited.
9. Members of Congress rely heavily on committee staff for assistance in organizing hearings, selecting witnesses, drafting bills and many other key support functions. The chairman's control of

committee staff is therefore an important resource in his control of the legislative process.

10. Richard Bolling, *House Out of Order* (New York: E.P. Dutton & Co., 1965), pp. 85-86.

11. Congressional Quarterly *Weekly Report,* September 10, 1977, p. 1905.

12. Members unable to attend a committee session frequently assign committee staffers to attend the meeting and brief them later. Staff aides can ask questions of witnesses if authorized by the committee rules or the chairman.

13. *The Listener,* August 26, 1976, p. 232.

14. *The Washington Post,* January 31, 1978, p. A1.

15. Dennis W. Brezina and Allen Overmyer, *Congress in Action* (New York: The Free Press, 1974), p. 65.

16. Executive sessions are committee meetings closed to the public. With movement in the 1970s to open committee meetings, most markup sessions are now open to the public.

17. John W. Baker, ed., *Member of the House* (New York: Charles Scribner's Sons, 1962), pp. 13-15.

18. *The Washington Post,* February 6, 1976, p. A6.

19. *Ibid.*

20. Congressional Quarterly *Weekly Report*, April 2, 1977, pp. 608-609.

21. Reports also provide the courts and executive agencies with a detailed explanation of the legislative history and intent of a bill. The explanation gives the courts and agencies some guidance when a bill is enacted into law and becomes the subject of litigation before the courts or interpretation by the agencies.

4

Scheduling Legislation
In the House

Scheduling legislation for floor debate may be simple or complex. As we have seen, relatively few bills ever emerge from committee; for these, legislative priorities are established by the majority leadership — the Speaker, majority leader and majority whip — sometimes in consultation with the minority leader. Numerous factors influence their decisions: House rules, the pressure of national and international events, the substance of committee reports and the actions of the Rules Committee. All these elements interact as legislators, pressure groups, and executive agencies maneuver to put favored legislation on the floor. The Congressional Budget and Impoundment Control Act of 1974 established a rigid timetable for considering money bills.

Scheduling involves many considerations: advance planning of annual recesses and adjournments, coordinating committee and floor activity, providing a predictable weekly agenda of business, and regulating the flow of bills to the floor during slack or peak periods. The procedures for managing the flow of bills to the floor have evolved throughout the history of Congress and still undergo frequent change. At first glance, they may appear needlessly complex and cumbersome, but they have an internal logic and, over the years, have served the needs of the House.

The focus in this chapter is on how bills reach the floor, through one of three basic scheduling procedures: special calendar days for speedy action on minor legislation; privileges (facilitated access to the floor) for certain categories of important legislation; and activities of the Committee on Rules, which is charged with responsibility for scheduling most major legislation.

MINOR AND NONCONTROVERSIAL LEGISLATION

Measures reported from committee are assigned by the parliamentarian (acting for the Speaker) to one of several "calendars." These list bills in the chronological order in which they are reported from the various committees. Legislation dealing with raising or spending money is assigned to the *Union Calendar*. Non-money measures of major importance are put on the *House Calendar*. Noncontroversial measures may appear on either of these, but, at the request of a member, they may be assigned to the *Consent Calendar* or brought to the floor by *suspension of the rules*. Bills dealing with the *District of Columbia* may be brought to the floor on special calendar days. Bills of a private nature — usually dealing with individuals or small groups — are assigned to the *Private Calendar*.

When the House is in session, members receive a daily document, *Calendars of the U.S. House of Representatives and History of Legislation,* shown on page 81, which lists all measures reported from the committees.[1] The document is a handy reference source, but there is no guarantee that the measures it lists will be debated or voted upon.

The Consent Calendar

Noncontroversial measures, such as the provision of a staff assistant for the Chief Justice of the United States, are assigned to the Consent Calendar. A bill assigned to the House or Union Calendars may be transferred to the Consent Calendar at the request of the member who introduced it. The first and third Mondays of the month are Consent Calendar days. Measures must be entered on the Consent Calendar at least three days before consideration by the House. Bills may be amended on motion of the reporting committee.

NINETY-FIFTH CONGRESS

FIRST SESSION { CONVENED JANUARY 4, 1977
{ ADJOURNED DECEMBER 15, 1977
SECOND SESSION { CONVENED JANUARY 19, 1978

CALENDARS
OF THE UNITED STATES
HOUSE OF REPRESENTATIVES
—AND—
HISTORY OF LEGISLATION

LEGISLATIVE DAY 85   CALENDAR DAY 85

Friday, June 16, 1978

HOUSE MEETS AT 10 A.M.

SPECIAL ORDERS

SUPPLEMENTAL APPROPRIATIONS, FEDERAL GRAIN INSPECTION SERVICE — On motion of Mr. Mahon, by unanimous consent, *Ordered*, That it may be in order on Tuesday, June 6, 1978, or any day thereafter, to consider H.J. Res. 944, joint resolution making urgent grain inspection supplemental appropriations for the Department of Agriculture, Federal Grain Inspection Service, for the fiscal year ending Sept. 30, 1978. (*Agreed to May 31, 1978.*)

LEAVE TO ADDRESS HOUSE — On motion of Mr. Evans of Delaware, by unanimous consent, *Ordered*, That on Friday, June 16, 1978, immediately after all legislative business of the day, Mr. Grassley be permitted to address the House for 30 minutes. (*Agreed to June 14, 1978.*)

(SPECIAL ORDERS CONTINUED ON P. 2)

PREPARED UNDER THE DIRECTION OF EDMUND L. HENSHAW, JR., CLERK OF THE HOUSE OF REPRESENTATIVES;

JOHN P. JENKINS, Tally Clerk; MAXINE W. SNOWDEN, JOHN R. GREGORY, Assistant Tally Clerks

Calendars shall be printed daily— } *Index to the Calendars will be printed on Monday of each week the House is in session;*
Rule XIII; clause 6 } *otherwise first day of session thereafter*

U.S. GOVERNMENT PRINTING OFFICE : 1978—O-29-038

There is minimal explanation, if any, and the bills must be passed without objection (i.e., by unanimous consent). A single objection returns the bill to the Calendar for consideration the next Consent Day. If three or more members object when the bill is again called, the bill is stricken from the Consent Calendar for the rest of the congressional session. When members anticipate that objections will be made, they may secure unanimous consent that the bill be "passed over without prejudice" and remain on the Consent Calendar.

The Consent Calendar is supervised by six official "objectors," three members from each party appointed by the majority and minority leaders. Bills are removed from the Consent Calendar by the objectors if they involve expenditures of more than $1 million, if they involve changes in domestic or international policy, or if they appear to be sufficiently controversial or substantive enough to require floor debate. Sponsors of Consent bills are asked to contact the objectors at least 24 hours before Consent Day to clear up questions the objectors may have and to expedite the legislation.

Suspension of the Rules

A legislative short cut is available to all bills, major and minor. By a two-thirds vote, the House may suspend its regular procedural rules for any bill. The vote to suspend the rules is simultaneously a vote to pass the measure in question. Debate is limited to 40 minutes before the vote, and amendments are not permitted. Bills that fail to gain the necessary two-thirds support may be considered again under regular House procedure. By and large, the suspension procedure is used for minor measures, but in the mid-1970s it has come to be used more frequently for important bills.

Until the 94th Congress (1975-77), motions to suspend the rules were in order only during the first and third Mondays of the month (following the call of the Consent Calendar) and during the last six days of a session when the backlog of bills awaiting floor debate is heavy. In 1975 the number of days for suspension of the rules was doubled by adding the first and third Tuesdays. In addition, the House instituted "cluster" voting to save still more time. Under the "cluster" voting rule, the Speaker announces that votes on suspensions will be postponed until later in the day when all can be consecutively voted on during five-minute voting intervals.

In 1977, the suspension rule was changed again — over the objections of many Republicans, to permit the Speaker to entertain motions to suspend the rules every Monday and Tuesday. The Republican minority saw this as an effort by Democrats to steamroll legislation through the House. Representative Bill Frenzel, R-Minn., declared that numerous bills, some important and controversial, are hastily scheduled "under these abnormal, unnecessary, and high-risk procedures."[2] Majority Leader Jim Wright of Texas replied that the change makes "it possible for the business of the House to be facilitated."[3] Democrats, to be sure, were also interested in limiting the ability of the minority party to obstruct the flow of legislation.

The Speaker is in absolute charge of the measures to be considered under the suspension procedures. Committee chairmen, usually with the concurrence of their ranking minority colleagues, write the Speaker requesting that certain bills reported from their panels be taken up via the suspension route. The Speaker may choose whether or not to recognize representatives who wish to offer suspension motions. In 1976, for example, Representative Donald Fraser, D-Minn., authored a proposal, unanimously approved by the International Relations Committee, that criticized the human rights policies of the South and North Korean governments. Fraser wanted the measure considered under suspension of the rules. Speaker Carl Albert refused to recognize Fraser because he considered the measure too controversial.

Major legislation is sometimes passed under suspension of the rules. After the harsh winter of 1977, President Carter asked for emergency powers to meet the nation's energy crisis. "Our people are suffering," the president said, urging quick action.[4] After one day of hearings and a day of markup by the Interstate and Foreign Commerce Committee, the

Table 4-1 The Consent Calendar and Suspension of the Rules

Consent Calendar	*Suspension of the Rules*
1st and 3rd Mondays	Every Monday and Tuesday, and during the last six days of the session
Bills placed on Consent Calendar three days before House consideration	No time limit
Bills may be amended	No amendments; 40 minutes of debate
Official party objectors	No objectors
Ground rules	No limit on substance of bills
Unanimous consent required	Two-thirds of the members voting, a quorum being present, is required to pass a bill

Emergency Natural Gas Act of 1977 was approved by a large majority, under suspension of the rules. But major legislation can also flounder along the suspension route. Late in the 94th Congress, a bill authorizing congressional disapproval of federal agency regulations failed to muster two-thirds support because many members objected to the "consideration of such a far-reaching and controversial bill under the suspension procedure."[5]

Most public measures are enacted either by the consent or suspension procedure. The Consent Calendar and suspension of the rules are compared in Table 4-1.

District of Columbia Legislation

The federal capital is a unique governmental unit. Residents of the District of Columbia have no voting representation in Congress. (They have a nonvoting delegate in the House, and no representation in the Senate.) Only in 1964, subsequent to the 1961 ratification of the 23rd Amendment to the Constitution, did they become eligible to vote in presidential elections.

For decades District residents have pressed hard for "home rule." In 1968, they were permitted an 11-member elected school board. In 1973, President Nixon signed the Charter Act, granting an expanded measure of local autonomy to the D.C. government. The Charter became effective January 2, 1975, following November 1974 elections of a mayor and a 13-member legislative council. Nonetheless, Congress remains constitutionally responsible for managing the affairs of the District. Even under the Home Rule Charter, Congress must approve all D.C. revenue measures.

The House exercises control over the District principally through its standing Committee on the District of Columbia and the Subcommittee on the District of Columbia of the Appropriations Committee. House rules set aside the second and fourth Mondays of each month for District of Columbia legislation. The Speaker usually recognizes the Chairman of the District Committee to call up bills previously reported by his panel. During the 94th Congress, the District Committee reported 15 such measures.

The Private Calendar

Private bills cover a range of purposes. For example, private bills have authorized payment to the family of a CIA agent who died while testing LSD for the agency, waived immigration requirements so a Philadelphia woman could marry a Greek man, and granted citizenship to an 111-year old Albanian woman so that she could vote in one free election before she died.

Under House procedures, the Speaker is required to call private bills on the first Tuesday of each month (unless the rule is dispensed with by a two-thirds vote) and may, at his discretion, consider the Private Calendar on the third Tuesday as well. Bills on the Private Calendar, unlike measures on the House or Union Calendars, are taken up in chronological order.

Few members have the time to review carefully all the private bills reported in each session. That job is done by a committee of "official objectors," composed of three members from each party, appointed by the majority and minority leaders (but these are not the same objectors who review the Consent Calendar). Bills must be placed on the Private Calendar seven days before being called up, to give the objectors time to screen them for controversial provisions. The objectors are on the floor on Private Calendar days to answer questions about the measures. If two or more members of the House object to a bill on the first Tuesday, it is automatically sent back to the reporting committee although, at the request of a member, it may be "passed over without prejudice" for later consideration. On the third Tuesday, the Speaker gives preference to omnibus bills, containing several previously rejected private measures. No objections to omnibus bills are permitted; they are either passed or rejected by the House. Private bills are debated and amended under strict rules.

PRIVILEGED LEGISLATION

Under House rules, six standing committees have direct access to the floor for selected measures. The committees and

Committee	Legislation
Appropriations	General appropriations bills
Budget	Budget resolutions under the Congressional Budget and Impoundment Control Act of 1974
House Administration	Printing resolutions and expenditure of the House contingent fund
Rules	Rules and the order of business
Standards of Official Conduct	Resolutions recommending action with respect to the conduct of a member, officer or employee of the House
Ways and Means	Revenue-raising bills

the types of legislation eligible to be called up for immediate debate are listed on page 86. Most of these bills, however, must observe a waiting period to give members time to read the committee's report; for example, reports on budget resolutions must be available for 10 days before coming to the floor.

Privileged measures are matters of special import to the House as an institution or to the federal government. The Appropriations, Ways and Means, and Budget panels report measures to finance the government; the Standards Committee is concerned with measures involving the public reputation of the House; the House Administration panel handles necessary housekeeping proposals; and the Rules Committee regulates much that the House considers.

Prior to 1974, the Committees on Interior and Insular Affairs, Public Works, and Veterans' Affairs also had privileged access to the floor. This was eliminated by the Committee Reform Amendments of that year in order to narrow the range of bills with a "green light" to the floor. Those remaining are subject to points of order (parliamentary objections) on the floor that may return them to committee. Frequently, committees with privileged access will ask the Rules Committee to waive points of order against their measures. The Committee on Appropriations, for example, occasionally violates the House rule against policy pronouncements in general appropriation measures, and protects its bills by asking the Rules Committee for a waiver on points of order.

MAJOR LEGISLATION

With the exception of privileged bills and occasional measures brought to the floor by suspension of the rules, most major legislation does not go directly from committee to the floor of the House. It is, instead, placed on a calendar, to await action by the House Rules Committee.

The Rules Committee is among the oldest of House panels. The First Congress appointed an 11-member rules group to draw up its procedures in April 1789. Each succeeding

Congress has done the same, although for nearly a century the Rules panel was a select (ad hoc) committee which prepared procedures for the incoming Congress and then went out of existence. In 1858, the Speaker became a member of the Rules Committee and, shortly thereafter, chairman of the panel. In 1880, the Rules Committee became a standing, or permanent, committee, and in 1883 initiated the practice of making special orders, or *rules*, which, when adopted by majority vote of the House, controlled the amount of time allowed for debate on major bills and the extent to which they could be amended on the floor.

From 1858 to 1910, the Speaker determined which bills reached the House floor. Because Speaker Joseph Cannon (Speaker from 1903 to 1911) abused this and other powers, the House "revolted" in 1910 and removed the Speaker from the Rules Committee. The House leadership, however, retained — and still retains, in cooperation with the House Rules Committee — considerable control over the flow of major bills to the floor.

The power of the Rules Committee lies in its scheduling responsibilities. As major bills are reported out of committee, they are entered in chronological order on one of two calendars, the Union Calendar or the House Calendar. The former deals with revenue measures and general appropriation bills. The latter contains all other major bills.

If measures were to be taken up in their calendar order, as was the practice in the early nineteenth century, many major bills would not reach the floor before Congress adjourned. Instead, a major bill reaches the floor in most instances by being granted precedence through a special order (rule) obtained from the Rules Committee. A request for a rule is usually made by the chairman of the committee reporting the bill. The Rules Committee debates the request in the same manner other committees consider legislative matters. The rule is considered on the House floor and voted on in the same fashion as regular bills.

A rule serves two principal purposes. It "bumps" a bill up the ladder of precedence, eliminating the waiting time that would be necessary if chronological order were observed;

and it governs the length of debate permitted on the floor and the extent to which a measure can be amended. The Rules Committee, in effect, shuffles the Union and House Calendars by holding back rules on some bills and reporting them for others.

In blocking or delaying legislation from reaching the floor, the Rules Committee is not necessarily playing an obstructionist role. It may actually be drawing fire away from the leadership, committees, and individual members. It is not uncommon for representatives to request the Rules Committee to prevent unwanted bills from reaching the floor. A former member of the committee, House Speaker Thomas P. O'Neill Jr., D-Mass., has said, "It takes the heat for the rest of the Congress, there is no question about that."[6]

The committee also acts as an informal arbiter of disputes among other House committees. Because of overlapping jurisdictions, one committee may report a measure that trespasses on the authority of another. In such a case, the Rules Committee may resolve the dispute by authorizing the second committee to offer amendments, or by refusing to waive points of order on the floor which may then be used by the second committee to strike the offending matter from the bill.

Powers of the Rules Committee

Because few pieces of major legislation would reach the House floor without a rule, action — or lack of it — by the Rules Committee generally determines whether a bill will be considered at all. The Rules chairman has wide discretion in scheduling the panel's order of business. By not setting a hearing on a rule for a particular bill, the chairman can, in most cases, effectively kill the measure. From 1965 to 1974, the Rules Committee denied hearings on 57 measures; none reached the House floor by other means.

Once hearings are underway, two common delaying techniques are sometimes used: (1) preventing quorums of the committee; and (2) scheduling a parade of witnesses to testify against issuing a rule for the bill.

The first technique involves manipulation of the rules governing a quorum. Opponents of a bill may persuade sympathetic Rules Committee members not to attend committee meetings. The Rules chairman may also either observe or ignore the rules for a quorum. Strict observance of the rules can be an effective delaying tactic. For example, in 1971 Rules Chairman William Colmer, D-Miss., and several Republican members opposed a Civil Service pay bill. During a committee meeting on the bill, Representative Ray Madden, D-Ind., left the session briefly to greet a visiting constituent. A Republican member observed that a quorum was not present. Chairman Colmer did not send for Madden, "who was within voice range in the adjoining hallway," but "promptly adjourned the meeting for lack of a quorum."[7]

In the second strategy, opponents of a bill can line up a series of witnesses to testify against it. Executive agency and pressure group witnesses do not testify at hearings of the Rules Committee that concern the granting of rules. The witness list is confined to legislators interested in the measure, usually the chairman and members of the committee reporting the bill, and legislators opposing it. Committee rules state that all members "will be provided a reasonable opportunity to testify." This provision, honored to the extreme, can open the way to a time-consuming flood of testimony. In 1974, two weeks of hearings were required before the Rules Committee finally granted a rule to a congressional committee reorganization plan.

After holding hearings, the Rules Committee can refuse to grant a rule. From 1965 to 1974, 38 measures were denied rules by committee vote and failed to reach the floor. Even during the voting, there is room for maneuver. The chairman may unexpectedly schedule a vote when certain committee members cannot attend. The Consumer Protection Act of 1970 failed to obtain a rule on a 7-7 tie because Representative Richard Bolling, D-Mo., a supporter of the measure, was out of town. The vote was scheduled on one-day notice, leaving little or no time for Bolling to return. The vote killed further action on consumer legislation in the 91st Congress and not until two years later did such a bill pass the House.

In 1968, the Rules Committee set a specific cutoff date after which no requests for rules would be heard. The policy was initiated by Rules Chairman Colmer and followed by successive committee leaders. Its purpose is to prevent logjams at the end of each session. Emergency and procedural measures are excluded from the cutoff provisions.

Types of Rules

The Rules Committee grants four main types of rules: open, closed, modified closed, and waivers of points of order.

The majority of bills are considered under an *open rule*. Of the 301 rules granted during the 94th Congress, 276 were open. Under an open rule, germane amendments may be offered from the floor. Amendments may be simple or complex. For example, an amendment may extend the funding of a program from two to four years or an amendment may rewrite whole sections of a bill. Open rules also provide a fixed number of hours of debate before amendments are in order.

A *closed rule* prohibits floor amendments, with exceptions occasionally made for the reporting committee, subject to chamber acceptance. Closed rules are rarely invoked; only three were reported during the 94th Congress. Critics say closed rules (also called "gag" rules) hamper the legislative process and violate democratic norms. Supporters of closed rules say they are necessary in the case of very complex measures and bills subject to intense lobbying pressures. In addition, certain national emergency bills need to be expedited by the closed rule procedure.

Tax bills illustrate the pressures surrounding closed rules. For decades the House considered tax measures under closed rules, agreeing with the argument of Wilbur Mills, D-Ark., chairman of the Ways and Means Committee from 1959 to 1974, that tax legislation was too complex and technical to be tampered with on the floor. If there were unlimited floor amendments allowed, Mills said, the internal revenue code would soon be in shambles and at the mercy of pressure groups.

For years, the members trusted the judgment of the Ways and Means Committee, but in the 1970s disenchantment began to set in. In 1973, the Democratic Caucus approved a change in procedures, requiring a committee chairman to give advance notice in the *Congressional Record* of a request for a closed rule. After such notice, a party caucus may be called on request of 50 Democratic members. The caucus discusses amendments and instructs Democrats on the Rules Committee to make those amendments "in order" for House debate.

The new procedure has had a significant impact on major legislation. During the 94th Congress, the Ways and Means Committee wanted to bar all amendments to the Tax Reduction Act of 1975, except one committee amendment. On February 25, 1975, the Democratic Caucus instructed Democrats on the Rules Committee to make in order two amendments, one repealing the oil and gas depletion allowance and the other exempting independent oil producers from the repeal. When the bill came to the floor two days later, the House voted to repeal the depletion allowance, rejected the proposed exemption, and passed the bill.

A third category of special order is the *modified closed rule*, permitting amendments to certain parts of a bill, but not others. The Legislative Reorganization Act of 1970 was considered under a modified closed rule permitting amendments to all parts of the bill except Title I dealing with the committee system. The modified closed rule was invoked to prevent an attempt to split the Committee on Education and Labor into two committees, a move opposed by Democratic members and trade union groups. Three such modified closed rules were granted during the 94th Congress.

Finally, there are *rules waiving points of order*. Under these rules, specific House procedures may be temporarily set aside. Without such waivers, measures in technical violation of House procedures could not be dealt with rapidly, and important parts of bills could be stricken for technical reasons. Waivers are frequently granted to the Committee on Appropriations. Appropriations bills sometimes touch on the jurisdiction of other committees in violation of House rules; waivers permit timely floor action on those measures. Waivers are not granted indiscriminately, and are generally confined to temporary exemptions from specific House procedures. Committee chairmen must "indicate any matter that they want a waiver on that may be subject to a point of order," Rules member Richard Bolling, D-Mo., has said.[8]

There are numerous variations of the four types of rules. Some identify the member who will offer specific amendments. Some accommodate the interests of several committees that have reviewed the same measure. Some permit the House to choose between conflicting proposals. All rules, however, must be approved by a majority of the House.

Rules are reported to the House by the Rules Committee and are debated for a maximum of one hour, with the time equally divided between the Rules Chairman or his designee, and the ranking minority member of the committee, or a designee. If there is no controversy, rules are adopted after a brief discussion. Under a 1977 procedural change, the Speaker may postpone votes on noncontroversial rules and permit them to be voted on at five-minute intervals later in the day. The procedure is similar to cluster voting under suspension of the rules.

The House seldom rejects a rule proposed by the Rules Committee. Speaker Thomas P. O'Neill Jr. once remarked, "Defeat of a rule on the House floor is considered an affront both to the [Rules] Committee and to the Speaker."[9] The Rules Committee generally understands the conditions the House will accept for debating and amending important bills. Only three of the 301 rules granted were rejected during the 94th Congress. One was a rule on a bill proposing federal loans for new energy technologies. Only a few days remained in the session, the measure had previously been turned down, several committees claimed jurisdiction, and confusion and controversy surrounded the bill. Such factors are usually involved when the House defeats a rule.

Changes in the Rules Committee

The Rules Committee, according to Representative Bolling, is "specifically designed to function as the responsible agent of the majority party, using its great discretionary authority over pending legislation to facilitate the consideration and adoption of the majority party's program."[10] As the agent of the majority party, the committee has generally come under the influence of the Speaker of the House.

It has not always worked this way, however. There have been "maverick" Rules chairmen. One of the best known was Howard W. Smith, D-Va., who presided over the committee with an iron hand from 1955 to 1967. Smith was no "traffic cop," simply regulating the flow of bills to the floor. He firmly believed the committee should "consider the substance and merits of the bills," and he often blocked measures he disapproved of and advanced those he favored, sometimes thwarting the will of the majority.[11]

The Rules Committee lacks authority to amend bills, but it can bargain for changes in return for rules. Smith frequently did this. To lessen his power and that of the conservative coalition of southern Democrats and Republicans that controlled the committee from the mid-1930s to the early 1960s, the House adopted a series of changes after World War II. These included several versions of the "21-day rule" and the 1961 enlargement of the committee.

First adopted in 1949 but revoked in 1951, the 21-day rule stipulated that if legislation had been before the Rules Committee for 21 days without being cleared for floor debate, the Speaker was obligated to recognize chairmen of the reporting committees to call up the stalled measures on the second and fourth Mondays of each month. The rule was resurrected in modified form in 1965 and was employed eight times during the 89th Congress, but was rescinded at the start of the next Congress. Some committee chairmen were accused of playing "both ends against the middle," by requesting a rule from the Rules Committee and simultaneously asking the Speaker to invoke the 21-day rule. The defeat in the 1966 Democratic primary of Rules Chairman Smith reduced the pressure for the 21-day rule. The House considered a 31-day rule in 1971, but rejected it 233 to 152.

Smith and the Rules Committee were still formidable obstacles at the beginning of the Kennedy administration in 1961. The two top Democrats on the committee regularly joined with the four Republican members to produce a 6-6 deadlock and prevent administration-sponsored bills from reaching the floor.

House Speaker Sam Rayburn, D-Texas, hit on the strategy of enlarging the Rules Committee membership from 12 to 15, adding two Democrats and one Republican member to weaken the conservative coalition. After a bruising legislative battle, the House approved the plan 217 to 212. Although critics called the move "committee packing," the enlargement was made permanent in 1963. Subsequently, a further enlargement took place; the committee's present composition is 11 Democrats and 5 Republicans.

The Speaker and the Rules Committee

The Rules Committee is no longer the independent fiefdom it was in the heyday of Chairman Smith; by the 95th Congress, the committee was closely tied to the Speaker and the Democratic Caucus.

Dormant for decades, the Democratic Caucus began to stir at the end of the 1960s. Starting in 1971, the caucus initiated procedures for secret ballot to elect committee chairmen, including the chairman of the Rules Committee. In January 1975, the caucus turned out three long-standing committee chairmen, replacing them with less senior members. At the same time, the Speaker was authorized to appoint, subject to caucus ratification, the 11 majority members of the Rules Committee.

Taken together, these actions have reduced the Rules panel's independence. The committee can still oppose the Speaker and sometimes — but not often — does. In 1977, several Democrats on the Rules Committee opposed parts of an ethics proposal favored by Speaker O'Neill. According to some observers, Speaker O'Neill handled the opposition as follows:

> O'Neill invited the Rules Committee Democrats to breakfast, at which he pounded the table, demanding their cooperation. They were not convinced. Next day, O'Neill got tougher. They were all his personal friends, O'Neill said, but by God they would find themselves on the District of Columbia Committee next year if they failed him on this one.[12]

Although the Rules Committee granted the rule requested by the Speaker in this case, the power of the committee should not be underestimated. The Speaker cannot track every major and minor bill. The caucus cannot convene to issue instructions each week. The history of the Rules Committee is "one of the committee's accommodating the leadership on the one hand and seeking independent status on the other."[13] For the time being, at least, the emphasis is on sharing power with the Speaker, the leadership, and the committee chairmen.

LEGISLATION BLOCKED IN COMMITTEE

What happens when a standing committee refuses to report a bill that many members support, or the Rules Committee does not grant a rule? Several procedures are available to bring unreported legislation to the floor. Which procedure is used depends on the nature of the legislation. Consent procedures and suspension of the rules, discussed earlier, are appropriate if the unreported measure is relatively uncontroversial or minor.

If, however, a major bill is blocked in a standing committee or in the Rules Committee, there are extraordinary procedures which can be employed to "spring" the bill from committee. These procedures are difficult to implement, but if the House is determined, committees can be compelled to yield legislation.

Legislation Stalled in a Standing Committee

The Discharge Petition. The discharge rule, adopted in 1910, provides that if a bill has been before a standing committee for 30 days, any member can introduce a motion to relieve the panel of its control over the measure. An appropriate clerk of the House then prepares a discharge petition, which is made available for members to sign when the House is in session. The names are not disclosed until the required 218 signatures (a majority of the 435-member House) are obtained. The names are then published in the *Congressional Record*. A member may withdraw his or her signature any time before the majority is secured.

When 218 members have signed the petition, the measure is put on the Discharge Calendar, where it is privileged business on the second and fourth Mondays of the month (but not during the last six days of a session). After the measure has been on the Discharge Calendar for seven days, any member who signed the petition may be recognized to offer a discharge motion. When a motion is offered, debate is limited to 20 minutes, divided between proponents and opponents. If the Discharge Motion is rejected, the bill is not eligible for discharge that session. If the motion prevails, any signer of the petition can move the bill's immediate consideration. It then becomes the business of the House until finally disposed of. A vote against immediate consideration assigns the bill to the appropriate calendar with the same rights as any bill reported from committee.

Few measures are ever discharged from committee. From 1909 to 1975, 860 discharge petitions were filed in the House; only 25 bills were actually discharged. Of those, 20 passed the House and only two became law: the Fair Labor Standards Act of 1938 and the Federal Pay Raise Act of 1960. Several factors account for this. Members are reluctant to second guess a committee's right to consider a bill. The discharge rule violates normal legislative routine and even members who support a bill may refuse to sign a discharge petition for this reason.

Legislators are also reluctant to write legislation on the floor without the guidance of committee hearings and reports. Particularly in the case of complicated legislation, many feel the need for committee interpretation. Then, too, it is not easy to obtain 218 signatures. Attempts to reduce the present requirement are regularly made, but none have been successful. Finally, members are hesitant to employ a procedure that may be used against committees on which they serve.

For all its limitations, the discharge rule serves important purposes. It focuses attention on particular issues; the threat of using it may stimulate a committee to report a bill. For some members, a discharge motion can demonstrate to constituents and pressure groups that an effort is being made to get an important measure to the floor. In 1975, for example, when school busing was a burning issue in her suburban Maryland district, Republican Marjorie Holt made several well-publicized, but unsuccessful attempts to discharge the Judiciary Committee of a controversial measure involving the busing of school children.

Rules Committee's Power of Extraction. The Rules Committee has an extraordinary authority that it rarely exercises: it can introduce rules for bills not yet reported by standing committees. The power of extraction is based on an 1895 precedent, which the committee has invoked only four times in the past three decades. Extraction is a highly controversial procedure and evokes charges of usurpation by the Rules panel of committee rights.

For example, it was used on February 9, 1972. The Committee on Education and Labor refused to report a dock strike measure, but the Rules Committee reported a rule to the floor anyway. With Speaker Albert in vigorous opposition, the House adopted the rule 203 to 170 and then enacted the bill. The threat of extraction in itself can break legislative logjams. In 1967, the Judiciary Committee balked at reporting an anti-riot bill. Rules Chairman Colmer announced that his committee would soon hold hearings on a rule for the bill; this was enough to prompt the Judiciary Committee to report the bill.[14]

Legislation Blocked by the Rules Committee

Discharging the Rules Committee. The discharge rule, with several variations, also applies to the Rules Committee, with one significant difference: a motion to discharge the Rules Committee is in order seven days, rather than 30 days, after a measure has been before that panel. Any member may enter the motion, which is handled like any other discharge petition in the House. If the required 218 signatures are secured, the House votes on the special order for consideration of the bill. The Rules Committee was last discharged on September 27, 1965, on a D.C. home rule proposal.

Calendar Wednesday. Every Wednesday is reserved for standing committees to call up measures (except privileged bills) that have been reported but held in the Rules Committee. The Speaker calls the roll of standing committees in alphabetical order; the chairmen (or designated members) either pass or bring up for House debate measures pending on the House or Union Calendars. The rule may be dispensed with by unanimous consent (i.e., without objection) or by a two-thirds vote of the House.

The Calendar Wednesday rule was adopted in 1909 to circumvent the scheduling power of Speaker Joseph Cannon. Today it is rarely used and is usually dispensed with by unanimous consent. In fact, it has been successful only on two occasions: the 1950 Fair Employment Practices Act and the 1960 Area Redevelopment Act. Four factors account for the limited use of this procedure. First, only two hours of debate are permitted, one for proponents and one for opponents. This may not be enough for complex bills. Second, a committee far down in the alphabet might have to wait weeks before its turn is reached. Third, a bill that fails on one Wednesday is not in order the following Wednesday, unless two-thirds of the members agree. Finally, the procedure is subject to dilatory tactics that stubborn minorities can use to forestall action.

In short, the Rules Committee performs a valuable service by assuring the orderly consideration of legislation. Although it generally works with the majority leadership, the committee can and sometimes does act contrary to its wishes and to the will of the House as a whole. Its actions in preventing or delaying bills from reaching the floor, or in negotiating changes in return for a rule, have led to periodic efforts to curb the committee's power. But the House is unlikely to endorse another mechanism to perform its functions. As recently as 1974, the House refused to bypass the Rules Committee by authorizing the Speaker to recognize committee chairmen to propose rules for their own bills.

FINAL SCHEDULING STEPS

After a bill has been granted a rule, the final decision on when it is to be debated is made by the majority leadership.

The leadership prepares daily and weekly schedules of floor debate, and adjusts them according to shifting legislative situations. A bill scheduled for debate may be withdrawn if it appears to lack sufficient support. President Carter's proposal to permit voter registration on election day, scheduled for May 1977 debate, was withdrawn when the majority leadership found only lukewarm support for it.

Nothing in House rules requires the majority leadership to provide advance notice of the daily or weekly legislative program. This is done as a matter of long-standing custom, in two principal ways. Floor announcements are made by majority party leaders, often in response to a query from the minority leader. The legislative program for each day is also printed in the *Congressional Record* in a section called "The Daily Digest." The Friday issue contains the "Congressional Program Ahead," which lists the following week's scheduled activities.

The majority leadership also sends "whip notices" to its members each week, or more frequently, if necessary. The whip notices describe the measures to be taken up each day. Although sent under the majority whip's signature, they are prepared mainly by the Speaker and majority leader. The schedule is often changed in response to unforeseen events or new circumstances. An example of a whip notice is on page 101.

The majority whip's office has several phone recordings describing the daily and weekly programs, actions taken on the floor, and changes in the schedule. Democratic and Republican members obtain similar information from their respective cloakrooms (located just off the chamber floor). The majority whip prepares one-page summaries of pending bills, called "Whip Advisories," and publishes "Whip Issue Papers," that describe activities of the House on one or more major issues. The minority whip prepares a weekly notice of floor business for all its members. The minority caucus publishes, each week, summaries of bills to be considered on the floor and the minority leader prepares "Legislative Alerts" for party colleagues highlighting measures reported from the committees.

JOHN BRADEMAS
INDIANA
MAJORITY WHIP

CHIEF DEPUTY WHIP
DAN ROSTENKOWSKI
ILLINOIS

DEPUTY WHIPS
BENJAMIN S. ROSENTHAL
NEW YORK
BILL ALEXANDER
ARKANSAS
GEORGE E. DANIELSON
CALIFORNIA

Congress of the United States
House of Representatives
Office of the Majority Whip
Washington, D.C. 20515

225-5604

May 5, 1978

WHIP NOTICE INFORMATION
Legislative Program — 51600
Floor Information — 57400
Whip Information — 55606

My dear Colleague:

The program for the House of Representatives for the Week of May 8, 1978 is as follows:

MONDAY

HOUSE MEETS AT NOON
District (No Bills)
Suspensions (6 Bills)

VOTES ON SUSPENSIONS WILL BE POSTPONED UNTIL END OF ALL SUSPENSIONS
1. H.R. 12481 — Omnibus Territories Authorization Act
2. H.R. 1920 — Refund Excise Tax on Alcoholic Beverages Destroyed by Vandalism
3. H.R. 2852 — Refund Excise Tax on Aerial Applicators Fuels
4. H.R. 2984 — Exempt Certain Trailers from Excise Tax
5. H.R. 6503 — Intercoastal Shipping Act Amendments
6. H.Con.Res. 583 — American MIA's in Southeast Asia

H.J. Res. 873 — Supplemental Appropriations for SBA Emergency Disaster Loans

TUESDAY

HOUSE MEETS AT NOON
Suspensions (2 Bills)

VOTES ON SUSPENSIONS WILL BE POSTPONED UNTIL END OF ALL SUSPENSIONS
1. S.J. Res. 4 — Hawaiian Native Claims Study
2. H.R. 11998 — Insulation Safety Standards

H.Con.Res. 559 — Budget for the United States Government for FY'79
(COMPLETE CONSIDERATION)

WEDNESDAY

HOUSE MEETS AT 3 p.m.

H.R. 12222 — International Development and Food Assistance Act of 1978, Authorizations
(OPEN RULE, ONE HOUR)

H.R. 12157 — To Amend and Extend the Export-Import Bank Act
(SUBJECT TO A RULE BEING GRANTED)

THURSDAY

HOUSE MEETS AT 11 a.m.

H.R. 11686 — Department of Energy National Security Authorizations, FY '79
(SUBJECT TO A RULE BEING GRANTED)

H.R. 7814 — Flexible and Compressed Work Schedules for Federal Employees
(OPEN RULE, ONE HOUR)

FRIDAY

HOUSE MEETS AT 11 a.m.

H.R. 11291 — Fire Prevention and Control Act
(OPEN RULE, ONE HOUR)

H.R. 9400 — Civil Rights of Institutionalized Persons
(COMPLETE CONSIDERATION)

THE HOUSE WILL ADJOURN BY 3 p.m. ON FRIDAYS AND BY 5:30 p.m. ON
ALL OTHER DAYS EXCEPT WEDNESDAYS

********** CONFERENCE REPORTS MAY BE BROUGHT UP AT ANY TIME **********
ANY FURTHER PROGRAM WILL BE ANNOUNCED LATER

Sincerely,

John Brademas
Majority Whip

SUMMARY

Scheduling is a party function that is shared by the majority leadership and the Rules Committee. Bills reported from committees are assigned to one of several calendars (or are brought to the floor under suspension of the rules). Most bills must then receive a rule, granted by the Rules Committee, specifying the bill's priority and the conditions under which it will be considered on the House floor. Although they are seldom employed, there are special procedures to dislodge bills that are locked in either a standing committee or the Rules Committee.

Outside events and pressures often influence the timing of floor consideration. The approach of elections can be a critical factor in scheduling controversial bills. And the congressional work load is taken into consideration.

Bargaining and compromise are necessary at each stage of the scheduling process. Members, pressure groups, and executive officials all try to influence the shaping of the House agenda. Their efforts are directed principally to the Rules Committee and the majority leadership. Once an important proposal is granted a rule and placed on the House schedule by the Speaker, the focus shifts to the intricacies of floor procedure.

NOTES

1. *Calendars of the United States House of Representatives and History of Legislation* also contains short summaries of bills, the title of measures that have become public law, bills in and through conference committees, and measures that were vetoed by the president.
2. U.S. Congress, House, *Congressional Record*, 94th Cong., 2d sess., September 20, 1976, 122, H10469.
3. U.S. Congress, House, *Congressional Record*, 95th Cong., 1st sess., January 4, 1977, 123, H18.
4. Congressional Quarterly *Weekly Report*, February 5, 1977, p. 191.
5. U.S. Congress, House, *Congressional Record*, 94th Cong., 2d sess., September 21, 1976, 122, H10689-H10690.
6. Spark Matsunaga and Ping Chen, *Rulemakers of the House* (Urbana, Ill.; University of Illinois Press, 1976), p. 21.

7. *Ibid.,* p. 98.
8. U.S. Congress, House, *Congressional Record,* 93rd Cong., 1st sess., June 26, 1973, 119, H5375.
9. Congressional Quarterly *Weekly Report,* February 14, 1976, p. 313.
10. Richard Bolling, "The House Rules Committee," University of Missouri *Business and Government Review* (September-October 1961), p. 39.
11. *Nation's Business,* February 1956, p. 103.
12. *The Washington Post,* March 8, 1977, p. A1.
13. Matsunaga and Chen, *Rulemakers of the House,* p. 143.
14. *Ibid.,* p. 25.

5

House Floor Procedure

To a casual observer, the House floor may appear hopelessly disorganized. Legislators talk in small groups or read newspapers while a colleague drones on. People come and go in an endless stream. Motions are offered, amendments proposed, points of order raised — all evoking little apparent interest from the members present. The scene may not make much sense to visitors in the gallery.

If the visitors are there to see their representatives in action, they are likely to be disappointed. Attendance is often sparse during floor debate. Members may be in committee, meeting with constituents, or attending to numerous other tasks. Members can reach the floor quickly, however, to respond to quorum calls, participate in debate, or vote.

The House chamber has two levels. Above the floor itself are the galleries for visitors, diplomats, the press, and other observers. Visitors sit to the side or facing the Speaker's rostrum; the press sits above and behind. Unlike senators, representatives have no desks in the chamber. Their seats, which are unassigned, are arranged in semicircular rows in front of the Speaker. Aisles divide groups of seats, and a broad center aisle divides the majority and minority parties. Traditionally, the Democrats sit to the Speaker's right, the Republicans to the left. When a majority of the 435 members are present, as for a recorded vote, the floor becomes alive with activity.

Normally, the House convenes daily at noon.¹ Buzzers ring in committee rooms, members' offices, and in the Capitol, summoning representatives to the floor. Rules and procedures set the daily order of business: an opening prayer, approval of the *Journal* (a record of the last day's proceedings), receipt of messages from the Senate or the president, one-minute speeches and insertions in the *Congressional Record*, and other routine business.

Formally, a majority of the House (218 members) must be present for business to be conducted. Once a quorum has been established — usually at the beginning of the session — it is considered to be present until challenged by any member. A member may ask for a quorum call, provided he or she is recognized for that purpose by the Speaker. Informally, the House frequently operates with far fewer members.

The House is usually in session Monday to Friday. Mondays are mainly reserved for routine legislation. Fridays are generally light in workload because many members want to return to their home districts over the weekend. Most major proposals are taken up Tuesday to Thursday.

The previous chapter outlined the normal procedure by which major legislation reported by standing committees is routed to the House floor through the Rules Committee, as well as certain legislative short-cuts to the floor, such as the Consent Calendar, Private Calendar, and suspension of the rules. This chapter will discuss the most common routes and roadblocks on the House floor for those few hundred major bills that have been granted a rule by the Rules Committee. The major phases of floor consideration for these bills are: adoption of the rule, resolution of the House into the Committee of the Whole, general debate, the amending process, and final action by the full House. Along the way we shall examine some of the strategies used by proponents of bills to secure passage, and by opponents to defeat or modify bills, and how the rules can be used to delay or expedite proceedings.

ADOPTION OF THE RULE

As noted earlier, the first step in bringing a bill to the floor is adoption of a rule from the Rules Committee. A rule, or special order, sets the conditions under which a measure is to be considered, determining whether amendments will be permitted and how much debate will be allowed.

Rules are rarely rejected by the House, although attempts are occasionally made to do so. Challenging the Rules Committee is an uninviting task; members know that at some future time they will need a rule from the committee for their own bills. Rejection of a rule usually reflects: sharp divisions among members; heavy lobbying by pressure groups, the president, or agency officials; or general agreement that the reporting committee did a poor job of drafting a bill.

Voting down a rule is a "procedural kill." Opponents of a controversial 1974 committee reorganization proposal tried to defeat the reform by rejecting the special order from the Rules Committee, declaring that "everybody against any part of H. Res. 988 must stand together and vote against the rule."[2] The strategy was unsuccessful, but the example shows how procedural matters can have a critical impact on the legislative process.

A typical rule from the Rules Committee is reproduced on page 108. This is an open rule for a bill dealing with the Peace Corps. The decisionmaking process it outlines is used for most major bills.

Upon adoption of the rule, a motion is made by the majority committee member in charge of the bill (called the "floor manager") to resolve the House into the Committee of the Whole. There is an hour of general debate, after which the bill is open to amendment under the five-minute rule. In other instances, a rule may permit more debate, restrict amendments, waive points of order, or grant priority to committee or member amendments. Following the amending stage, the Committee of the Whole is directed to report back to the House. There, after a motion to recommit the bill to committee (with or without instructions to revise), the bill is voted on in its entirety.

In the Peace Corps rule, the five principal procedural steps governing House consideration of major legislation are spelled out. These are: resolution into the Committee of the

95TH CONGRESS
1ST SESSION

H. RES. 600

[Report No. 95–367]

IN THE HOUSE OF REPRESENTATIVES

MAY 26, 1977

Mr. DODD, from the Committee on Rules, reported the following resolution;
which was referred to the House Calendar and ordered to be printed

---

RESOLUTION

1   *Resolved*, That upon the adoption of this resolution it

2   shall be in order to move that the House resolve itself into

3   the Committee of the Whole House on the State of the Union

4   for the consideration of the bill (H.R. 6967) to authorize

5   appropriations for the Peace Corps for fiscal year 1978. After

6   general debate, which shall be confined to the bill and shall

7   continue not to exceed one hour, to be equally divided and

8   controlled by the chairman and ranking minority member

9   of the Committee on International Relations, the bill shall

10   be read for amendment under the five-minute rule. At the

11   conclusion of the consideration of the bill for amendment,

12   the Committee shall rise and report the bill to the House

1   with such amendments as may have been adopted, and the

2   previous question shall be considered as ordered on the bill

3   and amendments thereto to final passage without intervening

4   motion except one motion to recommit.

Whole; general debate; the five-minute rule; a recommittal motion; and final passage. Roadblocks usually occur during the amending stage in the Committee of the Whole.

COMMITTEE OF THE WHOLE

The Committee of the Whole is simply the House in another form. Every legislator is a member. House rules require all revenue or money bills to be considered first in the Committee of the Whole. Technically, there are two such bodies. One is the "Committee of the Whole House," which debates private bills. The other and more important is the "Committee of the Whole House on the State of the Union," commonly shortened to the Committee of the Whole, which considers public measures. The rules of the Committee of the Whole are designed to speed consideration of measures. Four rules or customs distinguish the conduct of business in the full House from proceedings in the Committee of the Whole.

First, a quorum is only 100 members in the Committee of the Whole; 218 constitute a quorum in the House. Second, the Speaker does not preside over the Committee but appoints a majority colleague to chair it. Third, it is common in the Committee, unlike the House, to close or limit debate on sections of the bill by unanimous consent or majority vote of the members present. Finally, amendments are debated under the five-minute rule (discussed below in connection with the amending process) rather than the hour rule.[3]

From the beginning, the House has observed the English precedent: The Speaker does not chair the Committee of the Whole, but generally selects a senior, knowledgeable member to chair each bill under debate. The member's role is to keep order, recognize members, and rule on points of order. The Speaker is permitted to remain in the chamber and take part in debate, but generally participates only to the extent of making closing remarks on a major bill. Except to break a tie, the Speaker almost never votes.

Visitors in the gallery can tell whether the House is in the Committee of the Whole by the position of the mace, a 46-inch column of ebony rods bound together by silver and topped by a silver eagle. The mace, symbol of the Sergeant at Arms' authority, is carried by him, if called upon, to enforce order on the floor. It rests in a pedestal on a table at the right of the Speaker's podium in the center of the chamber. It is taken down from the table when the Speaker hands the gavel to the chairman of the Committee of the Whole. When the Committee rises and the Speaker resumes the chair, the mace is returned to its place.[4]

GENERAL DEBATE

The first order of business in the Committee of the Whole is general debate on the entire bill under consideration. Two to four hours of debate are usually allowed, equally divided between the minority and majority. In the rule on the Peace Corps bill *(p. 108),* only one hour is authorized; for very complex legislation, as many as 10 hours may be scheduled.

Each side of the debate has a floor manager from the committee of original jurisdiction, who controls time, allotting segments to supporters or opponents, as the case may be. Almost without exception, the majority floor manager is spokesman for the bill; the opposing manager represents the minority party. Exceptions sometimes occur when both sides may favor passage of a bill, and both floor managers rise in support. During debate on controversial legislation, both floor managers may declare their support for the aims of a bill, but indicate divergence on specific sections or amendments.

The term "general debate" can be misleading, as most members deliver set speeches and engage in a minimum of give-and-take exchange. Because committees and subcommittees shape the fundamental character of most legislation, only a limited number of representatives actually participate in debate, and those who do are usually members of the committee that drafted the legislation. Yet general debate has an intrinsic value that is recognized by most House members and experts on the legislative process.

Purposes of General Debate

General debate is both symbolic and practical. It assures both legislators and the public that the House makes its decisions in democratic fashion, with due respect for majority and minority opinion. General debate forces members to come to grips with the issue at hand; difficult and controversial sections of the bill can be explained; constituents and interest groups can be alerted to a measure's purpose through press coverage of the debate; member sentiment can be assessed by the floor leadership; a public record, or legislative history for administrative agencies and the courts is built, revealing the intentions of proponents and opponents alike; legislators can take positions that may enhance their prospects for reelection; and, occasionally, fence-sitters may be influenced.

Not all legislators agree on the last point. Some doubt that debate can really change views or affect the outcome of a vote. But debate, especially by party leaders just before the vote, can change opinion. "Some votes are always changed by debate," Democratic Majority Leader Jim Wright of Texas has written.[5] Those who tell you "that debate is worthless are just cynical," former New York Representative Bella Abzug has said.[6] Certainly the remarks of influential members can sway votes. Former Speaker Sam Rayburn's "entire speech (on a bill) took only 44 words," a member recounted, "but it turned the tide."[7] Who speaks is sometimes more important than what is said.

The Job of Floor Managers

Long-standing customs govern much of the debate on the floor. But the floor managers direct the course of the debate. The floor manager for the majority side is often the chairman of the committee that reported the measure, or an appointed committee colleague. The ranking minority committee member, or an appointed surrogate, is usually the floor manager for the minority view. Many committees routinely name subcommittee chairmen to manage bills reported from their subcommittees. The floor managers are centrally located during debate at long tables near the center of the chamber, with the main aisle separating the Democratic from the Republican side.

The floor managers guide their bills through final disposition by the House. Their duties are varied:

- They plan strategy and parliamentary maneuvers to meet changing floor situations;
- They respond to points of order;
- They protect bills from weakening amendments (in the case of the majority), or promote such amendments (in the case of the minority);
- They alert supporters to be on the floor to vote for or against certain amendments;
- They advise colleagues on the meaning and importance of amendments;
- They judge when committee amendments should be offered or deferred;
- They inform party leaders of member sentiment and the mood of the House toward their bill;
- They control the time for general debate and can act to limit debate on amendments, sections or titles of the bill, or the entire measure.

The fate of much legislation depends on the skill of floor managers. Mistakes can kill, delay, or weaken proposed legislation. For example, on May 19, 1977, the House suspended debate on a bill revising the Hatch Act, which limits political activity by federal employees. The majority floor manager had inadvertently permitted adoption of an amendment which, among other provisions, prohibited the use of union dues for any political purpose. The amendment passed, with substantial support from Democrats who had overlooked the sweeping implications of the antiunion clause. After the vote, supporters of the bill realized the implications of the amendment and quickly withdrew the bill from floor consideration. Three weeks later, after the majority leadership had circulated the word on the amendment, debate on the bill was reopened. The controversial clause was rescinded and the Hatch Act reforms were subsequently approved.

Conversely, effective floor management increases the chances for smooth passage of a bill. The success of the landmark budget reform measure (the Congressional Budget and Impoundment Control Act of 1974) was credited in large part to its skillful floor manager, Richard Bolling, D-Mo.

Floor managers are given several advantages over their colleagues. They customarily lead off debate in the Committee of the Whole and have the first opportunity to appeal for support. During debate, they receive priority recognition from the chair. A floor manager may take the floor at critical moments ahead of other legislators to defend or rebut attacks on the bill or may offer amendments to coalesce support for the measure. The floor manager is also entitled, by custom, to close debate on an amendment, thus having the last chance to influence sentiment.

Floor managers can generally count on support from their party leadership. They are also permitted to have up to five standing committee staff members on the floor during debate, ready to research rules and precedents, draft amendments, or prepare statements. Finally, as a result of committee hearings, discussion, and markup, they have a reservoir of knowledge about the technical details of a measure, and are in a good position to judge which amendments to accept or reject, and what arguments to employ during debate.

Delaying Tactics

Despite the generally tighter rules on debate in the House than in the Senate, there are many ways to prolong or delay proceedings. Members may raise numerous points of order, make scores of parliamentary inquiries, or offer trivial amendments. They may demand record votes on every amendment, ask unanimous consent to speak additional minutes on each amendment, make certain that all time for general debate is used, or, if the chair declares amendments nongermane, appeal the ruling and demand record votes on each appeal. Until a rules change in 1971, a reading of the *Journal* was used as a delaying tactic. Prior to that time, reading could be dispensed with only by unanimous consent or by a motion to suspend the rules, requiring a two-thirds vote. Since then, the Speaker has been authorized to examine the *Journal* and approve it.

The purpose of such delaying tactics is to stall action on a measure, either to allow more time to gather support (for those who favor it) or to kill it (for those who oppose). Sometimes delay is intended to force action and other times to prevent it. For example, on October 8-9, 1968, Republican members kept the House in continuous session for 32 hours by employing a variety of delaying tactics. The Republicans claimed they were trying to force the reluctant Democratic leadership to bring to the floor two stalled measures: a campaign spending reform bill and a legislative reorganization proposal. Democrats said the Republicans were trying to prevent House consideration of a pending bill authorizing television debates between the two major 1968 presidential candidates. In the end, none of the three bills in question was passed by Congress.

THE AMENDING PROCESS

The amending process is the heart of decisionmaking on the floor. Under an open rule, amendments determine the final shape of bills. At times, amendments may become more important or controversial than the bills themselves. A good example is the 1974 Jackson-Vanik Amendment (named for its sponsors, Senator Henry Jackson, D-Wash., and Representative Charles Vanik, D-Ohio). The amendment was tacked on to the 1974 Trade Act after prolonged controversy in each house. It limited trade with the Soviet Union until that country lifts its restrictions on Jewish emigration.

Reading for Amendments Under The Five-Minute Rule

At the end of general debate, a bill is "read" for amendment under the five-minute rule. Under this rule, "any Member shall be allowed five minutes to explain any amendment he may offer . . . after which the Member who shall obtain the floor shall be allowed to speak five minutes in opposition to it, and there shall be no further debate thereon."[8] Actual practice differs from the rule. Amendments are regularly debated for more than the 10 minutes allowed by the rule. Members gain the floor by offering *pro forma* amendments, moving "to strike the last word," or "to strike the requisite number of words." Technically, these are amendments, but no alteration of the bill is contemplated; their purpose is to extend debate. (*Pro forma* amendments are not in order under a "closed" rule.) In addition, members may ask unanimous consent to speak longer than five minutes, and may yield part of their time to other legislators. Debate on amendments cannot extend forever, however, since the floor manager can move that discussion be terminated within a specified time. Motions to close or limit debate are seldom rejected.

House rules require all bills and joint resolutions to be "read" three times to ensure that members are familiar with the measures they are acting on. In practice, bills are not read word for word. Verbatim readings are generally dispensed with by unanimous consent, although a member, as a delaying tactic, may insist on a full reading of the title or section under consideration.

The first "reading" occurs when a measure is introduced and referred to committee. The bill is not read aloud; the bill's number and title are printed in the *Congressional Record*. The second reading occurs in the Committee of the Whole. The third occurs by title (i.e., the name of the bill) just prior to the vote on final passage.

Amendments are considered, or "read," as specified in the rule or special order from the Rules Committee, usually section by section. The Rules Committee might specify a reading by title rather than by section, to permit larger, interrelated parts of the measure to be open to amendment. The 1974 Land-Use Planning Act was read by titles to "insure more orderly consideration," according to one member of the Rules Committee.[9]

Amendments are in order after a section has been read, but must be proposed before the clerk starts to read the next section. If the clerk has passed on to a succeeding section, a member must ask unanimous consent to offer an amendment to the previous section. In addition to being timely, amendments must be germane to the bill and section under consideration. Reading by section or title helps structure rational consideration of complex bills, but on noncontroversial measures, it is common for the floor manager to ask unanimous consent that the entire bill be considered as read. In that case, the entire measure is open to amendment at any point.

The reading stage is often used to delay or prolong proceedings. Any member can object to a unanimous consent request to dispense with the reading of sections, titles, or amendments. Opponents of a bill may draft lengthy amendments, not with the expectation of their passage, but to cause delays by having them read in entirety.

During 1977 debate on amendments to the Clean Air Act, Representative Henry Waxman, D-Calif., objected repeatedly to requests that sections of the bill be considered as read, claiming that reading was necessary "because the chairman of the subcommittee (that considered the bill) is not here right at the moment. . . ."[10] Such delaying tactics are usually sparingly employed, as they invite retribution by other members. "There is not anything we can do about prolonging the reading of the [Clean Air Act]," Representative Gene Snyder, R-Ky., observed, "but when other big bills come up" requiring expeditious action, various legislators "can object to dispensing with the reading and can require that they be read."[11] Both the rules of the game and the expectation of retaliation in kind encourage moderation in the use of dilatory tactics.

Types of Amendments

Amendments serve diverse objectives. Some are offered in deference to pressure groups, executive branch officials, or constituents; others are designed to attract public notice, to stall the legislative process, to demonstrate concern for an issue, or to test sentiment for or against a bill. Some amendments are more technical than substantive; they may renumber sections of a bill or correct typographical errors. One common strategy is to load down a bill with so many objectionable amendments that it will sink of its own weight. "The House amended the [1975 energy tax] bill so long and weakened it so much," declared Representative Otis Pike, D-N.Y., "that this congressman felt that by the time we were through with it, it was not worth having, and voted against it on final passage."[12] Committee members themselves may vote against a bill they originally reported if objectionable amendments are added on the floor.

Three types of amendment are worth special attention: committee amendments, "riders," and previously noticed amendments.

Committee Amendments. Committees are frequently divided when they report important bills. Committee members may have amendments they want to offer on the floor. For the purpose of amendment, the chair customarily recognizes members of the committee that reported the legislation ahead of other members.

Delays often occur between the time a measure is reported, assigned to a calendar, and finally considered on the floor. The longer the delay, the more likely are committee members to come up with amendments to bring a bill up to date, or to present their colleagues with policy alternatives. The Rules Committee often specifies that committee amendments be taken up first, and sometimes that only committee amendments be considered.

In the past, the House was inclined to defer to committee recommendations.[13] That may be changing. "When I came here 10 years ago," reflected Representative Thomas Foley, D-Wash., "most of the Members would follow the committee. Now partly because of the [Vietnam] war and the breakdown of the legitimacy of leadership, the committee's 'aye' or 'nay' isn't enough."[14] There are also committees whose legislation is regularly revised on the floor, because of its controversial nature, poor drafting, sharp splits among the members, or other factors.

Riders. In a two-week period in June 1977, representatives voted against Veterans Administration benefits for Vietnam deserters, public housing for homosexuals, Medicaid funds for abortions, federal funding for busing children beyond their nearest school (under most circumstances), and a roll-back of a legislative pay raise approved four months earlier. All the votes were on unrelated amendments, or "riders," to general appropriation bills.

Riders are amendments that are extraneous to the subject matter of a bill. They are more common in the Senate, because House rules, in theory at least, require amendments to be germane or relevant to the bill itself. Any member can question the relevance of a proposed amendment by raising a point of order on which the chair must rule. Such questions are not always raised, however, either because of oversight, because members agree with the provision, or because the rule from Rules Committee waives them. "I don't make points of order on all [riders]," a member has said, "because some may be necessary due to changing conditions."[15]

Riders often express proposals that might not become law on their own merit, either because of resistance in the Senate, or the probability of a presidential veto. The strategy is to add riders to important bills that are almost certain to be enacted, such as appropriations measures funding the federal government or bills to raise the federal debt ceiling. If the House is tenacious enough in clinging to its rider, the chances are good that it will be accepted — grudgingly — by the Senate or the president, if it is attached to "must" legislation.

Previously Noticed Amendments. All amendments must be offered from the floor, but in the House there is no requirement for them to be submitted ("previously noticed") in advance to all members. Most amendments are in written form when they are offered, but they need not be printed ahead of time for review by members or staff. However, the Legislative Reorganization Act of 1970 provided that amendments printed in the *Congressional Record* at least one day prior to a bill's consideration in the Committee of the Whole are guaranteed ten minutes of floor debate, regardless of agreements to terminate discussion. The objective is to prevent arbitrary closing of debate when important amendments are pending, but the rule can still be used for dilatory purposes. During 1974 debate on a committee reform measure, Representative John Dingell, D-Mich., a foe of the plan, had 50 amendments "noticed" in the *Congressional Record* in accord with the rule. Eight hours could have been consumed had the Committee of the Whole been forced to debate each one. Dingell did not offer his amendments after the committee reform proposal was watered down to his satisfaction.

Degrees of Amendments

When a bill is open to revision, only four forms, or degrees, of amendment can be pending on the floor. The four forms are (1) an amendment itself, (2) an amendment to the amendment, (3) a substitute amendment, and (4) an amendment to the substitute. Once an amendment has been offered, either an amendment to the amendment, or a substitute amendment is in order.

When a substitute amendment has been offered, an amendment to the substitute is in order. Beyond these four forms, further degrees of amendments (e.g. an amendment to an amendment to an amendment) are out of order. "The line must be drawn somewhere," Thomas Jefferson wrote, "and usage has drawn it after the amendment to the amendment."[16]

Maneuvering for Advantage: Common Tactics

Proponents and opponents of measures are constantly seeking to advance their policy objectives through the amending process. Skillful use of various motions, dilatory tactics, or shrewd drafting of wording can influence which side carries the day. Timing is all important to the success of many maneuvers on the floor, especially preferential motions and amendments to "sweeten" a bill.

Striking the Enacting Clause. Certain motions take preference over other floor business. One is the motion to strike the enacting clause, the opening phrase of a bill that makes it an operative law, after approval by Congress and the president ("Be it enacted by the Senate and House of Representatives of the United States of America in Congress assembled, . . ."). Under House rules, approval of a motion to strike the enacting clause is equivalent to rejecting the measure. A motion to strike the clause is in order any time during the amending process; it is a privileged motion which must be disposed of before the House takes up any further business on the bill. The motion is in order only once, unless the bill is materially changed by adoption of major amendments, an interpretation made by the chair if a point of order is raised against a motion to strike.

A motion to strike the enacting clause may cause considerable excitement in the chamber, and it may be used, for psychological purposes, either by opponents or proponents of a measure.[17] In 1974, for example, Richard Bolling, floor manager of the bitterly contested committee reform bill, surprised foes of reform by inviting them to offer a motion to strike the enacting clause. Bolling's plan was to defeat such a motion so resoundingly that it would be clear to all members that committee reform was going to be considered to its conclusion.

Bolling gained an immediate psychological advantage when Joe D. Waggonner, D-La., one of the opposition leaders, observed that his side did not have the votes to pass the motion. It might be made, he said, "at a point in time when we think there is a chance for it to succeed." Ironically, a supporter of committee reform, disappointed by the course of debate on the floor, later offered a motion to strike. It was turned down overwhelmingly because most members did not want the measure abruptly killed.

"Sweeteners." Measures considered unpalatable can be made more acceptable, or "sweetened," by offering proposals to attract the support of large numbers of legislators. These might include amendments granting members more staff, additional office allowances, or "pork barrel" provisions for construction of dams, highways, port facilities, airports, and the like, in various constituencies. In 1974, many Republican legislators were won over to the committee reform plan (diluted, to be sure), by an amendment granting a staff aide to each ranking minority member of a subcommittee. "I recognize a pot sweetener when I see one," declared floor manager Bolling, who unsuccessfully opposed the amendment. It passed, 218 to 180, with the support of 63 GOP members.[18] Pot-sweetening is the opposite of a technique noted earlier, loading down a bill with enough unattractive amendments to kill it.

Notes on the Amending Process

A controversial bill is virtually always amended in the Committee of the Whole. The amending process is critical to legislative floor action and, as has been seen, quite complex. A few observations will highlight the main features of the process.

● Amendments in the Committee of the Whole are usually offered section-by-section under the five-minute rule;

● All amendments must be offered from the floor and are nearly always in writing;

● Amendments may not be repetitious. When an amendment is defeated, a member may not offer a similar proposal later;

● Any amendment may be challenged on a point of order before debate on the amendment has begun;

● Committee amendments are considered before those offered by other legislators;

● *Pro forma* amendments enable members to discuss the legislation under consideration for five minutes, even though no change in the bill is actually intended;

● Amendments must be germane to the subject under consideration. Occasionally, nongermane amendments may slip by because members are generally agreed on their intent, or because the Rules Committee has barred points of order against them.

VOTING IN THE COMMITTEE OF THE WHOLE

Until 1971, there were three methods of voting in the Committee of the Whole: voice, division, and teller. *Voice* voting is based on the volume of sound of members responding yea or nay. If the chair is in doubt about the result, or if any member requests it, a *division* is called for. First, those in favor, and then those opposed, are asked to stand while a head count is taken. Again, any member dissatisfied with the result as announced by the chair may say, "Mr. Chairman, I demand *tellers*." The member's demand must be supported by one-fifth of a quorum (20 members) before a teller vote is ordered. Under teller voting, the chair appoints members, usually one from each side of the question, to act as "tellers," or vote counters. Members file up the center aisle toward the rear of the House — the yeas first, followed by the nays — between two member tellers, who count them. Tellers then report their results to the chair, for example, "200 for and 100 against."

None of the three methods provides a public record of who voted, how they voted, or even whether they voted. Often crucial amendments were adopted in the Committee of the Whole without recorded votes. Traditional arguments for this procedure were that it facilitated compromise and permitted members to vote the national interest against regional or local interests. Secrecy was not absolute, since reporters monitored the voting, but newsmen often found it difficult to identify members whose backs were turned as they passed between the two tellers.

Many members, nonetheless, supported the institution of recorded votes in the Committee of the Whole. Secret voting, they said, enabled legislators to duck issues or vote contrary to publicly stated positions. Constituents could not trace their representatives' voting records and hold them accountable. "A member can vote for any number of amendments which may cripple a water pollution bill or render ineffective a civil rights bill or fail to provide adequate funding for hospital construction or programs for the elderly," Representative David Obey, D-Wis., explained, "and then he can turn around on final passage and vote for the bill he has just voted to emasculate by amendment."[19]

Frustration with "secret" voting in the Committee of the Whole mounted in the late 1960s. Some members believed they were coming under increasing pressure from committee chairmen and party leaders to vote the party's position, whereas with recorded voting they could argue that their reelection depended on voting as their constituents wished. In 1970, the movement for *recorded teller* votes succeeded.

Change to Recorded Teller Votes

Members of the Democratic Study Group (DSG), the largest *ad hoc* group in the House, with about 235 moderate-to-liberal members in 1978, were primarily responsible for promoting reform of the teller procedure. Attendance by members of the Democratic Study Group during Committee of the Whole proceedings had been poor. The DSG reasoned that if votes were recorded publicly, attendance would improve markedly, since excessive absences could be used against legislators in future campaigns.

To avoid a partisan label, the DSG joined forces with reform-minded Republicans and developed a bipartisan package of amendments to a major legislative reorganization act. The coalition developed an antisecrecy strategy to build public support for recording teller votes. Thousands of letters were mailed to newspaper editors. Editorials soon began appearing across the nation in support of recorded teller voting in the Committee of the Whole. Public attention helped convert formerly hostile members into supporters of the issue.

The campaign was helped — perhaps inadvertently — by the activities of "gallery spotters," observers, often members of antiwar groups, who sat in the visitors' area trying to recognize and record members as they walked up the center aisle. The information was shared with newsmen and others. Sometimes the spotters made mistakes, provoking protests from members who were identified in news reports as voting one way when they had actually voted another. Through a confluence of factors — public pressure, member dissatisfaction with the spotting system, and bipartisan backing — an amendment was added to the Legislative Reorganization Act of 1970 permitting recorded votes in the Committee of the Whole.

Voting Changes Since 1970

Recorded voting compelled members to take public stands on an increasing number of controversial issues. Under the new procedure, members had to sign and deposit green or red cards, signifying yea or nay, in ballot boxes in full view of the House and galleries. That simple procedure may have changed the outcome of voting on federal financing of the supersonic transport (SST). For months before the vote, environmental groups had been generating strong opposition to the SST, and public opinion appeared to be opposed to it. In Congress, however, sentiment seemingly leaned toward approval of the plane. Finally, on March 18, 1971, Representative Sidney Yates, D-Ill., stood and said, "Mr. Chairman, I demand tellers with clerk." Knowing their votes would be recorded and widely publicized, members voted 217 to 204 to cut off funds for the SST.

Electronic voting, also authorized by the 1970 Legislative Reorganization Act, began in 1973. Members insert a personalized card about the size of a credit card into one of the more than 40 voting stations throughout the House floor, and press one of three buttons: Yea, Nay, or Present. Votes are displayed on panels above the Speaker's desk and on other walls of the House. The system is also used to establish quorums. If electronic voting malfunctions, traditional methods are used.

The impact of the recorded teller procedure and electronic voting may be seen in the enormous increase in the number of recorded votes taken annually, shown in the chart below:

Year	Number of House Record Votes
1970	266
1971	320
1972	329
1973	541
1974	537
1975	612
1976	661
1977	706

The increase has caused scheduling conflicts and kept legislators running from committee meetings to the floor in response to calls for recorded votes. Many members complain that too many record (recorded) votes are taken on frivolous or unnecessary amendments. But some legislators find the new systems a boon because they can improve their attendance records simply by calling for recorded votes on even the most trivial matters.

The voting changes have placed additional pressures on the floor managers. Electronic voting has cut balloting time in half, from 30 minutes under the traditional roll-call method, to 15 minutes. Managers now have less time to coordinate floor activities during a vote. Members can enter the chamber through numerous doors, insert their cards to vote, and leave before the leadership can talk with them. As a result, both sides station monitors at the doors to furnish information as members enter and to urge them to vote with the floor manager or party leadership.

From the floor managers' standpoint, there are advantages and disadvantages to the new system. Managers have computer display terminals that show a continuous and changing record of the progress of a vote. There is less time to evaluate opposition to proposals and to line up votes, so floor managers now work to build support before bills reach the floor. Problems, such as the absence of a member, or the unexpected switch of a vote by another, can be spotted quickly on the computer consoles. Absent members can be summoned to the floor and vote-switchers can be approached by persuasive members of the party.

One other voting change is worth noting. On January 14, 1975, the House amended its rules to permit "pairs" in the Committee of the Whole. "Pairing" was previously limited to the House. Pairing is a voluntary arrangement between any two representatives on opposite sides of an issue. When there is advance knowledge of an amendment or other issue to be voted on, the paired representatives may express their preference, even though one or both are absent. Pairs are not counted in tabulating the final results of record votes.

Pairs take three forms. A *general* pair means that two members are listed without any indication as to how either might have voted. A *specific* pair indicates how the two absent legislators would have voted, one for and the other against. A *live* pair matches two members, one present and one absent. The member in attendance casts a vote, but then withdraws it to vote "present," announcing that he or she has a live pair with a colleague, identifying how each would have voted on the issue. A live pair subtracts one vote, yea or nay, from the final tally, and can influence the outcome of closely contested issues. Both parties have pair clerks to help arrange these informal agreements.

Factors in Voting

On any given day, legislators may be required to vote on measures ranging from foreign aid to abortions, from maritime subsidies to tax reform. It is nearly impossible for a member to be fully informed on every issue before the House. As a result, many rely on "cue-givers" for guidance on matters beyond their special competence. These may be committee or party leaders, members of the state congressional delegation, trusted colleagues or staff aides, or floor managers.[20] Party loyalty, constituency interests, and individual conscience are primary factors in determining a member's vote on any issue, but they are not the only factors. It is not unusual for members to vote for proposals they actually oppose, in order to prevent enactment of something worse, or in the expectation that, somewhere along the line, the proposal will go down to defeat.

Some votes are simply cast in error. "With 500 votes or more each year in the House, I'm sure there are some times when I've met myself coming and going," said Representative Abner Mikva, D-Ill.[21]

Other votes are carefully timed for impact. In 1977, the Democratic leadership was attempting to defeat an amendment repealing a 29 percent pay increase for members. The leaders "instructed congressmen who . . . found it politically impossible to support the $12,900 boost a year . . . to lay back and vote on it as late as possible so they wouldn't scare off others the leadership had convinced to vote for the raise."[22] During the first several minutes of the vote, there was substantial opposition to the amendment, which created the needed "steamroller" effect to defeat the proposal. Later votes in support of the amendment were largely for public consumption.

When voting on all amendments has been concluded, the Committee of the Whole "rises" (dissolves) and reports back to the full House. The chairman of the Committee of the Whole hands the gavel back to the Speaker who resumes the podium; the mace is returned to its pedestal on the table next to the podium, and a quorum becomes 218 members. As prescribed in the rule, there is a standard sequence of events that takes place prior to final passage of a bill.

FINAL PASSAGE IN THE HOUSE

After taking the chair, the Speaker announces that "under the rule, the previous question is ordered"; this means that no further debate is permitted on the measure or amendments. Then the House, sitting as the House, must approve the decisions of the Committee of the Whole. The Speaker asks all the members to identify amendments on which they want separate ballots. The remaining amendments are decided *en bloc* by voice vote, after which the contested amendments are voted on individually. Except for motions to send a measure back to the reporting committee with instructions, only amendments adopted in the Committee of the Whole can be considered in the full House.

When voting on amendments either individually or *en bloc*, the House, unlike the Committee of the Whole, permits any member to demand a record vote. The demand must be supported by only one-fifth of those present, whether or not there is a quorum. However, if a quorum fails to vote, any member can demand a quorum call which under House rules will simultaneously decide the proposal in question and the presence of a quorum.[23]

Following action on individual amendments, there are three more procedures before a measure is enacted by the House. The first is *engrossment* and *third reading*. "The question is on engrossment and third reading of the bill," the Speaker declares. This is a *pro forma* question, which is approved automatically by unanimous consent. House rules provide that the bill be read by its title. Before 1965, any legislator could demand that the bill be read in full, but the rules were changed to prevent this dilatory tactic.

Engrossment is the preparation of a final and accurate version of the bill by an enrolling clerk, for transmission to the Senate. This can be a complicated process, particularly if numerous amendments were adopted. On rare occasions, a mistake is made in engrossment, creating problems for both the House and Senate.

The second step is the *recommittal motion*, provided for in the rule from the Rules Committee. This is a privileged motion, protected and guaranteed by the rules, that gives the opponents one last chance to obtain a recorded vote on their proposals. Recommittal is a motion to return the bill to the committee that reported it, and is always made by a member opposed to the bill. Customarily, the Speaker recognizes a member of the minority party, usually the senior minority committee member, and specifically asks if that member opposes the bill. Recommittal is in order only in the House, not the Committee of the Whole. The motion may be a simple, or "straight" motion to recommit or it may contain instructions to the reporting committee. For example, certain amendments defeated in the Committee of the Whole could be reported back to the House. This is the only way amendments defeated in the Committee of the Whole can be brought before the full House. Until 1970, no debate was permitted on a recommittal motion. The Legislative Reorganization Act of that year authorized ten minutes of debate on recommittal motions with instructions.

If adopted, a simple recommittal motion kills the bill, although it may be returned again to the House later in the session. Recommittal motions with instructions commonly provide that the committee report "forthwith." If the recommittal motion is adopted, the committee chairman immediately reports back to the House in conformity with the instructions, and the bill, as modified by the instructions, is before the House again in a matter of seconds.

Recommittal motions are seldom successful, but much depends on the size of the minority party. Moreover, since recorded votes now permit the minority party to express its views openly on legislation, recommittal motions have become less important. On August 5, 1977, however, William Steiger, R-Wis., offered a significant recommittal motion to drop a key component of President Carter's national energy plan: a tax on domestic crude oil. The rule from the Rules Committee prohibited a separate vote in the Committee of the Whole on whether such a tax should be imposed. Steiger's motion permitted such a vote. It was cleverly drafted to attract bipartisan support and almost carried the day, losing by only 219 to 203. It provided a forum for Republicans to put their views on record.

If the recommittal motion is rejected, the Speaker moves to the third step, the final vote on the whole bill. "The question is on the passage of the bill," he says. Normally, final passage is by record vote. If the outcome is obvious, and the members are anxious to be done with it, the measure may be adopted by voice vote. When the results of the final vote have been announced, a *pro forma* motion to reconsider is made and laid on the table (postponed indefinitely), to prevent the bill from being reconsidered later. House rules state that a final vote is conclusive only if there has been an opportunity to reconsider it.

SUMMARY

Although the House decisionmaking process may appear quite complex, it accommodates varied institutional interests and members' needs. There are numerous restraints on what legislators can and cannot do. Success often depends on one side gaining an advantage through use of the rules. Infinite variations are possible within the process, but basic House procedures are the same on almost all important bills:

- A "rule" from the Rules Committee;
- Consideration in the Committee of the Whole;
- General debate;
- Amendments under the five-minute rule;
- Recorded teller votes;
- Return of the bill from the Committee of the Whole to the House;
- Separate votes, if requested, on any amendment adopted in committee;
- A recommittal motion, with or without instructions;
- Final passage.

The intensity of debate may vary; the complexity of the rule may change; and a host of other factors may differ from issue to issue, but the pattern of decisionmaking is the same no matter the range or scope of the legislation.

After approval by the House, the bill moves on to the Senate. There, the legislative process is quite different. If the House is characterized by devotion to rules and parliamentary procedures, the Senate is much more informal, often transacting its business by "gentlemen's agreements," with the rules often ignored or set aside. Chapter 3 treated introduction of a bill, referral, and committee action in the Senate. The following chapter begins with a bill that has been reported by a Senate committee and discusses the scheduling procedure for moving a bill on to the Senate floor.

NOTES

1. During the 95th Congress, the House developed a more refined system of scheduling floor sessions. This was done in response to the desires of members, committees, and party leaders. Members complained about problems in arranging their personal schedules and their inability to make firm commitments for meetings in their districts; committees wanted more time early in the session to work on legislation without being interrupted by floor meetings; and party leaders wished to better synchronize committee and floor activities and utilize the time in session more effectively. As a result, the House approved the following convening hours for 1977: Noon on all Mondays and Tuesdays; Wednesdays at 3 p.m. until May 15, 10 a.m. until July 1, and Noon thereafter; Thursdays and Fridays at 11 a.m. until May 15, 10 a.m. until July 1, and Noon thereafter. The House also adjourned by 3 p.m. on Fridays and 5:30 p.m. on all days except Wednesdays until May 15.

2. Roger H. Davidson and Walter J. Oleszek, *Congress against Itself* (Bloomington, Ind.: Indiana University Press, 1977), pp. 193-194.

3. In the House sitting as the House, an hour is permitted for debate on amendments. "No member," the rule states, "shall occupy more than one hour in debate on any question in the House." Technically, then, all matters could be debated for 439 hours — one hour each for the 435 representatives, three delegates (from the District of Columbia, the Virgin Islands, and Guam), and one resident commissioner (from Puerto Rico). In practice, measures are debated for only *one* hour in total and then voted on.

4. For a description of the 17th century English origins of the Committee of the Whole, see DeAlva Stanwood Alexander, *History and Procedure of the House of Representatives* (Boston: Houghton Mifflin, 1916), pp. 257-258.

5. Jim Wright, *You and Your Congressman* (New York: Coward-McCann, 1965), p. 153.

6. Bella W. Abzug, *Bella* (New York: Saturday Review Press, 1972), p. 11.

7. Wright, *You and Your Congressman,* p. 153.

8. *Constitution, Jefferson's Manual and Rules of the House of Representatives,* 94th Congress, 2d Session, House Document No. 94-663, p. 597.

9. U.S. Congress, House, *Congressional Record,* 93rd Cong., 2d sess., June 11, 1974, 120, H 5020. This is one of the relatively rare cases of rules being rejected by the House, but not because the bill was to be read by titles rather than sections. The measure was controversial, and involved control of private property.

10. U.S. Congress, House, *Congressional Record,* 95th Cong., 1st sess., May 26, 1977, 123, H 5148.

11. *Ibid.,* p. H 5151.

12. U.S. Congress, House, *Congressional Record,* 94th Cong., 2d sess., February 19, 1976, 122, H 735.

13. Randall B. Ripley, *Congress, Process and Policy* (New York: W. W. Norton, 1975), pp. 116-118.

14. Michael J. Malbin, "House Democrats Are Playing With A Strong Leadership Lineup," *National Journal,* June 18, 1977, p. 946.

15. Richard F. Fenno Jr., *The Power of the Purse* (Boston: Little, Brown, 1966), p. 74.

16. *Constitution, Jefferson's Manual and Rules of the House of Representatives,* House Document No. 94-663, p. 226.

17. Customarily, the motion to strike is also used by members to obtain five more minutes of debate time.

18. Davidson and Oleszek, *Congress against Itself,* p. 239.

19. Congressional Quarterly *Weekly Report,* January 22, 1972, p. 153.

20. On factors influencing votes, see John W. Kingdon, *Congressmen's Voting Decisions* (New York: Harper & Row, 1973).

21. *Chicago Tribune,* April 4, 1976, p. 24.

22. *The Washington Star,* June 30, 1977, p. D-8.

23. To summarize: there are several ways of voting in the House. These include: voice, division, unrecorded teller, record teller, and electronic. There are two other ways of demanding a record vote that do not apply in Committee of the Whole: the constitutional yeas and nays and the "automatic" record votes. One fifth of a quorum, 44 members, must support requests for record votes in the House.

6

Scheduling Legislation
In the Senate

The pace of Capitol Hill places enormous demands on the time of legislators. Representatives and senators work long days, not only on the legislative floor and in committees, but also in meetings with executive branch officials, constituents, pressure groups, and the press. They are also in contact with the diplomatic community, party leaders, and state and local officials. It is not uncommon for a representative or senator to average 11 or more working hours a day while in Washington. To that must be added periodic trips home to attend important political functions, or merely to "press the flesh" with constituents.

Of the two branches of Congress, members of the Senate may lead the more harried existence. There are fewer senators — 100 compared with 435 House members — and in most cases senators represent a larger number of constituents. Senators are more in the public eye and are called upon more frequently to comment on national and international policy. The legislative and committee workload is as heavy in the Senate as in the House, but must be carried out by fewer people. During the 94th Congress, the Senate was in session 2,210 hours; the House was in session 1,788 hours. The Senate averages an estimated 2,700 committee and subcommittee meetings a year, and interviews more than 8,000 witnesses.[1]

The workload is heaviest for senators from the larger states, not only because of the greater number of constituents

SCHEDULE FOR SENATOR GARY HART
Thursday, April 27, 1978

8:15 AM	Breakfast with Jean Galloway, Senator Floyd Haskell's, D-Colo., campaign manager—Senators' Dining Room
9:30 AM	Resource Protection Subcommittee Hearing
10:00AM	Armed Services Committee Markup
10:00 AM	Senate Convenes
10:30 AM	Senator Hart testifies before the Senate Appropriations Subcommittee on Clean Air Funding
11:30 AM	Meeting with Jack Eatherton, manager of Energy Fuel Co. in Colorado
2:00 PM	Meeting with Allen Merson, Regional Director, Environmental Protection Agency
2:30 PM	Armed Services Committee Meeting
2:30 PM	Environment and Public Works Hearing
4:00 PM	Meeting with Barbara Schlei, Administrator, Agricultural Marketing Service
5:00 PM	Meeting organized by Senator Alan Cranston, D-Calif. Debriefing by Marshall Shulman, Special Advisor to the secretary of state on SALT, re: trip to Moscow
5:00 PM	Reception hosted by Senator John Chafee, R-R.I., for A. Bartlett Giamatti, new president of Yale University
5:30 PM	Reception hosted by Representative Timothy Wirth, D-Colo.—Wirth Workshop for Colorado Business People

to attend to, but also because of the multiplicity of political and economic interests in those states. "I don't see how senators from big states like New York and California, Illinois and Pennsylvania do it [all]," commented former Majority Leader Mike Mansfield, D-Mont.[2] The schedule *(above)* of a senator from a medium-sized state, Senator Gary Hart of Colorado, shows the varied and conflicting demands that arise on any given day. As is true of all his colleagues, Senator Hart is frequently expected to be in two or more places at the same time. In such a case, a senator must select the top priority event to attend in person, and delegate staff members to cover the rest or, in the last resort, rely on a fellow senator for a fill-in on what took place. "I pick up my [schedule] card in the evening and I find that the next day I've got three subcommittees who have hearings scheduled at the same time," commented Senator James Pearson, R-Kan. "You can't even be at all of them, let alone do a good job on them," he said.[3]

In response to the manifold pressures on members, the Senate has evolved a highly flexible legislative scheduling system that responds to individual, as well as institutional, needs. The system bears little resemblance to what the formal rules specify and rests largely on usage and informal practice. Unlike House members, all senators have an opportunity to participate in scheduling legislation for floor action. Minor or noncontroversial bills are expedited to save time for major and controversial measures. Insofar as possible, consideration of important bills is scheduled to suit the convenience of members and to reduce to a minimum conflicts with other legislative activity that takes place off the Senate floor.

SCHEDULING MINOR LEGISLATION

The Senate's system for classifying measures to be debated on the floor is simpler than the system used by the House. In contrast to the House with its five calendars, the Senate has only two: the *Calendar of General Orders* and the *Executive Calendar*. All legislation, major or minor, controversial or noncontroversial, is placed on the former; treaties or nominations under the Senate's "advice and consent" authority are placed on the latter.[4]

The Senate, by motion or unanimous consent, resolves into "executive session" to consider treaties or nominations.

Within the course of a single day, the Senate may consider measures on both the Executive and General Orders Calendars. It may go from executive session to legislative session before finishing the Executive Calendar item before it. It did this in April 1978, for example, when it temporarily suspended debate on the Panama Canal treaties (executive session) to take up an emergency farm bill (legislative session).

As discussed in Chapter 4, minor legislation in the House comes up under the Consent Calendar, suspension of the rules, or the Private Calendar. Specific days of the month are even designated for consideration of minor legislation. The Senate has no comparable procedure. Senate rules for calling up legislation — both major and minor — are cumbersome and, as a result, are generally ignored. One rule, for example, requires a daily calendar call with measures to be debated in order; were the Senate to follow that rule, it would lose virtually all flexibility in processing its workload.

Practically all noncontroversial measures are "called up by unanimous consent and enacted without debate," commented Senate Majority Leader Robert C. Byrd of West Virginia. "In this regard," he has said, "I have reference to private bills, most nominations on the Executive Calendar — which run into the thousands — and bills that are not of general interest."[5] Party leaders on both sides check with senators to clear minor or noncontroversial legislation before such measures reach the floor. A single pre-floor dissent will hold up action until the roadblock is cleared away. But once cleared, minor and noncontroversial bills generally take only several seconds or a few minutes to pass.

In 1977, Senate Majority Leader Byrd introduced an informal "Unanimous Consent Calendar" which lists bills cleared to be considered by unanimous consent a day in advance of floor consideration. Before that, minor or noncontroversial measures were frequently "reported out one day and cleared for consent (by interested senators) and acted upon the following day."[6] Not every senator was familiar with the bills being passed. Now all members can keep abreast of scheduled action on consent measures and be present on the floor to ask questions or offer amendments.

This scheduling innovation highlights a difference between the House and Senate. Senate party leaders simply have greater opportunities than House leaders to implement informal procedural changes. The Senate's smaller size and its tradition of cooperation, comity, and flexibility facilitate procedural experimentation. If such changes prove unworkable after a trial period, they can be discarded easily. The larger House, on the other hand, is bound more tightly by formal rules and precedents.

Minor and noncontroversial measures may also reach the Senate floor on the motion of any individual senator. However, the majority and minority leaders normally try to reach agreement on the floor schedule, and are likely to oppose action that will bring bills to the floor without prior clearance from them. In 1976, for example, Senator J. Bennett Johnston, D-La., indicated he wanted to bring a private bill to the floor during the final days of the 94th Congress. "I will be constrained to move to table (kill) any motion that has not been cleared with me," declared Senator Robert Byrd, then majority whip.[7] Johnston did not offer the motion to bring his bill to the floor.

SCHEDULING MAJOR LEGISLATION

Major legislation also reaches the floor by unanimous consent. Majority Leader Byrd has characterized the Senate's rules as an "untidy mess."[8] If they were strictly observed, the Senate would become mired in a bog of parliamentary complications.

As a result, the Senate expedites its business by setting aside the rules with the unanimous consent of all members on the floor. Any senator can object to a unanimous consent agreement, but this seldom occurs because members recognize the importance of keeping legislation moving. By long-standing tradition, the business of the Senate is "largely transacted through unanimous-consent agreements," Massachusetts Senator Henry Cabot Lodge said in 1913, "not only the important unanimous-consent agreements which are reached often with much difficulty on large and generally contested measures, but constantly on all the small business of the Senate we depend on unanimous consent to enable us to transact the public business."[9] The statement holds true today. Unanimous consent agreements are accepted as binding on all senators and are not violated unless the Senate, by unanimous consent, agrees to modify them.

Simple Unanimous Consent Requests

There are two types of unanimous consent requests: simple and complex. Simple requests are made on the floor by any senator and almost always deal with routine business or noncontroversial actions. The simple requests are made orally and are normally accepted without objection. For example, senators regularly ask permission for staff members to be with them on the floor during debate. Permission is sought for committees to meet while the Senate is in session, which is sometimes contrary to Senate rules. Simple unanimous consent agreements may also rescind quorum calls, add senators as cosponsors of bills, insert material in the *Congressional Record*, or limit the length of time members have to be recorded on roll-call votes. Some Senate rules even contain built-in unanimous consent provisions. One rule requires the full reading of the *Journal* of the previous day's proceedings at the beginning of each session; the same rule permits the reading to be dispensed with by unanimous consent. Objections are seldom raised to such a motion.

Complex Unanimous Consent

Complex agreements usually set the guidelines for consideration of specific major legislation. They are proposed orally, usually by the leadership, and are recorded in writing after protracted negotiation among party leaders and key senators.[10] They may establish the sequential order in which measures will be taken up, pinpoint the time period when measures are to reach the floor, and set rules for debate, including a frequent requirement that all amendments must be germane to the bill under consideration. Prior to 1975, most unanimous consent agreements were worked out during floor debate on a measure. They were offered to extricate the

Senate from a difficult parliamentary situation. Now such agreements are regularly worked out in advance of floor debate, approved by the Senate, and then transmitted in written form to all senators.

Below are two examples of unanimous consent agreements (also called "time-limitation agreements"). They identify the bills and their position (Order No.) in relation to all other measures on the General Orders Calendar.

The agreement specifies which senators are to control time for debate on amendments and final passage and also limits debate on various motions and points of order. These are common features of most such agreements. Common,

PENDING BUSINESS

H.R. 7555 (ORDER NO. 261)

An act making appropriations for the Departments of Labor, and Health, Education, and Welfare, and related agencies, for the fiscal year ending Sept. 30, 1978, and for other purposes. (*June 27, 1977.*)

UNANIMOUS CONSENT AGREEMENTS

H.R. 7589 (ORDER NO. 273)

1.—*Ordered*, That when the Senate proceeds to the consideration of H.R. 7589 (Order No. 273), an act making appropriations for military construction for the Department of Defense for the fiscal year ending Sept. 30, 1978, and for other purposes, DEBATE on any amendment shall be limited to 30 minutes, to be equally divided and controlled by the mover of such and the manager of the bill, and that debate on any debatable motion, appeal, or point of order which is submitted or on which the Chair entertains debate shall be limited to 20 minutes, to be equally divided and controlled by the mover of such and the manager of the bill: *Provided*, That in the event the manager of the bill is in favor of any such amendment or motion, the time in opposition thereto shall be controlled by the Minority Leader or his designee.

Ordered further, That on the question of FINAL PASSAGE of the said bill, debate shall be limited to 1 hour, to be equally divided and controlled respectively, by the Senator from Louisiana (Mr. Johnston) and the Senator from Alaska (Mr. Stevens): *Provided*, That the said Senators, or either of them, may, from the time under their control on the passage of the said bill, allot additional time to any Senator during the consideration of any amendment, debatable motion, appeal, or point of order. (*June 24, 1977.*)

H.R. 7558 (ORDER NO. 274)

2.—*Ordered*, That when the Senate proceeds to the consideration of H.R. 7558 (Order No. 274), an act making appropriations for Agriculture and related agencies programs for the fiscal year ending Sept. 30, 1978, and for other purposes. DEBATE on any amendment (except an amendment dealing with saccharin and any amendments thereto on which there shall be no time limit) shall be limited to 30 minutes, to be equally divided and controlled by the mover of such and the manager of the bill, and that debate on any debatable motion, appeal, or point of order which is submitted or on which the Chair entertains debate shall be limited to 20 minutes, to be equally divided and controlled by the mover of such and the manager of the bill: *Provided*, That in the event the manager of the bill is in favor of any such amendment or motion, the time in opposition thereto shall be controlled by the minority leader or his designee.

Ordered further, That on the question of FINAL PASSAGE of the said bill, debate shall be limited to 1 hour, to be equally divided and controlled, respectively, by the Senator from Missouri (Mr. Eagleton) and the Senator from Oklahoma (Mr. Bellmon): *Provided*, That the said Senators, or either of them, may, from the time under their control on the passage of the said bill, allot additional time to any Senator during the consideration of any amendment, debatable motion, appeal, or point of order. (*June 27, 1977.*)

too, is the provision permitting only germane amendments. Senate rules do permit nongermane floor amendments, but unanimous agreements often prohibit them to prevent extraneous issues from being taken up. Some agreements also set the date and time when a measure will be voted upon.

The Track System

Another device used to move legislation to the floor is of relatively recent origin. The track system was instituted in the early 1970s by Majority Leader Mike Mansfield, with the concurrence of the minority leadership and other senators. It permits the Senate to work on several pieces of legislation simultaneously, by designating specific time periods during the day when each proposal will be considered. The system is particularly beneficial when there are numerous important bills awaiting floor action, or when there is protracted floor conflict over one bill.

Prior to the initiation of the track system, legislative business came to an abrupt halt during filibusters. The "two track system enables the Senate to circumvent that barrier," commented Majority Whip Alan Cranston, D-Calif. The Senate "can now continue to work on all other legislation on one 'track' while a filibuster against a particular piece of legislation is . . . in progress on the other 'track.' "[11]

The track system is used at the instigation of the majority leadership or by unanimous consent of the Senate. On July 18, 1972, Majority Leader Mansfield announced the legislative program for the next five weeks. There was a substantial backlog of major bills at the time. The majority and minority leaders agreed "to go ahead with the multiple track system" so more than a dozen "must" bills could be acted upon before the Senate recessed for the Republican National Convention. Mansfield further announced he was prepared to hold up scheduling all other legislation until action on the "must" bills was completed.[12]

The use of unanimous consent agreements and the track system impose a measure of discipline on the Senate. Formerly, senators could arrive in the midst of a debate on a banking bill, obtain recognition from the chair, and launch

into a lengthy discussion of the wheat harvest prospects. Today, complex agreements and the track system prevent that
from happening. Now senators generally know what measure
will be considered during a specific time period, when they
can arrive to speak, and how long they will have the floor.

Comparing "Rules" and Unanimous Consent Agreements

With regard to scheduling, the Senate has nothing to
compare with the Rules Committee of the House.[13] That panel, as previously described, regulates the flow of major bills
to the floor, specifies the time for general debate, stipulates
whether amendments can be offered, and decides if points of
order should be waived. The legislative route in the House is
clearly marked by firm rules and precedents, but that is not
so in the Senate. "Rules are never observed in this body,"
one president pro tempore observed, "they are only made to
be broken."[14]

Nonetheless, unanimous consent agreements and
"rules" from the House Rules Committee are similar in several respects. Each waives the rules of the respective chambers to permit timely consideration of important measures
and amendments. Each must be approved by the members,
the former by unanimous consent of the senators present on
the floor and the latter by majority vote of the representatives. Each effectively sets the conditions for debate on measures and amendments. And rules and unanimous consent
agreements are also formulated with the significant involvement of party leaders, although participation in the House is
generally limited to the majority leadership and only for
rules on selected measures.

Among the more important differences between rules
and unanimous consent agreements are that rules are drafted
in public session by a standing committee; unanimous consent agreements are usually negotiated privately by senators
and staff aides. Measures given a rule in the House are commonly taken up almost immediately; unanimous consent
agreements generally involve prospective action on bills.

The amendment process also differs between the two
houses. Rules from the House Rules Committee may limit

Table 6-1 Comparison of House Rules and Senate Unanimous Consent Agreements

House Rule	*Senate Unanimous Consent Agreement*
Specifies time for general debate	Specifies time for debating amendments and on final passage
Permits or prohibits amendments	Usually restricts only the offering of nongermane amendments
Formulated by Rules Committee in public session	Formulated by party leaders in private sessions or sometimes on the floor
Approved by majority vote of the House	Approved by unanimous approval of senators present on the floor
Adoption generally results in immediate floor action on bills	Adoption geared more to prospective action
Covers more aspects of floor procedure	Limited primarily to debate restrictions on amendments and final passage
Does not specify date and exact time for vote on final passage	May set date and exact time for vote on final passage
Effect is to waive House rules	Effect is to waive Senate rules

the number of permissible amendments or prohibit them altogether; Senate unanimous consent agreements, except those prohibiting nongermane amendments, do not limit amendments. Interestingly, Senate practices regard an amendment as germane if it is specifically enumerated in the unanimous consent agreement, even if it is really not germane at all.

Finally, rules specify almost every significant floor procedure that will affect consideration of important bills. Complex agreements primarily cover two points: limitations on debate of amendments, motions, points of order and appeals from rulings of the chair; and debate limitations on final passage. Table 6-1 summarizes the principal characteristics of rules and unanimous consent agreements.

Unanimous Consent and Senate Leadership

Complex agreements are formulated in informal negotiations between party leaders and interested senators. The job of the leadership is to insure that the interests of all senators are protected. One scholar has written: "Because the system of unanimous consent would collapse if even one senator were habitually mistreated, Senate leaders strive to identify those senators interested in a given measure and to give them ample opportunity to express their interest."[15] If members were to lose confidence in the unanimous consent procedure, the Senate would be in danger of reversion to hide-bound observance of cumbersome rules. It would almost certainly lose the informality and flexibility that sets it apart from the more rules-conscious House. Informal norms such as courtesy and fairness to all senators buttress trust in the wide use of unanimous consent agreements. The party leaders who negotiate complex unanimous consent agreements hold the key to the continued smooth operation of the Senate.

Two recent majority leaders — Democrats Mike Mansfield (1961-1977) and Robert C. Byrd (1977-   ), are largely responsible for refining and extending the use of unanimous consent agreements. Each had his own style. Mansfield was a mild-mannered leader who viewed himself as only "one among my peers"; Byrd is an activist, who works diligently to control all procedural phases of floor action. The two approached the negotiation of unanimous consent agreements in differing fashion, but each was successful in achieving agreement even, at times, in the face of fierce opposition to particular bills. Table 6-2 shows that complex unanimous consent agreements are used more frequently in the 1970s than in previous Congresses. They are also more complicated and govern many more measures.

The majority leader generally has an important ally in the minority leader. In contrast to the House, where scheduling is the sole prerogative of the majority leadership, Senate scheduling is most often a bipartisan effort. The Senate

143

Table 6-2 Trends in the Use of Complex Unanimous Consent Agreements, 1950-1977*

	1950	1955	1959	1965	1970	1975	1976	1977
Number of agreements	40	20	20	41	50	66	54	67
Number of measures affected	29	9	14	25	24	62	53	63
Number of days in session	203	105	140	177	208	178	142	170
Average number of lines per agreement	11.4	7.5	7.7	10.0	10.0	17.1	17.2	16.9

* This information was compiled by Robert Keith of the Congressional Research Service from the Senate Calendar of Business and made available to the author.

system is not merely a question of equity, but of necessity, as Senate rules confer on each individual member formidable power to frustrate the legislative process by objecting to unanimous consent requests. Majority Leader Byrd and Minority Leader Howard Baker of Tennessee constantly consult with one another and their top assistants, other senators, and key staff members on legislative scheduling. Majority Leader Byrd also seeks the advice of his party's policy committee, a 15-member party group which he chairs.

In short, scheduling involves numerous considerations. Party leaders must balance their interest in planning the Senate's business on a daily, weekly, and annual basis with (1) the needs of committees, which require concentrated periods of time, particularly early in the session, to process legislation assigned to them and (2) the needs of senators, who prefer some measure of predictability and certainty in the legislative agenda so they can plan the efficient use of their time. This often means that no matter how carefully Senate leaders plan when and in what order measures are to be taken up, they still must juggle the schedule to suit senators and political circumstances or to influence policy outcomes.

Breakdowns in Unanimous Consent Scheduling

There are times when intense divisions and strong feelings make unanimous consent agreements impossible to reach. The effect of a breakdown in unanimous consent is most apparent on the floor, where opponents of legislation have a vast array of obstructionist tactics — including the filibuster — at their disposal. (Floor action will be discussed in the next chapter.)

A failure to reach an agreement also delays bringing legislation to the floor, for varying lengths of time. Two examples illustrate this point. The first involves the emotional and discordant issue of abortion. On April 27, 1976, then Majority Whip Robert Byrd offered a unanimous consent request on a proposed constitutional amendment guaranteeing unborn children the right to life. Objections were raised to his request, even though the leadership, according to Majority Leader Mansfield, "thought it had cleared the way with the parties most interested in this legislation."[16] Taken aback, concerned senators continued private negotiations to reach an agreement. An attempt later in the day to secure unanimous consent was again blocked.

Negotiations went on during the evening of April 27 and continued until the Senate convened the next day. A compromise was finally reached, under which Senator Birch Bayh, D-Ind., a strong opponent of the amendment, asked and received unanimous consent that Senator Jesse Helms, R-N.C., author of the joint resolution on abortion, be recognized to make a motion to call up his proposal. The agreement limited debate on Helms' motion and provided for an intervening motion to table (kill) before the original motion was voted on. The compromise satisfied both sides. Proponents of the amendment were able, for the first time, to secure debate, however limited, on an anti-abortion amendment. Opponents were given the opportunity to vote the proposal down on procedural, rather than substantive, grounds. On April 28, the motion to table was adopted 47 to 40.

In the second example, there was a much longer delay. "For about five months," said Senator Gaylord Nelson, D-Wis., the 1977 Legal Services Corporation Act "has been on the Senate Calendar awaiting consideration of the full Senate." It was not called up during that time because it faced a certain filibuster by several senators. The threat of a filibuster gave opponents leverage to force several important changes in the proposed legislation and, after lengthy bargaining, a compromise was reached; the bill was brought to the floor and approved on October 12 by a vote of 77 to 15.

Unlike the House, where failure to secure a rule from the Rules Committee spells almost certain defeat for important bills, the Senate, with its greater flexibility, has a variety of ways to secure action on legislation. Any senator can move to take measures off the General Orders Calendar. If such a move has the backing of party leaders and a majority of the Senate, the proposal will almost certainly reach the floor. Alternatively, a senator may offer a blocked measure as a nongermane amendment on the floor to almost any measure. Finally, a senator can resort to the threat of a filibuster or of objection to all unanimous consent requests until the measure is scheduled for floor action.

KEEPING SENATORS INFORMED

At the end of each day, the majority leader announces the program for the next day or subsequent days. Periodically, he indicates what the legislative agenda looks like for longer periods of time. Senators are kept informed of the legislative program through summaries of measures to be introduced, which are distributed by both parties, and by weekly "whip" notices (issued more frequently as needed by each party) listing the measures to be considered each day.

Senators and staff aides also monitor the *Congressional Record*, committee calendars, the daily Calendar of Business, newspapers and other publications. Most senatorial offices (like House offices) have computer terminals with access to an assortment of legislative information banks. These video terminals display summaries of bills, show when they were introduced, list their sponsors, the committees to which they were referred, and actions, such as hearings and markups, taken on them. Legislative support agencies, such as the Congressional Research Service, continually prepare reports for members, committees, and staff aides on current and prospective legislative activities.

SUMMARY

The informality of unanimous consent does not mean that Senate procedure is less complex than that of the House. On the contrary, unanimous consent requests are unique to each bill and are arrived at only after careful and sometimes difficult negotiations. The differences between House and Senate scheduling procedures are summarized in Table 6-3.

Similarities in scheduling between the two chambers are also worth noting. Scheduling is essentially a party function in both the House and Senate. As in the House, privileged legislation — measures dealing with general and supplemen-

Table 6-3 House and Senate Scheduling Compared

House	Senate
Important role for the Rules Committee	No equivalent
Majority party leaders are the predominant force in scheduling, but, on occasion, they confront a Rules Committee that opposes their decisions	Majority party leaders control the flow of business to the floor in close consultation with minority party leaders
More formal process	Less formal process
Only key members are consulted in scheduling measures	Every reasonable effort is made to accommodate the scheduling requests of the senators
Elaborate systems of calendars and special days for calling up measures	Heavy reliance on informal practice in scheduling
Party leaders can plan a rather firm schedule of daily and weekly business	Party leaders regularly juggle several measures to suit events and senators

tal appropriation bills, conference reports, revenue bills, vetoed bills, and Senate bills with House amendments — can be brought to the floor at almost any time on the motion of a member. But in the Senate, to a greater degree than in the House, party leaders decide when such motions will be made.

Standing committees provide the legislation for floor consideration in both chambers. Although party leaders largely set the agenda, they are dependent on committees to process legislation for floor consideration. "I have said to the press time and time again this week that it was my intention to bring [an assistance bill for Southeast Asia] up once it reached the calendar and before we recessed," said Majority Leader Mansfield. "Now it is too late. It is not on the calendar."[17]

As in the House, there are a number of ways in the Senate to bring up stalled bills, including measures never even considered in committee. Senate rules provide for discharge of committees, suspending rules, placing measures directly on the General Orders Calendar, or offering nongermane amendments on the floor. These are discussed in the following chapter.

In the Senate, the strength of the support for or opposition to a bill is the critical factor. If a voting bloc is large enough, and intensely committed to a bill, it can usually overcome the resistance of even the most intransigent committee chairman.

When there is a strong political consensus, bills may sail smoothly through the Senate. In the absence of such a consensus, the rules of the body can be applied to bring virtually any measure to a screeching halt on the floor. The art of legislating in the Senate requires an understanding of the procedural dynamics of floor action. The interplay of issues, rules, and personalities affect floor strategy and the eventual outcome of all bills.

NOTES

1. *Legislative Activity Sourcebook: United States Senate,* Prepared for the Commission on the Operation of the Senate, 94th Congress, 2d Session (1976), pp. 1-49.
2. *U.S. News and World Report,* August 16, 1976, p. 28.
3. *The Washington Star,* October 21, 1977, p. A-5.
4. Each calendar is printed separately. There are also separate executive and legislative *Journals.* The General Orders Calendar is found in the "Calendar of Business," which is printed each day the Senate is in session. Measures on the Calendar are assigned a Calendar Order Number. The Executive Calendar appears whenever there is executive business on it.
5. U.S., Congress, Senate, *Congressional Record,* 93rd Cong., 1st sess., January 26, 1973, 119, S 1391. Byrd was then Majority Whip. It should be noted that Senate rules state: "Any rule may be suspended without advance notice by unanimous consent of the Senate...."
6. U.S., Congress, Senate, *Congressional Record,* 95th Cong., 1st sess., March 10, 1977, 123, S 4012.
7. U.S., Congress, Senate, *Congressional Record,* 94th Cong., 2d sess., September 30, 1976, 122, S17258-S17259.
8. *The Wall Street Journal,* May 12, 1975, p. 21.

9. U.S., Congress, Senate, *Congressional Record,* 62nd Cong., 3rd sess., January 11, 1913, 59, 1388.

10. Unlike simple requests, which are completed orally, complex agreements are formalized in writing and reported to senators via the *Congressional Record,* the front page of the daily *Calendar of Business,* and in party whip notices.

11. U.S., Congress, Senate, *Congressional Record,* 94th Cong., 1st sess., January 21, 1975, 121, S612-S613.

12. U.S., Congress, Senate, *Congressional Record,* 92d Cong., 2d sess., July 18, 1972, 118, 24227-24230. For a more recent discussion of the processing of "must" bills, see *Congressional Record,* 95th Cong., 1st sess., April 25, 1977, 123, S6311-S6313. This involved prospective scheduling of energy and welfare legislation.

13. The Senate's Rules and Administration Committee has jurisdiction over internal Senate matters but is not involved in scheduling bills for floor debate.

14. Quoted in Floyd M. Riddick, *Congressional Procedure* (Boston: Chapman and Grimes, 1941), p. 322.

15. Robert Keith, "The Use of Unanimous Consent in the Senate," *Committees and Senate Procedures,* A Compilation of Papers Prepared for the Commission on the Operation of the Senate, 94th Congress, 2d session, p. 161. This excellent study covers the history, trends, and contemporary use of unanimous consent agreements. Much of the information on unanimous consent agreements was developed by Mr. Keith and is used here with his permission.

16. U.S., Congress, Senate, *Congressional Record,* 94th Cong., 2d sess., April 27, 1976, 122, S6039.

17. U.S., Congress, Senate, *Congressional Record,* 94th Cong., 1st sess., March 21, 1975, 121, S4641.

7

Senate Floor Procedure

A visitor who moves from the House Gallery to the Senate Gallery is immediately struck by the contrast in atmosphere. The Senate's atmosphere is more formal and quiet than that of the House. The chamber is smaller and more intimate, the members fewer and more easily identifiable. Typically, only a handful of senators are present on the floor at any one time. The remainder are busy in committee meetings or with other constituent or legislative business. All senators, however, generally arrive on the floor quickly in response to buzzers announcing roll-call votes or quorum calls.

There are four semicircular tiers of desks; each of the 100 senators has an assigned desk, complete with snuffbox and open inkwell. There are no electronic voting machines in the Senate; each senator responds aloud as the roll is called. As in the House chamber, there are microphones in the Senate.

The chamber is ringed by an upper level of galleries for the press, visitors, and dignitaries. On the floor, a broad aisle separates the Republicans, on the right (facing the podium), from the Democrats, on the left. Depending on the makeup of the Senate, there may be more desks on one side than the other.

The senators face a raised platform. One of several different people may occupy the chair and preside over the session. When he is in attendance, the constitutional president of the Senate, the vice president of the United States, sits there. He may vote only to break a tie. Usually, of course, the vice president is not present. The Constitution also provides for a president pro tempore of the Senate to preside in the vice president's absence. The president pro tem is usually the most senior senator of the majority party. In practice, each day's session is chaired by several temporary presiding officers, senators chosen by the majority leader and president pro tem to serve for a particular period of time. Neither the president pro tem nor the presiding officer is analogous to the Speaker of the House.

The principal elective leaders of the Senate are to be found at the front two desks on the center aisle, those assigned to the majority and minority leaders. To the left of the majority leader and the right of the minority leader sit the party whips, second in command in the Senate party hierarchy. These party leaders, or their designees, remain on the floor at all times to protect their party's interests. Also in the chamber may be some of the assistant whips — in the 95th Congress, four on the Democratic side and 16 for the GOP.

There is frequent contact between the leadership and individual senators. To a much greater extent than in the House, each member has the power to influence the course of the legislative process. Any senator can disrupt legislation more easily and with more telling effect than any one representative in the House. A senator, declared former Majority Leader Mike Mansfield, "if he wants to exercise his power, can tie up the Senate for days, and if he allies himself with a few other senators, he can tie up the Senate for weeks."[1]

That this happens only infrequently is a tribute to the smooth operation of the Senate's system of unanimous consent and to the long tradition of trust among members, accommodation and reciprocal courtesy that characterizes that body. Smaller in size than the House, and more flexible, the Senate normally functions by suspending its own rules in order to process legislation efficiently. This chapter describes how the Senate processes legislation each day and what commonly happens during floor action. Four main topics are discussed: the daily order of floor business, consideration of major bills under a unanimous consent agreement, consideration of bills without a unanimous consent agreement, and special floor procedures to bypass Senate committees. Throughout the chapter various procedural devices used to delay or expedite legislation will be examined, and comparisons with House procedure will be highlighted.

THE DAILY ORDER OF BUSINESS

Under resolutions adopted at the start of each Congress, the Senate generally convenes each day at noon. The leadership, by a unanimous consent request, may modify the time on a day-to-day basis to accommodate the Senate workload. During spring 1978, having lost time debating the Panama Canal treaties, and facing a filibuster on a labor bill, the leadership frequently convened the Senate at 10 a.m.

The regular order of business begins, as in the House, with a prayer and the reading of the *Journal* of the previous day's activities. The *Journal* reading is almost always dispensed with by unanimous consent, except when a member wishes to use the reading as a delaying tactic. Then follows the "morning hour," which technically runs for two hours. "Morning business" is conducted during this time, including the receipt of messages, reports, and communications from the president, the House, and heads of executive branch departments. Bills and resolutions are introduced and referred, committee reports presented, statements inserted in the *Congressional Record*, and brief speeches delivered. Bills and resolutions must be read twice — each reading on a different day — before they can be referred to committee. But rarely is this rule invoked; unanimous consent is obtained to dispense with it.

The leadership may, by unanimous consent, restrict or change the "morning hour." Former Majority Leader Mansfield once observed, "There will be no morning hour tomorrow for the conduct of morning business, unless it occurs late in the afternoon."[2]

Following morning hour business, the leadership schedules "special orders," for up to 15 minutes. Under special orders, members are given permission to speak for a limited time on any subject. The Senate then proceeds to "unfinished business," legislation pending from a previous day. If there is no unfinished business, the majority leader or another senator offers a motion to take up a new measure that the majority leader has scheduled after consultation with the minority leader and other interested senators. This may be a critical juncture in the proceedings, for it is at this point that the opponents of a bill could begin delaying tactics — for example, a filibuster to prevent the bill from being considered.

This sequence of activities is subject to change by unanimous consent. It may also be affected by the method by which the previous daily session was ended — either by recess or by adjournment. The distinction is important because if the Senate recesses, it can resume consideration of unfinished business at its next session, with no intervening activity, such as morning business. If it adjourns, it normally must begin its next session with morning business, following the prayer and approval of the *Journal.*

The decision to adjourn or recess is made either by unanimous consent or by majority vote on a motion made by the majority leader. If a quorum cannot be obtained, the Senate must adjourn. Adjournment favors senators trying to delay business, as it may trigger a series of time-consuming tactics the next day. The majority leader's decision to ask for a recess or an adjournment can therefore have a significant effect on any controversial bill before the Senate.

Recess or adjournment also determines the sequence of "legislative days" and "calendar days." If the Senate adjourns at the end of a daily session, the legislative day ends with that calendar day. If, however, it should recess, rather than adjourn, the legislative day is carried over into the next calendar day. As an example, when the Senate met on Friday, November 4, 1977 (the calendar day), it was in the legislative day of Tuesday, November 1, because it had recessed, rather than adjourned, at the close of business on Tuesday, Wednesday, and Thursday. The longest legislative day on record ran from April 20 through August 2, 1922, a total of 105 calendar days, when the Senate was considering the Fordney-McCumber Tariff Act of 1922. Once the Senate adjourns after a series of recesses, the legislative day and calendar day become the same. Hence, the legislative day leaped forward by more than three months when the Senate met for the first time after August 2, 1922. (The House does not normally observe the distinction between "legislative" and "calendar" days.)

CONSIDERATION OF MAJOR BILLS
UNDER UNANIMOUS CONSENT AGREEMENTS

A unanimous consent agreement governing consideration of a major farm bill is shown in item 1 below:

UNANIMOUS CONSENT AGREEMENTS

S. 275 (ORDER NO. 153)

1.—*Ordered*, That when the Senate proceeds to the consideration of S. 275 (Order No. 153), a bill to provide price and income protection for farmers and assure consumers of an abundance of food and fiber at reasonable prices, and for other purposes, DEBATE on any amendment shall be limited to 1 hour, to be equally divided and controlled by the mover of such and the manager of the bill; debate on any amendment to an amendment, debatable motion, or appeal shall be limited to 30 minutes, to be equally divided and controlled by the mover of such and the manager of the bill; and debate on any point of order which is submitted or on which the Chair entertains debate shall be limited to 20 minutes, to be equally divided and controlled by the mover of such and the manager of the bill: *Provided*, That in the event the manager of the bill is in favor of any such amendment or motion, the time in opposition thereto shall be controlled by the minority leader or his designee: *Provided further*, That no amendment that is not germane to the provisions of the said bill shall be received: *Provided further*, That no vote on the bill or any amendment or motion thereto shall occur on Monday, May 23, 1977.

Ordered further, That on the question of FINAL PASSAGE of the said bill, debate shall be limited to 4 hours, to be equally divided and controlled, respectively, by the Senator from Georgia (Mr. Talmadge) and the Senator from Kansas (Mr. Dole): *Provided*, That the said Senators, or either of them, may, from the time under their control on the passage of the said bill, allot additional time to any Senator during the consideration of any amendment, debatable motion, appeal, or point of order. (*May 18, 1977*.)

2.—*Ordered*, That when the Senate proceeds to the consideration of S. 725 (Order No. 103), a bill to extend certain programs under the Education of the Handicapped Act, DEBATE on any amendment shall be limited to 1 hour, to be equally divided and controlled by the mover of such and the manager of the bill, and debate on any amendment in the second degree, debatable motion, appeal, or point of order which is submitted or on which the Chair entertains debate shall be limited to 30 minutes, to be equally divided and controlled by the mover of such and the manager of the bill: *Provided*, That in the event the manager of the bill is in favor of any such amendment or motion, the time in opposition thereto shall be controlled by the minority leader or his designee: *Provided further*, That no amendment that is not germane to the provisions of the said bill shall be received.

Ordered further, That on the question of FINAL PASSAGE of the said bill, debate shall be limited to 1 hour, to be equally divided and controlled, respectively, by the Senator from West Virginia (Mr. Randolph) and the Senator from New York (Mr. Javits): *Provided*, That the said Senators, or either of them, may, from the time under their control on the passage of the said bill, allot additional time to any Senator during the consideration of any amendment, debatable motion, appeal, or point of order.

Ordered further, That if in the judgment of the manager of the bill, once S. 725 has been read the third time, it would be desirable to call up H.R. 6692, the House bill, and substitute the language of the Senate bill therefor, such shall be in order without any intervening motion or debate, and that the Senate then shall proceed immediately to vote on the House bill as amended by the Senate bill. (*May 18, 1977*.)

This complex agreement, like most others controlling major legislation, reflects standard operating procedure for the Senate: No day is specified when the bill will be taken up; debate on any amendment is limited to one hour; 30 minutes are allocated to consider amendments to amendments, debatable motions, and appeals; 20 minutes for points of order; nongermane amendments are prohibited; and debate on final passage is restricted to four hours. Its only unique feature is a prohibition against any votes on Monday, May 23 — apparently to accommodate certain senators who expected to be absent that day.

As noted in the previous chapter, unanimous consent agreements are printed in the *Congressional Record*, the daily Senate *Calendar of Business* (illustrated on page 157), and party whip notices. Senators check with party leaders, committee members, and staff to learn when bills are to be considered. The majority leadership also announces the next day's or week's program at the close of each daily session.

Measures governed by unanimous consent agreements may be called up by the presiding officer at the conclusion of the 15-minute special order speeches. Customarily, the presiding officer briefly summarizes the terms of the agreement, then recognizes the majority floor manager, usually a committee or subcommittee chairman, for a short description of the bill and its intent. The majority floor manager is followed by the minority manager, who presents similarly brief opening remarks. The Senate is then ready to debate.

Debate in the modern Senate consists primarily of prepared speeches, perfunctorily read, or inserted in the *Congressional Record* without having been formally delivered.[3] When intensive debate occurs, it is often among only a handful of senators with special interest in the legislation. Senator Ernest Hollings, D-S.C., has protested: "We get in here working hot and heavy in debate, but there is no one here to listen."[4] As in the House, even though only a scattering of members are on the floor, a quorum is technically present until a member suggests its absence.

Early Senates were characterized by protracted debates and great orators: Daniel Webster, John Calhoun and Ste-

SENATE OF THE UNITED STATES
NINETY-FIFTH CONGRESS

FIRST SESSION { CONVENED JANUARY 4, 1977 ADJOURNED DECEMBER 15, 1977 } DAYS IN SESSION 178

SECOND SESSION { CONVENED JANUARY 19, 1978

Daily Session No. 266   Issue No. 258

CALENDAR OF BUSINESS

Monday, June 26, 1978

(LEGISLATIVE DAY, MAY 17, 1978)

SENATE CONVENES AT 9 A.M.

(IN RECESS)

UNANIMOUS CONSENT AGREEMENTS

S. 1476 (ORDER NO. 638)

1.—*Ordered*, That when the Senate proceeds to the consideration of S. 1476 (Order No. 638), a bill for the relief of the estate of Harry Eugene Walker, deceased, formerly of Anniston, Ala., time for DEBATE on this bill shall be limited to 2 hours, to be equally divided and controlled, respectively, by the Senator from Alabama (Mr. Sparkman) and the Senator from

(SPECIAL ORDERS CONTINUED ON P. 2)

PREPARED UNDER THE DIRECTION OF J. S. KIMMITT, SECRETARY OF THE SENATE
By HAROLD G. AST, LEGISLATIVE CLERK

phen Douglas on slavery, or Henry Cabot Lodge on the League of Nations. Today, senators are so busy and the legislative agenda so crowded that extended debate is the exception, rather than the rule. On occasion, debate still serves to publicize issues, build constituencies, and influence Senate votes. After one spirited floor session, Senator Spark Matsunaga, D-Hawaii, declared, "I was really undecided on the pending amendment, but Senator Hart so ably presented his case that I will join him" in opposing the amendment.[5] Then, too, there are still "great debates" that capture national attention and mobilize national sentiment on critical issues, such as civil rights, arms limitation, the Vietnam War, and the Panama Canal treaties. In the latter instance, the Senate, for the first time, authorized live radio coverage of floor debate.

The Floor Manager's Role

Floor managers have the major responsibility for guiding legislation to final passage. "I lean on the manager of the bill and the ranking [committee] members to carry the load" on the floor, Majority Leader Byrd has said.[6] The skill of the floor manager often determines the fate of legislation.

Senate floor managers, like their House counterparts, have varied responsibilities. They offer amendments to strengthen their measures or to win support, oppose weakening amendments, respond to points of order and alert proponents when their support is needed on the floor. Staff aides often assist floor managers. Senator Herman Talmadge, D-Ga., for example, received unanimous consent to have more than a dozen aides on the floor during consideration of the farm bill mentioned above. Senators rely more heavily on staff assistance during floor debate than do representatives. Aides draft amendments and arguments and negotiate with aides of other senators to marshal support for legislation under consideration.

The Amending Process

Unlike the House, the Senate has no five-minute rule for debating amendments. There are no "closed" rules in the

Senate. Any measure is open to virtually unlimited amendments. On occasion, a floor manager may ask that a measure pass unamended. Opponents are still likely to offer amendments, but if the floor manager has sufficient support, they will be defeated.

Senators, unlike representatives, can modify their own amendments without the unanimous consent or the majority approval of the Senate.[7] During debate on the farm bill, Senator Jesse Helms, R-N.C., offered an amendment requiring the secretary of agriculture to establish a stockpile of peanuts. Floor manager Talmadge said that if Senator Helms would make such a stockpile discretionary rather than mandatory, he would support the proposal. Senator Helms made the change on his own authority and the Senate adopted the amendment.

Mechanics of the Amending Process. Senators must be recognized by the presiding officer to offer amendments. Committee amendments take precedence over those offered from the floor by other senators. These are often offered in response to new developments occurring after a bill has been placed on the calendar.

Senators can propose amendments to any portion of a bill. This approach differs from the more orderly routine of the House, where the rule specifies that each part of a measure be considered in sequential order, usually section-by-section. Amendments must be read by the Senate clerk, but this is usually dispensed with by unanimous consent unless an attempt is being made to delay the bill. As in the House, only amendments in the first and second degree are permitted. Roll-call votes may be ordered if the motion is supported by one-fifth of a quorum (51 members), or 11 senators.

Strategic Uses of the Amending Process. Timing, strategy, lobbying, and skillful drafting are all important parts of the amending process. Party leaders often try by unanimous consent to arrange the order in which senators can call up their amendments. On important measures, senators regularly jockey for position in offering proposals. Whether an amendment is accepted or rejected sometimes depends on its purpose, and its purpose may not be to amend the bill under consideration. A few examples will illustrate the point.

1. Raising Novel Ideas. During 1977 consideration of an urban transit bill, Senator S. I. Hayakawa, R-Calif., proposed an amendment calling for the easing of state and local transportation regulations to permit more minority citizens to enter the taxicab business. Senators uniformly praised the idea, but noted that it raised numerous questions that needed further study. The senators asked such questions as: How much would the proposal cost? Who would pay the automobile insurance of the participants? Should the federal government move into an area traditionally regulated by the states? The floor manager, Harrison Williams, D-N.J., while favoring the idea, urged that it be taken up by the appropriate committee. After receiving assurances of an early committee hearing, Senator Hayakawa withdrew his amendment. Not uncommonly, a commitment to hold congressional hearings is what the author of an amendment is seeking.

2. Defeating Legislation. One strategy of opponents of a bill is to load it with controversial amendments, to ensure that it gets bogged down in extended debate and possibly recommitted to the committee that reported it — sometimes a fatal blow. "All I know," Senator Russell Long, D-La., has observed, "is that when you get the package too big, what happens is that the whole package goes under."[8]

There are other, more subtle, ways to defeat measures through amendments. In 1964, an opponent of proposed Medicare legislation offered an amendment to provide *increased* cash payments to Social Security recipients. It was an appealing proposal, particularly in an election year, but would have required additional payroll taxes to fund the increase. As former Senator Clinton Anderson, D-N.M., noted, the proposal contained an "ambush. . . . [I]f such an amendment was approved, it would make the levying of still more taxes for Medicare all but impossible."[9]

Medicare supporters, meeting in the majority leader's office, developed a counterstrategy, drafting an amendment that combined *reduced* cash payments for retirees with a program of hospital insurance for the aged through Social Security. The revised amendment passed the Senate, the first time either house had approved a Medicare proposal.

3. Defusing Controversial Issues. A timely amendment can prevent potential embarrassment to committees, members, and even presidents. In 1977, President Carter announced that U.S. troops would gradually be withdrawn from South Korea. Subsequently, the Foreign Relations Committee endorsed the withdrawal plan in a provision of a bill concerning the State Department. Minority Leader Baker, who opposed the plan, said he would offer an amendment on the floor to delete the language supporting troop withdrawal.

Majority Leader Byrd sensed that there was strong opposition to the withdrawal plan and that Baker's amendment might receive strong support and embarrass the new president. He asked the floor manager, George McGovern, D-S.D., to yield to him soon after debate began. Then Byrd first proposed an amendment emphasizing the impact of troop withdrawal on other Asian countries (the first degree amendment) and followed it immediately with an amendment specifying the need for regular consultation with and reporting to Congress by the president on troop withdrawal policy (the amendment in the second degree) to forestall Senator Baker's proposal. For three hours, Byrd "fought a holding action against any conservatives who objected that the language implicitly endorsed the Carter plan."[10] After Senator Byrd had modified his amendment seven times to meet floor objections, the Senate finally adopted the modest declaration "that U.S. policy toward Korea should be arrived at by joint decision of the president and the Congress."[11] An effort was made to recommit the whole bill to the Foreign Relations Committee, but Byrd successfully moved to table (kill) the recommittal motion.

Voting on Amendments

The Senate has three types of voting: voice, division and roll call. Voice and division voting are similar to House procedures, but there is nothing comparable to the recorded teller vote or the electronic voting procedures of the House. The system of buzzers that summons senators to the floor is much like that of the House. During the roll call members respond "yea" or "nay" as their names are called alphabetically. A time limitation of 15 minutes is placed on roll-call votes; it is sometimes reduced further by unanimous consent. Also by unanimous consent, votes on amendments may be grouped back-to-back, and voting times arranged to accommodate senators.

Party leaders and floor managers make every effort to ensure that their supporters are on the floor when needed for a vote. "My experience convinces me," commented Majority Leader Byrd, that voting "is the most critical step in the legislative process. . . . [The leaders and the floor managers must] "have the right members at the right place and at the right time."[12]

Party leaders give advance notice of impending votes in whip notices and on the floor. Occasionally, complex unanimous consent agreements specify the exact date and time for votes on final passage of a bill. The times for votes on amendments may often be agreed to during debate by unanimous consent. For example, during consideration of the 1977 farm bill, floor manager Talmadge, in a successful effort to expedite action, obtained unanimous consent "that any record [roll-call] votes we order between now and 12:15 be deferred until 12:15, and that all votes that we order between now and 12:15 begin at 12:15, back to back at that time."[13]

Over the years there has been a steady increase in the number of roll-call votes. Recall that recorded votes can be obtained quite easily with the support of 11 senators. If that number is not obtained at the time the request is made, a member can summon other colleagues to the floor through a quorum call, get their support, and then renew his request for a roll-call vote. Most roll calls occur on amendments. The growth in the number of recorded votes may occur for several reasons: pride of authorship, evidence of having taken a position, and demonstration of Senate support for a measure that may go to a conference committee. The increase can be illustrated as follows:

Year	*Number of Roll Calls*
1965	259
1966	238
1967	315
1968	280
1969	245
1970	422
1971	423
1972	532
1973	594
1974	544
1975	611
1976	700
1977	636

Senators, like representatives, rely on numerous "cue-givers" for guidance on voting because of the range and complexity of legislation. "When it comes to voting," former New York Senator James Buckley has written, "an individual senator will rely heavily not only on the judgment of staff, his own and his committee's, but also on a select number of senators whose knowledge he has come to respect and whose general perspectives he shares."[14] The position of the reporting committee is an important factor to many senators. "A lot of members of the Senate," commented Senator Edmund Muskie, "will arrive on the floor, and there's an amendment up that they really haven't had a chance to look at, and they'll just come up and ask, 'What's the committee position?' "[15]

On controversial amendments, members often maneuver for procedural, rather than substantive, votes. Majority Leader Byrd has explained the difference:

A motion to table is a procedural motion. It obfuscates the issue, and it makes possible an explanation by a Senator to his constituents, if he wishes to do so, that his vote was not on the merits of the issue. He can claim that he might have voted this way or he might have voted that way, if the Senate had voted up or down on the issue itself. But on a procedural

> motion, he can state he voted to table the amendment, and he
> can assign any number of reasons therefore, one of which
> would be that he did so in order that the Senate would get on
> with its work or about its business.[16]

Therefore, if a procedural vote can be arranged to kill or
delay a bill, it is more likely to win support of senators who
might prefer to duck a substantive issue.

As in the House, the Senate permits vote "pairing," either in "live" or "dead" pairs. In a live pair, one senator is
present on the floor during the vote. The practice is for such
a senator to cast his vote, yea or nay, then withdraw it and
announce, "I have a pair with the senator from. . . . If he
were present and voting, he would vote [yea or nay]. If I were
at liberty to vote, I would vote [yea or nay]." In a dead pair,
both senators are absent from the floor. Their positions are
printed after each recorded vote. Live and dead pairs are not
tabulated on roll-call votes, but a live pair can affect the
outcome of a vote. When the Senate passed its first Medicare
proposal in 1964, several senators first voted against the proposal, producing a 42 to 42 split; then these senators nullified
their negative votes by pairing with absent colleagues.[17] The
result was that the measure carried. (On the vote there was
no vice president to cast a tie-breaking vote, Lyndon B.
Johnson having succeeded to the presidency on the death of
John F. Kennedy in 1963.)[18]

The Final Vote on the Bill

The normal procedure for setting the time of the final
roll-call vote on a bill is by unanimous consent. In theory,
any senator can continue talking and delay the vote. In practice, once the amending process is completed, the Senate
proceeds by unanimous consent immediately to final passage, unless a unanimous consent agreement has been made
setting a later date and time for a final vote. The floor manager announces that there are no further amendments and
requests a "third [and final] reading of the bill." The presiding officer orders the bill engrossed — put in the precise form
in which it emerged from the amending process — and
"read" a third time, a procedure that takes only a few

seconds. Technically, any senator could demand a full reading of the engrossed bill, but this delaying tactic happens only in the rarest of circumstances.

After the result of the final vote on the bill has been announced, there is yet another parliamentary step required — a step available only to the side that prevailed on the final vote. For example, if the bill passed on the vote, a senator who voted for the bill makes a motion to reconsider the vote. Then immediately thereafter, another proponent of the bill will move to table (kill) the motion to reconsider. By this procedural device Senate rules protect the bill from further consideration, and rarely does the motion to table fail. This procedure is also used after a vote on any amendment; the House procedure, as noted in chapter 5, is identical.[19]

To summarize, the usual floor procedure for major legislation is the following: First, there is a unanimous consent agreement negotiated by the majority leader; second, the bill is called up by the floor manager after being scheduled by the joint leadership; third, the bill is amended, with debate regulated by the unanimous consent agreement; finally, there is a roll-call vote on final passage. But what happens when a major bill reaches the floor in the absence of a unanimous consent agreement? By and large, the procedural sequence is much the same, but bills are much more vulnerable to obstructionist tactics on the floor.

CONSIDERATION OF BILLS WITHOUT UNANIMOUS CONSENT AGREEMENTS

Sometimes party leaders are unable to achieve unanimous consent agreements. This may happen for a variety of reasons — intense opposition to the bill, a general desire for unrestricted debate and amendment, commitments by some senators to protect the interests of absent colleagues, or even simply the temporary personal pique of some senators against party leaders. The passage of legislation then becomes a much more difficult task. At the very least, debate will be extensive and amendments numerous; this process, under the Senate's rules, will be extremely time-consuming.

If there is intense opposition to the bill on the part of one or more senators, moreover, the well-known tactic of the filibuster may be threatened or used.[20] It is sometimes difficult to tell when "extended debate" becomes a filibuster — a senator does not make a motion to "filibuster." Typically, the filibuster is viewed as the last recourse, forcing an almost complete stoppage of normal floor business, and a situation most senators try to avoid if possible. Nevertheless, it is the most distinctive feature of Senate floor procedures and deserves careful consideration here.

The Filibuster

Generally characterized in the public mind as a nonstop speech, a filibuster in the fullest sense employs every parliamentary maneuver and dilatory motion to delay, modify, or defeat legislation. More has been written for and against extended debate than any other senatorial procedure. Hollywood even glamorized the filibuster in a 1930s movie, "Mr. Smith Goes to Washington," starring Jimmy Stewart.

The filibuster, politely called "extended debate," has been part of the Senate from its earliest days. It is a formidable weapon that can be used by any senator or group of senators. Defenders of the filibuster say it is necessary to prevent bad bills from becoming law, protect minority rights against majority steamrollers, ensure thorough analysis of legislation, and dramatize issues for the public. Opponents argue that the filibuster thwarts majority rule, brings the Senate into disrepute, and permits small minorities to extort unwarranted concessions in bills supported by the majority.

These pro and con arguments highlight a dilemma: How to strike a balance between the right to debate and the need to decide.[21] There is no easy answer. What is apparent is that the filibuster is a powerful bargaining device. Even the possibility of its use can force compromises in committee or on the floor. Senators of widely diverse viewpoints have resorted to the use or threat of use of the filibuster to influence legislation, as a few examples will illustrate.

Use of the Filibuster. Before the 1970s, filibusters were most frequently used by southern Democrats to defeat or delay civil rights measures. The 1957, 1960, and 1964 Civil Rights Acts were the objects of systematic filibusters by southern senators, each of whom held the floor for several hours, yielding to colleagues for long questions, while others remained in their offices or left Capitol Hill until their turn to talk. The southern senators demanded periodic quorum calls, keeping the pressure on opponents who had to stay near the chamber to prevent the Senate from adjourning rather than recessing.

Adjournment would have played into the hands of the senators conducting the filibuster by requiring the series of routine procedures at the opening of the next session. The senators supporting the filibuster would certainly refuse unanimous consent to dispense with any of the elements of daily procedure — thereby delaying even further consideration of the bill being filibustered. During an extended filibuster, the Senate may remain in day and night sessions with opponents of the filibuster remaining near the Senate floor — sometimes sleeping on couches and cots — to be ever ready for the threat of a quorum call.

Each bill faces two potential filibusters: the first on the motion to take up the legislation and the second during consideration of the bill itself. The 1964 filibuster consumed 16 days on the motion to take up and 57 days on the measure itself. The 1964 Act was unique on further grounds. For the first time in history, the Senate voted to end the filibuster on a civil rights bill.

Moderate and liberal senators have traditionally opposed use of the filibuster, but times change. During the 1970s, Senators Alan Cranston, D-Calif., Frank Church, D-Idaho, Charles McC. Mathias, R-Md., and others conducted filibusters against the Vietnam War; military spending; extension of the draft; President Nixon's nominations of Clement Haynsworth, G. Harrold Carswell, and William Rehnquist to the Supreme Court; funding the supersonic transport (SST); the 1972 anti-busing bill; and a loan to the Lockheed Aircraft Corporation. While liberal and moderate senators have employed the filibuster in the past (on the 1948 Taft-Hartley Act, for example), the "recent obstructionism represents, in frequency alone, a significant departure from past liberal practice."[22] Conversely, senators who have unswervingly supported the filibuster, often as a matter of principle, have become more flexible. In 1971, Senator John Stennis, D-Miss., a traditional defender of the practice, urged his colleagues to terminate extended debate on a draft extension bill, in the name of national security.

Ending the Filibuster. There are two interrelated ways to end a filibuster: by informal compromise and by cloture, a formal Senate procedure to terminate debate. Frequently, cloture cannot be obtained unless compromises are made.

1. Compromise. In 1971, the Senate took up President Nixon's proposal to guarantee a $250 million loan to the Lockheed Aircraft Corporation, which was in serious financial trouble. Supporters of the Nixon plan expanded the measure into a $2 billion loan program for all failing companies deemed necessary to national security, in the belief that such a measure would be more palatable. Senator William Proxmire, D-Wis., charged the expanded measure was a "giveaway of the worst sort," and led an extended filibuster against it. Finally, Senator Proxmire agreed to end debate if the Senate bill were withdrawn in favor of the original Nixon plan of aid to Lockheed alone. By unanimous consent, the Senate agreed to debate the Lockheed bill for two hours and all amendments for 20 minutes. On August 2, 1971, the Nixon plan was approved.

There is a danger in altering bills by proposing amendments in order to placate those who are filibustering. Senators favoring a strong version of the bill may be unwilling to accept a weaker substitute. During the filibuster, senators may meet in the cloakroom — off the Senate floor — or in the offices of the party leaders to conduct negotiations which can go on day and night. The process may take several days or weeks, depending on how controversial the bill may be. If there are no compromises, opponents of the bill may win the battle, and the measure dies. Alternatively, proponents may manage to invoke cloture.

2. Cloture. After decades of determined resistance by many senators, the Senate adopted Rule XXII in 1917, permitting limitation of debate (cloture). Until that time, debate could only be ended by unanimous consent, an impossibility in the face of a filibuster.

What finally prompted the Senate to adopt the rule was a filibuster which defeated a bill to arm U.S. merchant ships against attacks by German submarines. President Wilson strongly criticized the filibuster and called a special session of the Senate, which adopted the cloture rule March 8, 1917, five weeks before war was declared.

Under Rule XXII, a cloture petition signed by 16 senators must first be filed. Two days after the petition is filed, one hour after the Senate convenes, the presiding officer is obliged to ask, "Is it the sense of the Senate that the debate be brought to a close?" A vote immediately follows. If three-fifths of the entire Senate (60 of 100 members) vote for cloture, cloture is invoked. This effectively limits further debate because no senator may speak for more than one hour after cloture has been invoked. Prior to 1975, when the current three-fifths rule was adopted, a cloture vote required two-thirds of those senators present and voting. (This two-thirds requirement still applies to proposals to amend the Senate's rules.)

Once cloture is invoked, only germane amendments may be offered and the presiding officer may rule out of order dilatory motions. The cloture rule has helped ease some types of delaying tactics, but has not finally ended them, as will be seen in the discussion of "post-cloture filibusters" beginning on page 170.

There is no limit to the number of times cloture can be sought on a single piece of legislation. The record for unsuccessful cloture votes is six, on the question of recognizing the winner of the disputed 1975 New Hampshire senatorial election and the 1978 labor law revision bill.

Cloture may be tried immediately after a bill is brought to the floor, but in general senators respect and value the tradition of extended debate. Former Senator George Aiken, R-Vt., once said he would refuse "to vote for cloture until discussion and debate on an important measure has been carried on for at least two weeks."[23] Occasionally, however, cloture *is* sought soon after a bill is called up to block a threatened filibuster, test sentiment for or against a measure, or expedite action on the legislation because following cloture, amendments must be germane to the bill. A cloture motion was filed on December 2, 1975, as soon as the Senate began debate on the Rail Services Act and cloture was invoked two days later. Anxious for final action on the bill, the leadership announced on December 4 that the Senate would stay in continuous session until the bill was acted on. "Now if it means midnight, it means midnight," said Senator Robert C. Byrd, then majority whip.[24]

On the theory that some bill is better than no bill, supporters of legislation are frequently willing to compromise with filibustering senators. Yet there are controversial measures where both sides are open to very little bargaining. When possible, cloture is the preferred tactic of the majority in such cases. The device was increasingly employed in the early 1970s reaching a high of 23 cloture votes in 1975, of which 11 were successful — both figures the highest since 1917. Only four cloture votes occurred in 1976 and five in 1977. The drop-off in cloture use after 1975 is perhaps explained by the relative ease of invoking cloture under the three-fifths rule, the increased use under Majority Leader Byrd of unanimous consent agreements, and the use of yet another dilatory tactic — the post-cloture filibuster.

The Post-Cloture Filibuster

Filibusters try to defeat or weaken bills by talking them to death. The post-cloture filibuster attempts to do the same by employing an array of parliamentary tactics to delay final action. The technique involves extensive use of roll calls, quorum calls, and reading of amendments, none of which counts against the one hour of floor time allotted to each member after cloture. It is particularly effective if opponents have had the foresight to offer a large number of germane amendments prior to the invoking of cloture, which are still pending after the cloture vote has passed.

For the most part, the post-cloture filibuster is a contemporary and innovative dilatory tactic. Senators were long aware of its availability, but seldom employed it. Members apparently believed that it violated the spirit of fair play. Once the battle had been fought and cloture invoked by a large majority, the informal rules of the game dictated that further delaying actions be ended. The post-cloture filibuster, however, was used three times in 1976 and once in 1977.

In 1977, Senators James Abourezk, D-S.D., and Howard Metzenbaum, D-Ohio, prolonged consideration of an intensely controversial natural gas deregulation bill for two weeks after cloture had been invoked. Party leaders even scheduled the Senate's first all-night session in 13 years in an attempt to break the post-cloture filibuster. The story of the efforts of the two senators and the extraordinary countertactics employed to combat them is a classic example of the use of the post-cloture filibuster.

As part of his 1977 national energy plan, President Carter proposed that the federal ceiling on the price of natural gas be continued, although at a higher level. A Senate committee divided, nine-to-nine, on the issue, but still voted to send the matter to the Senate because of its national importance. Deregulation appeared reasonably certain to pass the Senate, because many senators believed that this would provide an incentive for increased exploration. Senators Abourezk and Metzenbaum said that deregulation would harm the American consumer. They directed their staffs to prepare dozens of amendments to be introduced before an expected cloture vote on the gas bill.

Under Senate rules, any senator who offers a germane amendment before an announcement of a cloture vote is eligible to propose it after cloture. Senator Metzenbaum introduced 212 printed amendments in one day alone. They were a mixture of substance and technicalities. There were numerous alternate dates for deadlines in the bill, alternate amounts of money, redefined terms, and various deletions and additions to the bill. Altogether, 508 amendments were pending when cloture was invoked.

With so many amendments pending, the two senators had plenty of ammunition to stall the Senate. Here is how their strategy was carried out:

● Senator Abourezk or Metzenbaum would call up any amendment and object to a unanimous consent request to suspend the required reading. In one case, the clerk took 55 minutes to read an amendment.

● Occasionally the senators would demand two roll-call votes on a single amendment, one on the proposal itself and another on the motion to reconsider. In such instances, the two senators shrewdly voted with the majority to reject the amendments, so they were eligible to offer the motion to reconsider.

● Although debate on the amendments was minimal under cloture, the two senators would demand roll-call votes on each amendment, a process requiring 15 minutes. They made repeated quorum calls to insure that 51 senators were present on the floor. Each quorum call could take an hour or more.

These relatively simple steps enabled Senators Abourezk and Metzenbaum to tie the Senate into knots. Frustration and bitterness grew as the post-cloture filibuster rolled on. "In the course of the last few days," commented Minority Leader Howard Baker, "we have gone through a torture that the Senate has seldom encountered, including not just an all-night session, but an all-night session that was unique and different from others, as we painfully knew, because the roll calls and quorum calls came at 15-, 30-, and 45-minute intervals."[25]

Finally, Majority Leader Byrd and several members and staff aides devised a counterstrategy. The aim was to rule out of order the bulk of the Abourezk-Metzenbaum amendments pending at the desk. Byrd enlisted the cooperation of Vice President Mondale, the constitutional presiding officer of the Senate.

When the Senate convened on October 3, 1977, Vice President Mondale recognized Majority Leader Byrd, who made the point of order "that when the Senate is operating under cloture, the Chair is required to rule out of order all amendments which are dilatory or which on their face are out of order." Under previous Senate precedents, the chair had to wait for a point of order to be raised against each individual amendment before ruling that it is or is not dilatory.

Mondale sustained Byrd's point of order. Abourezk appealed the decision, but lost on the 79 to 14 vote. The stage was then set for a pre-arranged plan. Reading from a typed script given him by Byrd, Mondale recognized the majority leader, who called up 33 of the amendments. Each was quickly ruled out of order by the presiding officer, who ignored the senators who wanted to appeal the chair's ruling, a customary right of members.

Bedlam broke out on the floor. Cries of "dictatorship" and "steamroller" were heard. "The Senate of the United States has just seen an outrageous act," declared Senator Gary Hart, D-Colo. Abourezk and Metzenbaum, feeling betrayed by the administration, ended their filibuster. With 9 days and 129 roll-call votes behind it, the Senate enacted the natural gas deregulation measure. Several new precedents had been set for strengthening enforcement of the cloture rule and studies of reform of Rule XXII were proposed.

Final Vote on A Bill

Once cloture is invoked, filibusters-by-amendment broken, and other obstructive tactics ended, the Senate proceeds to a final vote on the legislation under consideration. If obstructionist tactics cannot be ended, the leadership may withdraw the bill and proceed to other business. Even when the post-cloture filibuster on the gas bill was broken, several senators used some of the time authorized them under Rule XXII to discuss the deregulation bill and call up germane amendments.

On other measures not regulated by complex agreements, and not the subject of deliberate obstructionist tactics, the floor managers and party leaders try to fashion *ad hoc* agreements under which amendments will be debated and voted on. Because of the strong commitment in the Senate to giving every member ample opportunity to be heard, this can be a lengthy process. The 1976 Tax Reform Act, which was not filibustered, nevertheless consumed 25 days of debate. There were 209 amendments or motions on the bill and 129 roll-call votes. The length of time debating this issue reflected its significance and complexity.

Paradoxically, while it is relatively easy to frustrate floor activity, Senate rules make it difficult for committees to bottle up legislation and prevent it from reaching the floor. The means by which senators can move bills to the floor are discussed in the following section.

PROCEDURES TO CIRCUMVENT COMMITTEES

In an earlier chapter, it was seen that the House has a number of ways to bring bills blocked in committee to the floor. These include Calendar Wednesday, the discharge petition, the power of extraction by the Rules Committee, and suspension of the rules. Except for suspension, which is generally used for minor bills, the House procedures are seldom employed and rarely successful.

Bypassing committees, while not an everyday occurrence in the Senate, is easier to accomplish than in the House. At least four techniques are available to senators: (1) nongermane amendments, (2) placing House-passed bills immediately on the calendar, (3) suspension of the rules, and (4) the discharge procedure. The first two are the most effective.

Nongermane Amendments

Unlike the House, the Senate has never had a rule requiring amendments to be germane to pending legislation. "Amendments may be made," Thomas Jefferson wrote in the parliamentary manual he prepared during his service as president of the Senate (1797-1801), "so as totally to alter the nature of the proposition."[26] A classic case occurred in 1965 when Senator Everett Dirksen, R-Ill., tried to add a proposal for a constitutional amendment on reapportionment to a joint resolution designating August 6 to September 6 as "National American Legion Baseball Month." An opponent called Senator Dirksen's attempt a "foul ball." More recently, portions of Carter's 1977 energy legislation were attached to several House-passed private bills.

When Congress extended the Voting Rights Act in 1970, the Senate agreed to a nongermane amendment reducing the voting age requirement for federal, state, and local elections to 18 years. Although the Judiciary Committee had studied the 18-year-old vote for years, no such legislation had been reported out of the committee in the 91st Congress. Backers, including Majority Leader Mike Mansfield and Senator Edward Kennedy, D-Mass., reasoned the proposal could only be brought to the floor as a nongermane amendment. Subsequently, the measure became the 26th Amendment to the Constitution.

Another nongermane amendment was not so successful. In 1977, Senator Pete Domenici, R-N.M., offered a nongermane amendment dealing with the stockpiling of copper to a bill on endangered wilderness areas. "I know this is not an ordinary procedure," he said, "but time is running out for economical purchases of copper."[27] Opponents disagreed. Resistance came from the subcommittee that had drafted the wilderness bill and from the Armed Services Committee, which has jurisdiction over the stockpiling of strategic material. "This is not the time nor the way to get to this problem," declared Armed Services Chairman John Stennis, D-Miss. "Beware of handling matters of this kind on floor amendments where no hearings have been held," he warned.[28] The Senate tabled the amendment 48 to 44.

The voting age amendment had widespread popular support, plus the backing of the Senate leadership, the White House, and key members of the Judiciary Committee, where legislation on the subject was bottled up. Its passage was relatively easy. But the copper proposal was opposed by the majority leadership and by the chairman of the committee with jurisdiction. Moreover, there was no broad public constituency for the proposal. Only the narrowness of its defeat was a surprise. Both proposals, however, illustrate the value of nongermane amendments in permitting both popular and unpopular issues to be raised by any senator, and in protecting against arbitrary committee action.

House-Passed Bills

When measures pass the House and are sent to the Senate, they are customarily referred to a Senate committee. As noted earlier, all measures, including House-passed bills, must be read twice on different legislative days before being referred to committee. Under Senate Rule XIV, if any senator objects to the second reading, the committee stage is bypassed and the House-passed bill is placed directly on the calendar. This procedure was used by supporters of the 1957 and 1964 Civil Rights Acts (the 1960 Civil Rights Act was introduced as a nongermane amendment), who wanted to avoid sending the bills to the Judiciary Committee, which had an unbroken record of never reporting out civil rights bills.

Although effective, Rule XIV is used sparingly because of the general deference to committee prerogatives. It *is* used when the proponent of a bill feels intensely enough about it to flout the jurisdiction of a committee that is known to oppose it. For example, in 1977 the waterway toll bill passed the Senate and was sent to the House. The House dropped an "inland waterway charge" and substituted a "fuel tax" on barge operators. When the bill returned to the Senate, it was headed for the Finance Committee, which handles all tax matters. Finance Committee Chairman Russell Long was known to oppose the bill, sponsored by Pete Domenici. In fact, as noted in chapter 3, Domenici had originally drafted the bill in a way to prevent it from being referred to Long's committee when it was first introduced in the Senate.

To prevent the House-passed version of the bill from being referred to the Finance Committee, Domenici used Rule XIV, and the measure was placed directly on the calendar for floor action. The result was that the Senate eventually adopted a toll on the barge operators.

More commonly, House-passed measures are held at the clerk's desk by unanimous consent. When the House passed President Carter's 1977 energy package, it was held at the desk until Senate leaders decided how the package was to be handled by various committees. Similarly, the 1975 House-passed bill providing financial assistance to New York City was held at the desk with the proviso that the leadership could call it up at any time.

House-passed measures are also held at the desk when similar Senate bills are already pending on the Calendar or are expected shortly to be reported out of committee. Senate Finance Chairman Long asked unanimous consent to hold the House-passed version of the 1977 Social Security Financing Amendments at the desk. "I would think the best way to proceed," he said, "would be just to report the [Finance] committee's recommendations and then proceed to substitute the committee's recommendations for the House Social Security financing bill."[29] The Senate agreed.

Suspension of the Rules

Senate rules can be suspended, provided there is one day's notice in writing and the terms of the suspension motion are printed in the *Congressional Record*. The rules are silent on the number of votes needed to suspend. Precedents require two-thirds of those present and voting to approve suspensions. The procedure is rarely used because it represents a challenge to the committee system and is open to dilatory attack. In effect, three filibusters are possible on suspension motions: the first, on the motion to suspend the rules; the second, on the motion to take up the bill; and the third, on the bill itself. Suspension motions are occasionally made by senators who want to offer policy amendments to general appropriations measures. Policy amendments to appropriation measures are forbidden by Senate rules and can only be made in order by unanimous consent or the suspension procedure.

The Discharge Procedure

Discharge of a committee has taken place only 14 times in the history of the Senate; it was last done in 1964. The prevailing sentiment is that the procedure undercuts the committee system. In addition, rules governing its use are cumbersome. The discharge motion can only be made during the "morning hour" and must remain at the clerk's desk one legislative day. Party leaders can forestall discharge motions for days or weeks simply by recessing, thus keeping the Senate in the same legislative day. If debate on the motion is not concluded within the morning hour, the motion is placed on the Calendar where it faces a serial of potential filibusters.

There is technically yet another way to bypass a Senate committee — unanimous consent, because the Senate can do almost anything by unanimous consent. However, unanimous consent will not be obtained if a single member — presumably a member of the committee that would be bypassed — objects, so this procedure is seldom used.

SUMMARY

There are more differences than similarities between Senate and House floor procedures, mainly as a result of the smaller size and greater opportunity for informal arrangements in the Senate. Senate procedures such as unanimous consent agreements, the track system, cloture, filibusters, nongermane amendments, morning business, legislative days, and executive sessions have no real counterpart in the House. Conversely, the five-minute rule, rules from the Rules Committee, recorded teller votes, and electronic voting cannot be found in the Senate.

The larger, more complex, House emphasizes formal rules and precedents. The Senate functions in a largely *ad hoc* fashion, emphasizing reciprocity and courtesy among senators. House procedure is relatively straightforward, with few detours. The Senate changes its procedures to meet new contingencies, accommodate members, and resolve unforeseen problems. The Senate occasionally observes its formal rules, but more commonly waives them by unanimous consent and modifies arrangements to suit each bill.

Senate rules emphasize the influence of individual members and, as Senator Byrd has observed: "The rules of the Senate are made for the convenience of those who wish to delay."[30] As a result, it is often more difficult to create winning coalitions in the Senate than it is in the House. The discipline imposed by House rules aid party leaders in forming and sustaining majorities. The Senate's informality requires leaders to negotiate new majorities constantly.

There are also more opportunities to revise legislation on the Senate floor than in the House. Senators feel freer to offer amendments to legislation coming from committees other than their own than do members of the House, who are more likely to defer to the committee decision. And to a far greater degree in the Senate than in the House, members are assured that the party leaders will make every effort to accommodate their scheduling needs.

A crucial legislative arbiter on virtually all important measures is the conference committee. Composed of a handful of legislators from each chamber, this "third house of Congress" reconciles differences between similar measures passed by both houses. The next chapter examines this important institution and other ways of resolving differences in bills passed by the House and the Senate.

NOTES

1. *The Wall Street Journal,* November 11, 1977, p. 14.
2. U.S. Congress, Senate, *Congressional Record,* 91st Cong., 2d sess., February 27, 1970, 116, S5207.
3. A Senate rule requires three hours of germane debate following morning business. Called the Pastore Rule after its sponsor, former Senator John Pastore of Rhode Island, its purpose is to confine debate to pending business.
4. *The Wall Street Journal,* September 17, 1973, p. 10.
5. U.S. Congress, Senate, *Congressional Record,* 95th Cong., 1st sess., June 9, 1977, 123, S9289.
6. U.S. Congress, Senate, *Congressional Record,* 95th Cong., 1st sess., October 28, 1977, 123, S18130.
7. Such modifications are permissible until the Senate takes any action on the amendment, such as agreeing to a roll-call vote on it.
8. U.S. Congress, Senate, *Congressional Record,* 94th Cong., 2d sess., September 29, 1976, 122, S17007.
9. Clinton P. Anderson, *Outsider in the Senate* (New York: The World Publishing Company, 1970), p. 283.
10. Congressional Quarterly *Weekly Report,* June 18, 1977, p. 1204. See U.S. Congress, Senate, *Congressional Record,* 95th Cong., 1st sess., June 16, 1977, 123, S9938-S9969.
11. *Ibid.*
12. U.S. Congress, Senate, *Congressional Record,* 94th Cong., 1st sess., September 23, 1975, 121, S16543.
13. U.S. Congress, Senate, *Congressional Record,* 95th Cong., 1st sess. May 24, 1977, 123, S8382-S8384.
14. James L. Buckley, *If Men Were Angels* (New York: G.P. Putnam's Sons, 1975), p. 129.

15. Bernard Asbell, *The Senate Nobody Knows* (Garden City, New York: Doubleday & Co., 1978), p. 267.

16. U.S. Congress, Senate, *Congressional Record,* 94th Cong., 1st sess., September 23, 1975, 121, S16543.

17. Anderson, *Outsider in the Senate,* pp. 284-285.

18. The Twenty-Fifth Amendment, providing for appointment of a vice president in such a case, was ratified February 10, 1967.

19. On May 24, 1976, the Senate voted against the confirmation of an individual for a seat on the Consumer Product Safety Commission. Opponents of the nomination, however, failed to offer the motion to reconsider so it could be tabled. Two days later, the Senate agreed to a motion to reconsider and approved the nomination.

20. The word derives from the Dutch word *Vrijbuiter,* meaning freebooter. Passing into Spanish as *filibustero,* it was used to describe military adventurers from the United States who in the mid-1800s fomented insurrections against various Latin American governments. The first legislative use of the word is said to have occurred in the House in 1853, when a representative accused his opponents of "filibustering against the United States." By 1863, filibuster had come to mean delaying action on the floor, but the term did not gain wide currency until the 1880s.

21. The longest speech in the history of the Senate was made by Strom Thurmond, D-S.C., during a filibuster against passage of the Civil Rights Act of 1957. He spoke for 24 hours and 18 minutes in a round-the-clock session, August 28-29, 1957.

22. Allan L. Damon, "Filibuster," *American Heritage,* December 1975, p. 97.

23. George D. Aiken, *Aiken: Senate Diary* (Brattleboro, Vermont: The Stephen Greene Press, 1975), p. 325.

24. U.S. Congress, Senate, *Congressional Record,* 94th Cong., 1st sess., December 4, 1975, 121, S21022.

25. Congressional Quarterly *Weekly Report,* October 1, 1977, p. 2070.

26. *Constitution, Jefferson's Manual and Rules of the House of Representatives,* 94th Congress, House Doc. No. 93-663, p. 235.

27. U.S. Congress, Senate, *Congressional Record,* 95th Cong., 1st sess., October 20, 1977, 123, S17401, S17409.

28. *Ibid.*

29. U.S. Congress, Senate, *Congressional Record,* 95th Cong., 1st sess., October 27, 1977, 123, S17919.

30. U.S. Congress, Senate, *Congressional Record,* 94th Cong., 2d sess., August 31, 1976, 122, S15039.

8

Resolving House-
Senate Differences

Before legislation can be sent to the president to be signed, it must pass both houses in identical form. House-and Senate-passed versions of the same bill frequently differ, sometimes only slightly, but at other times on critical points. The two versions must be reconciled by mutual agreement. Whenever possible, this is done informally; but about 10 percent of all bills passed by both chambers require action by a House-Senate conference committee — an ad hoc joint committee composed of members selected from both chambers to iron out differences between the House- and Senate-passed bills.[1] Most major or controversial legislation requires conference committee action.

The conference committee process is older than Congress itself. State legislatures used conference committees prior to 1789 to reconcile differences between the chambers of their bicameral legislatures. The conference committee system was taken for granted when the first Congress convened and has been used ever since.[2] Nevertheless, the conference committee is — compared to other aspects of the legislative process — little known or understood by many citizens.

The relative obscurity of the conference process is explained by the fact that up until the 1970s, conference committees almost always met in secret session with no published record of their proceedings. The conference committees produced a conference committee report that showed the results of the secret negotiations, but the bargaining and deliberations that led to these results were not formally disclosed.

In one of the most significant reforms of congressional procedure in this decade, both chambers in 1975 adopted rules requiring open conference committee meetings unless a majority of the members of the conference committee (called conferees or managers) from either chamber voted in public to hold secret sessions. In 1977 the House went a step further, adopting a rule requiring the full House to vote approval of a closed conference.

The conference committee is one of the most critical points in the legislative process. The natural gas bill involved in the 1977 post-cloture filibuster described in chapter 7 ran into even more trouble in the conference committee than it had on the Senate floor.

The bills passed by the House and Senate differed radically, the House opting for President Carter's plan for continued price controls at a higher level — and the Senate approving a deregulation plan ending price controls. The two bills went to conference on October 18, 1977; but the differences were so profound that by summer 1978, the bills were still in conference.

For several reasons members of Congress normally try to resolve House-Senate differences over legislation without recourse to the conference committee process. They want to hasten the passage of legislation. They are concerned that a bill might be watered down by conferees of the other chamber. And they want to preclude the possibility of a deadlocked conference committee — particularly in the weeks and days before a final adjournment of Congress. Failure of the conferees to reach agreement prior to adjournment means that a bill dies.

This chapter explores, first, the resolution of House-Senate differences without a conference; second, the complexities of the conference committee process; and, finally, the last steps of the legislative process — presidential approval or veto of legislation with subsequent congressional action on the veto.

RESOLUTION WITHOUT A CONFERENCE

There are two principal methods of resolving House-Senate differences without a conference: (1) informal consultation prior to or after the passage of a bill by one chamber and (2) the adoption by one chamber of a bill and its amendments passed by the other.

It is usual for House and Senate committee staff to communicate regularly on legislation of mutual interest. Drafts of measures are exchanged for comment and reconciliation, companion bills are compared, and strategies are devised to facilitate passage of identical legislation in each chamber. Executive branch officials and pressure groups often participate in such informal consultation. This kind of prior consultation frequently helps clear away obstacles to passage of identical bills in each chamber.

Consultation may also take place after one or both chambers have passed a bill. In August 1976, the House passed its version of a bill to strengthen enforcement of antitrust legislation. The Senate was expected to go to conference to resolve the differences. However, in September, Senator James Allen, D-Ala., announced his intention to filibuster both the required motion to appoint conferees and the conference report itself. House and Senate staff aides met informally to discuss ways to reconcile differences between the bills. As a result of those negotiations, the Senate passed a substitute version of the original antitrust bill and sent it to the House, thereby avoiding the filibusters by Allen. "What we're hoping," said Senate Majority Leader Mike Mansfield, "is that the House will accept what the Senate has done and send it to the President. In the short time we have left [before final congressional adjournment], any other course is suicidal."[3] The House followed Mansfield's advice and passed the Senate measure with no changes. The president signed the bill into law.

Another approach is for one house to accept the amendments of the other chamber. In 1972, for example, the House passed and sent to the Senate a joint resolution regarding limitation of strategic weapons by the United States and the

Soviet Union. The Senate approved several amendments and sent the measure back to the House. At that point, Chairman Thomas Morgan, D-Pa., of the House Foreign Affairs (renamed International Relations in 1975) Committee urged his colleagues to accept the Senate amendments "in the interest of expediting the initiation of the second phase of the Strategic Arms Limitations Talks [SALT]." To go to conference, he said, "would almost certainly be an additional delay, perhaps a protracted one."[4] The House passed the joint resolution as amended by the Senate.

THE CONFERENCE COMMITTEE PROCESS

It is often clear from the outset that controversial measures will go to conference. Members plan their floor strategy accordingly, frequently adding expendable amendments for use as bargaining chips in conference. Such amendments can be traded away for other points considered more important. Senate Finance Committee Chairman Russell Long, D-La., "usually comes to conference with a bill loaded up with amendments added on the Senate floor. . . . Long has plenty of things he is willing to jettison to save the goodies."[5] For this reason, it is difficult to identify the "winners" or "losers" in conference simply by counting the number of times one house gave in to the other.[6]

Sometimes amendments are added to ensure that certain points of view are heard in conference. In 1972 Massachusetts Senator Edward Kennedy offered an amendment to an appropriations bill to delete $100,000 provided for the National Board for the Promotion of Rifle Practice and also to delete the authority of the secretary of defense to supply ammunition to gun clubs. Although it was clear the House opposed such deletion, the floor manager of the bill, Senator John McClellan, D-Ark., said he was "willing to take that to conference, so that both sides of the argument can be fully developed."[7]

There are also instances when members prefer that certain issues be resolved in conference, rather than on the floor. Former Speaker Sam Rayburn once explained:

My position is this: I should like to see this bill in conference. I have pointed out a great many things in both bills. I think there are frailties in the House measure and also in the Senate measure, but I think we can do a better job in conference than we can here.[8]

A small group of conferees may be able to reach compromises that are impossible in the full House or Senate during floor debate on controversial bills.

Finally, measures are sometimes sent to conference for the political convenience of members. Legislators may vote for a bill, fully aware that it contains special interest provisions, in the expectation that conferees from the other house will kill items that constitute a costly "raid on the Treasury," or are simply ill-advised. When one chamber "passes the buck to the other," former Senator George Aiken, R-Vt., wrote, "the conference committees simply get together and straighten things out. Then every member of Congress can tell his constituents that he voted for the things they wanted and against the things they opposed, and they will never know the difference."[9]

There are five major steps in the conference committee process: first, requesting a conference; second, selecting conferees; third, conference committee bargaining; fourth, the conference committee report; and, fifth, House and Senate consideration of the report.

Requesting a Conference

When the House passes a bill, and it is returned with amendments by the Senate, the House has several options. It can take no further action and let the measure die. It can pass an entirely new version of the bill and send it to the Senate. It can agree to the Senate's amendments, negating the need for a conference, or it can amend the Senate's amendments and return the measure once again to the Senate. More commonly, though, on major legislation, a member will ask and receive unanimous consent for the House to disagree to the Senate's amendments and request a conference with the Senate. The Speaker may also recognize an appropriate committee member to offer a motion (which requires majority approval) to go to conference.

When a Senate-passed bill is amended by the House and returned, it is referred to the committee having jurisdiction over the bill. From committee, the bill goes to the floor where the House amendments may be agreed to, making a conference unnecessary. Alternatively, the House amendments to the Senate's bill may be objected to, in which case a conference is requested by motion or unanimous consent.

Selecting Conferees

The selection of conferees is governed in both chambers by rules and precedent. The House Speaker and the presiding officer of the Senate formally appoint their respective conferees. In fact, both chambers rely on the chairman and ranking minority member of the committee that originally reported the bill to make the selection. The Speaker and the presiding officer almost never deviate from the list of conferees given them by committee leaders, who generally select members of their own committees. A member of another committee may be appointed when he or she has special knowledge of the subject matter, or the bill is of particular interest to the member's state or district. Where a bill has been multiply referred to several commitees, it is common to have conferees from these committees.

Seniority used to be a dominant criterion in the appointment of conferees. But in the wake of the legislative reforms of the 1970s, junior members, especially those with particular expertise or interest in the legislation going to conference, are now often selected. "We used to select conferees by seniority," commented Senate Finance Chairman Long, but "now we try to get more balance ideologically and geographically while still including those who made the biggest contribution to the bill."[10]

Increasingly, members of the subcommittee that reported the bill are being appointed to conference committees, as they are most directly acquainted with the legislation in question. Rules of several House committees, in fact, require conferees to be named from appropriate subcommittees.

Party ratios on conference committees generally reflect the party makeup of the full House or Senate. In the nineteenth century it was common for each chamber to select three conferees — two majority party members and one member of the minority. Today the number of conferees usually ranges from 7 to 11, but there is no limit. On the natural gas portion of President Carter's massive 1977 energy bill, the Senate included all 18 members of the Energy and Natural Resources Committee as conferees along with ten other senators. The House appointed 25 conferees (17 Democrats and 8 Republicans) to consider the energy bill. The conferees from each house vote as a unit, with a majority deciding issues in each delegation. The House and Senate have, in effect, one vote each.

The rules require that a majority of conferees must have "generally supported" the bill in question. "The child is not to be put to a nurse that cares not for it," is how Thomas Jefferson described the tradition;[11] and in 1960, Senator Richard Russell, D-Ga., expressed a view that is still strongly held by most members today:

> When I go to a conference as a representative of the Senate, I represent the Senate viewpoint as vigorously as possible, even though it may not be in accord with the vote or votes I cast on the floor of the Senate. I conceive that to be the duty of the conferee.[12]

Selecting conferees according to this criterion is not always easy, particularly in the case of highly controversial bills that have passed one or the other chamber by narrow margins. One stumbling block on the natural gas bill mentioned above was that both the Senate and House conference delegations were divided among themselves on deregulation versus price controls. Usually, a member's vote on final passage is taken as evidence of an overall position on a measure. Yet a member who votes for a final bill may have voted against critical amendments that were adopted, or for amendments intended to cripple the bill. In case of a clash of interest or views, conferees are permitted to resign from conference committees. The latter step was taken by Senator Robert C. Byrd in 1975, when he explained:

> I was named as a Senate conferee. I do not feel — after thinking overnight about the matter — that I can conscientiously serve as a conferee on that amendment. Although there is no

rule that would bind me to support the Senate position on the amendment, I would not wish to go to the conference and oppose the Senate position, because in so doing I would be putting myself and my will above the Senate and the majority will of the Senate.[13]

Senator Byrd's remarks illustrate another important point concerning conferees. The House or Senate may approve motions instructing conferees to sustain the majority position of the chamber. This places additional political and moral pressure on the conferees and normally hardens their position in conference committee bargaining. However, these instructions are not binding. Conferees may disregard them, particularly when they feel the need for room to maneuver or compromise. The House and Senate may, of course, still accept or reject the conference committee report, and another conference may be requested if conferees have grossly violated their instructions.

The House and Senate seldom reject conferees designated by the Speaker or the presiding officer. The House requires unanimous consent to change the Speaker's choices. The Senate's rules provide several ways to overrule the presiding officer. Senators can offer substitute motions naming conferees other than those appointed by the presiding officer. Or senators can filibuster or threaten to filibuster the motion to appoint conferees in an effort to change the list.[14] Finally, a senator may challenge the conferees at the time they are actually appointed. These procedures are rarely invoked because challenging the presiding officer's decision is tantamount to questioning the basic prerogative of committee leaders to select the conferees, who are only *formally* designated by the presiding officer. Challenging conferees is even more difficult in the House where the Speaker not only has endorsed the nominees of the committee leaders, but is also the leader of the majority party.

Bargaining in Conference

Conferees usually convene in the Capitol building itself rather than in one of the Senate or House office buildings. An overall conference chairman is selected in ad hoc fashion, as there are no rules governing the procedure. On recurring measures that go to conference annually, such as appropriations and revenue bills, the chairmanship often rotates between the two houses. Despite the informal selection process, the chairman plays an important role in the conference procedure, arranging the time and place of meetings, the agenda of each session, and the order in which issues are discussed. The chairman sets the pace of conference bargaining, proposes compromises, and recommends tentative agreements.

Conference committee bargaining, like bargaining throughout the legislative process, is subject to outside pressure. Even before the 1975 "sunshine" rules required open conference meetings, conferees were heavily lobbied by special interest groups, executive agency officials, and the president. On important measures, the president or presidential aides "write letters to conferees; . . . administration personnel show up at conference meetings; and the president freely threatens to use his veto unless conferees compromise."[15]

Two key objectives underlie bargaining in conference committees. Conferees want to sustain the position of their respective chambers on the bill, and they want to achieve a result acceptable to a majority of both chambers. Normally bargaining and compromise are necessary. The conferees may agree to split their differences — particularly on bills funding federal programs. Or logrolling may occur with House conferees agreeing to certain Senate-passed provisions in order to gain leverage on House-passed provisions that are strongly supported by members of their own chamber.

One tactic to break a deadlock is for the conferees of one chamber to threaten to break off negotiations and return to their chamber for instructions — thereby reinforcing their position when negotiations resume. A member of the House once described this ploy as follows:

Last year there was a difference of about $400 million between the House and Senate versions of the foreign aid appropriations [bill]. The chairman of the House delegation in the conference took a very firm position that we had to end up with slightly less than 50 percent of the difference as a matter of prestige. It was the day we [Congress] were to adjourn. We were in conference until about 10:30 p.m., and the Senate [conferees] wouldn't give in. I think the difference between conferees was only five or ten million dollars. The Senate was fighting for its prestige, and our chairman for his. At 10:30 he started to close his book [staff papers prepared for the conference] and he got up saying he would get instructions from the House. All the rest of our [House] conferees did the same. That prospect was too much for the senators. They capitulated.[16]

This example illustrates a number of factors in conference bargaining — the importance of timing and leadership, the threat of yet another protracted meeting after instructions, the role that fatigue can play in resolving hotly contested issues, and the investment that both senators and representatives have in upholding the prestige of their respective chambers.

Restrictions on Bargaining. The conference bargaining process is carefully limited by rule and precedent. Conferees may not go beyond the scope of the bills agreed to by the House and Senate. If, for example, the House authorizes $5 million for a program and the Senate $10 million, an agreement must be sought within those limits. Equally important, conferees can consider only the points of disagreement between the two Houses; they may not reconsider provisions agreed to by both bodies.

Conferees are also limited to the specific matters committed to them, and may not insert new provisions into the conference report. This precedent was formalized in the Legislative Reorganization Act of 1970. Like many rules and precedents, this one is sometimes waived, and new material in fact appears in conference reports. A report containing new provisions not previously agreed to or acted upon can be rejected on a point of order raised by any member on the floor.

A conference committee has maximum flexibility when one of the houses takes a bill from the other and, instead of passing it with amendments, strikes out everything after the enacting clause and inserts a completely new version of the bill. This is called an "amendment in the nature of a substitute." In such a case, the conference committee can consider the versions of both houses and actually draft a third version of the legislation, provided, of course, that it is a reasonable (that is, germane) modification of either the House or Senate bill.

The new congressional budget process places further constraints on conferees. Discipline and coordination have replaced the piecemeal, uncoordinated approach of the past. The House and Senate budget committees monitor the recommendations of all committees, including those of conference committees, to see that they conform to overall budget guidelines. In 1975, for example, Senate Budget Chairman Edmund Muskie persuaded the Senate to send a military procurement measure back to conference because the conferees had exceeded the budget objectives for defense previously adopted by Congress.

Nongermane Senate Amendments. As noted in chapter 7, the Senate's greater flexibility enables it to add amendments that are considered nongermane under House rules. House conferees long opposed amendments of this kind, contending that they undercut the role of House committees and enabled important and controversial measures to be adopted with minimum consideration because House rules permitted only one hour of debate on conference reports.

Frequently, the House was faced with a "take it or leave it" proposition — accept the nongermane Senate amendments, or lose the bill in its entirety including, of course, House-passed provisions. Many members of the House were frustrated by this recurring dilemma. "I have chafed for years," declared Rules Committee Chairman William Colmer, D-Miss., in 1970, "about the other body violating the rules of this House by placing entirely foreign, extraneous, and nongermane matters in House-passed bills."[17] As a result, the House finally acted against the Senate practice during the 1970s by taking several procedural steps including a 1972 rules change permitting separate votes on the nongermane parts of conference reports.

The effect of these House procedural changes was to cut back the addition of nongermane Senate amendments to conference reports. House conferees are now able to request that certain Senate nongermane amendments be dropped in conference, as they would be voted down in the House in any event. The new procedures have also apparently reduced the introduction of nongermane amendments on the Senate floor.

The Conference Committee Report

When the conferees have reached agreement, they instruct committee staff aides to prepare a report explaining the conference decisions. When a majority of the conferees from each house sign the report, the conference committee has concluded its work. Conferees disagreeing with the report may refuse to sign it; but unlike reports of standing committees of each chamber, precedent prohibits minority or additional viewpoints on conference committee reports. Conference reports must be printed in the *Congressional Record* before they can be considered on the House or Senate floor. In addition, the 1970 Legislative Reorganization Act requires conference reports to be accompanied by a statement explaining specific changes made by the conferees.

House-Senate Consideration of the Report

Once conferees report the final bill, it must be acted upon by both chambers. Customarily, the chamber that requests a conference acts last on the conference report, but only if the "papers" are in its possession. The papers are official documents, such as the bill originally introduced and the amendments added to it by the other chamber. Normally, the papers are held by the chamber which passed the initial legislation; however, they may be transferred to the other house by agreement of the conference committee.

Conference reports are privileged, and may be brought up at almost any time in the House and Senate, with the approval of the leadership. The senior House or Senate conferee is usually the floor manager. Both chambers require a conference report to be accepted or rejected in its entirety. A conference report cannot be amended. If conferees cannot agree on certain amendments, these are submitted to each chamber for separate action. They are called "amendments in disagreement." In such cases, the conference report is debated first and the amendments in disagreement are considered separately. Every amendment must be reconciled before the bill can be sent to the president.

Conference reports are seldom rejected because rejection of a report kills the bill and requires a repetition of the entire legislative process. This becomes particularly significant prior to the final adjournment of a Congress when members face the choice of either accepting the bill as it is, recommitting it to conference committee, or killing the bill knowing that there is no time to move a revised bill through Congress. Conference reports also benefit from the same deference that members grant the reports of their own standing committees; the conferees are the experts on the legislation and the sanctity of their decision is general respected.[18]

Once the conference report is approved by both houses, the papers are delivered to the house that originated the measure. A copy of the bill as finally agreed to is prepared by an enrolling clerk. The "enrolled bill" is signed by the Speaker and presiding officer of the Senate, or other authorized officers, and sent to the president.

PRESIDENTIAL APPROVAL OR VETO

Under the Constitution (Article I, section 7), the president has a qualified veto power. The president can disapprove of legislative acts, subject to the ability of Congress to override the vetoes by a two-thirds vote of the members present and voting in each house. Once an enrolled bill is sent to the White House, the president has 10 days, excluding Sundays, to sign or veto a measure. If no action is taken within the 10-day period, and Congress is in session, the bill automatically becomes law without the president's signature. If the final adjournment of a Congress takes place before the 10-day period ends, the legislation dies as a "pocket veto."[19]

Woodrow Wilson wrote that the president, in using the veto power, "acts not as the executive but as a third branch of the legislature."[20] The president can use the veto, or the threat of a veto, to advance legislative and political goals. Often, the threat of a veto is itself enough to persuade Congress to change its legislative course. In 1976, for example, President Ford indicated he would veto a railroad revitalization and regulatory measure. "Because of this certain veto," Representative Harley Staggers, D-W.Va., said, "the Senate did not send the bill to the White House in the usual manner." Instead, certain members of the House and Senate met with administration officials to find ways of modifying the bill to make it "acceptable to both the House and Senate as well as the administration."[21] More recently, in 1978, the House voted down a farm bill already passed by the Senate, in part because President Carter had said he intended to veto it.

In little more than two years in office, President Ford vetoed 62 public bills. Congress overrode 12 vetoes, but the remainder never became law, emphasizing the potency of the president's veto power. Many Democrats were so frustrated by what some called the "veto tyranny" of President Ford that Representative Jonathan Bingham, D-N.Y., in 1975 proposed a constitutional amendment to limit the veto power of nonelected presidents. Congress took no action on Bingham's proposal.

The frustration is not entirely one-sided. Presidents can be tied up by adroit congressional maneuvering. Congress can virtually force the president to approve measures by attaching them as "riders" to legislation regarded as essential by the president. "Almost everyone has heard of . . . the practice indulged in by Congress," former Representative Emanuel Celler, D-N.Y., said, "of coercing the President to approve a bill that he does not want by coupling it with one that is necessary or highly desirable."[22]

Presidents veto measures for a variety of reasons: they regard them as unconstitutional; they believe they encroach on the president's powers and duties; or they hold them to represent ill-advised policies. When President Nixon vetoed the 1973 War Powers Resolution (which Congress subsequently overrode), he cited all three factors as the basis of his disapproval.

Public Law 95-192
95th Congress

An Act

To provide for furthering the conservation, protection, and enhancement of the
Nation's soil, water, and related resources for sustained use, and for other
purposes.

*Be it enacted by the Senate and House of Representatives of the
United States of America in Congress assembled,* That this Act may
be cited as the "Soil and Water Resources Conservation Act of 1977".

Nov. 18, 1977
[S. 106]

Soil and Water
Resources
Conservation Act
of 1977.
16 USC 2001
note.

FINDINGS

SEC. 2. The Congress finds that:

(1) There is a growing demand on the soil, water, and related
resources of the Nation to meet present and future needs.

(2) The Congress, in its concern for sustained use of the resource
base, created the Soil Conservation Service of the United States
Department of Agriculture which possesses information, technical
expertise, and a delivery system for providing assistance to land users
with respect to conservation and use of soils; plants; woodlands;
watershed protection and flood prevention; the conservation, development, utilization, and disposal of water; animal husbandry; fish and
wildlife management; recreation; community development; and
related resource uses.

(3) Resource appraisal is basic to effective soil and water conservation. Since individual and governmental decisions concerning soil and
water resources often transcend administrative boundaries and affect
other programs and decisions, a coordinated appraisal and program
framework are essential.

16 USC 2001.

DEFINITIONS

SEC. 3. As used in this Act:

(1) The term "Secretary" means the Secretary of Agriculture.

(2) The term "soil, water, and related resources" means those
resources which come within the scope of the programs administered
and participated in by the Secretary of Agriculture through the Soil
Conservation Service.

(3) The term "soil and water conservation program" means a set of
guidelines for attaining the purposes of this Act.

16 USC 2002.

DECLARATIONS OF POLICY AND PURPOSE: PROMOTION THEREOF

SEC. 4. (a) In order to further the conservation of soil, water, and
related resources, it is declared to be the policy of the United States
and purpose of this Act that the conduct of programs administered
by the Secretary of Agriculture for the conservation of such resources
shall be responsive to the long-term needs of the Nation, as determined
under the provisions of this Act.

(b) Recognizing that the arrangements under which the Federal
Government cooperates with State soil and water conservation agencies and other appropriate State natural resource agencies such as those
concerned with forestry and fish and wildlife and, through conservation districts, with other local units of government and land users,

16 USC 2003.

A Public Law

195

Presidents may use vetoes as a political technique to gain public support for administration policies. President Roosevelt dramatized his disapproval of a 1935 measure by personally delivering his veto message to a joint session of Congress. President Nixon vetoed a 1970 appropriations bill on nationwide television. In 1975, President Ford announced that he would veto 100 bills "if necessary to prevent unnecessary and inflationary spending increases" by Congress.[23]

When the president vetoes a measure, the Constitution provides that "he shall return it with his objections to that House in which it shall have originated." Neither chamber is under any obligation to schedule an override attempt. Party leaders may realize they have no chance to override and simply not schedule a vote. If an override attempt fails in one chamber, the process ends and the bill dies. If it succeeds, the measure is sent to the other chamber, where a second successful override vote makes it law.

Whether signed by the president or passed over a veto, the "bill" has now become a "public law" and is sent to the General Services Administration, the government's housekeeping department, for deposit in the National Archives and publication in the *Statutes at Large,* an annual volume which compiles all bills that have passed the Congress and been signed into law, or have become law through a veto override.

SUMMARY

Both chambers must approve identical versions of a bill before it can be sent to the White House. Usually, House-Senate differences over legislation are resolved by informal consultation or by the adoption by one chamber of a bill passed by the other. Major legislation, however, generally contains controversial provisions passed in differing forms by each chamber. Resolution of these differences is achieved through the conference committee process. A conference committee, composed of members usually selected from the appropriate standing committees of each chamber, is appointed to iron out House-Senate differences.

The conferees are expected to support their chamber's bill regardless of their personal views; sometimes, their bargaining positions are reinforced by instructions from their parent chamber. Conference committee bargaining resembles bargaining elsewhere in the legislative process; it includes the traditional techniques of compromise and logrolling. There are, however, some restrictions that are unique to the conference process. Conferees are not, for example, supposed to go beyond the scope of the bills agreed to by their respective chambers.

Until the 1970s, flexible Senate floor procedure permitting nongermane amendments to House-passed bills enabled the Senate to force the House to accept many unrelated amendments. House floor procedure on conference reports did not permit the chamber to vote separately on the nongermane amendments. The House responded to the Senate procedure by amending its own procedures during the 1970s, with the result that the nongermane Senate amendment is a less effective device for obtaining congressional approval of provisions of bills that have not been passed by the House.

Conference reports are generally accepted by both chambers for two important reasons — the members' disinclination to repeat the entire legislative process and their deference to the expertise of the conferees. The final step of the legislative process is presidential action, but the president's veto power influences the entire legislative process. The extraordinary majority (two-thirds) required to override a veto forces Congress to consider the White House's position from the moment a bill is introduced until it is finally passed by both houses. Congress occasionally tries to achieve certain objectives by attaching "riders" opposed by the president to legislation that the administration regards as essential.

The enactment of legislation does not bring the legislative process to a close. Once a bill becomes law, it may set in motion a new federal program, redefine the role of executive branch agencies, or change the responsibilities of federal, state, and local governments in numerous program areas. All these new activities generated by legislation become — in time — the subject of renewed congressional scrutiny as Congress endeavors to monitor the implementation and the effects of the laws it has passed. The next chapter turns to this broad area of congressional activity, usually termed "legislative oversight."

NOTES

1. Ada G. McCown, *The Congressional Conference Committee* (New York: Columbia University Press, 1927), p. 12. Also see Gilbert Steiner, *The Congressional Conference Committee, Seventieth to Eightieth Congresses* (Urbana: University of Illinois Press, 1951), and David J. Vogler, *The Third House, Conference Committees in the United States Congress* (Evanston: Northwestern University Press, 1971).

2. Roy Swanstrom, *The United States Senate, 1787-1801,* Senate Document No. 64, 87th Cong., 1st sess. (Washington: U.S. Government Printing Office, 1962), p. 232.

3. *The Washington Post,* September 14, 1976, p. D8. Also see *National Journal,* September 25, 1976, pp. 1353-1355; Congressional Quarterly *Weekly Report,* September 18, 1976, pp. 2578-2579.

4. U.S. Congress, House, *Congressional Record,* 92d Cong., 2d sess., September 25, 1972, 118, 8714-8715.

5. *National Journal,* May 22, 1976, p. 694.

6. John Ferejohn, "Who Wins in Conference Committee?" *Journal of Politics,* (November 1975), pp. 1033-1046. Walter J. Oleszek, "House-Senate Relationships: Comity and Conflict," *The Annals,* (January 1974), pp. 80-81.

7. U.S. Congress, Senate, *Congressional Record,* 92nd Cong., 2d sess., October 2, 1972, 118, 16549-16552.

8. U.S. Congress, House, *Congressional Record,* 74th Cong., 1st sess., July 2, 1935, 79, 10635.

9. George D. Aiken, *Aiken: Senate Diary, January 1972-January 1975* (Brattleboro, Vermont: The Stephen Greene Press, 1975), p. 303.

10. *Los Angeles Times,* November 14, 1977, p. 15.

11. Jefferson quoted in U.S. Congress, Senate, *Congressional Record,* 86th Cong., 1st sess., May 12, 1959, 105, 7975.

12. U.S. Congress, Senate, *Congressional Record,* 86th Cong., 2d sess., August 26, 1960, 106, 17831.

13. U.S. Congress, Senate, *Congressional Record,* 94th Cong., 1st sess., December 11, 1975, 121, 21736.

14. Senator James Allen's threat to filibuster the appointment of conferees — mentioned on page 183 — represented a threat to

defeat the bill itself, not an attempt to obtain the appointment of other conferees.

15. Ted Siff and Alan Weil, *Ruling Congress* (New York: Grossman Publishers, 1975) p. 184.

16. Quoted in Charles L. Clapp, *The Congressman* (Washington: Brookings Institution, 1962), p. 249.

17. U.S. Congress, House, *Congressional Record,* 91st Cong., 2d sess., September 15, 1970, 116, 31842.

18. There are, however, exceptions; the 1976 clean air bill fell victim to a filibuster on the eve of the 94th Congress' final adjournment.

19. Under the Constitution, Congress does not have the opportunity to override a pocket veto. The question of whether a president could pocket veto legislation during a congressional recess or recesses between the first and second sessions of Congress became an issue in 1970 when President Nixon used the veto during a six-day recess. The pocket-vetoed measure, a medical training bill, had passed both houses by nearly unanimous votes, indicating that a regular veto would have been overridden. Senator Edward M. Kennedy, D-Mass., challenged Nixon's use of the pocket veto in court. The U.S. Court of Appeals for the District of Columbia upheld Kennedy's challenge and declared that Nixon had improperly used his pocket veto power. *Kennedy* v. *Sampson,* 511 F. 2d 430 (D.C. Cir. 1974).

20. Woodrow Wilson, *Congressional Government* (Boston: Houghton Mifflin Company, 1885), p. 52. Later in his book, Wilson wrote that the "president is no greater than his prerogative of veto makes him; he is, in other words, powerful rather as a branch of the legislature than as the titular head of the Executive." (p. 260)

21. U.S. Congress, House, *Congressional Record,* 94th Cong., 2d sess., January 20, 1976, 122, 92.

22. U.S. Congress, House, *Congressional Record,* 82d Cong., 2d sess., February 25, 1952, 98, A1152.

23. *Los Angeles Times,* October 15, 1975, p. 23.

9

Legislative Oversight

Congress "sometimes gets in the habit of 'pass it and forget it' lawmaking," former Senator Hubert Humphrey of Minnesota once said.[1] Efficient government, however, requires careful attention by Congress to the administration of laws. A thoughtful, well-drafted law offers no guarantee that the policy intentions of legislators will be carried out. The laws passed by Congress are general guidelines, sometimes deliberately vague in wording. The implementation of legislation involves development of administrative regulations by the executive agencies, and day-to-day program management by agency officials. These are the subject of "legislative oversight" — the continuing review by Congress of how effectively the executive branch is carrying out congressional mandates.[2]

Congress formalized its legislative oversight function in the Legislative Reorganization Act of 1946. The act required congressional committees to exercise "continuous watchfulness" of the agencies under their jurisdictions and divided oversight functions into three areas. First, authorizing committees (such as Agriculture, Education and Labor, and Commerce) were required to review federal programs and agencies under their jurisdictions and propose legislation to remedy deficiencies they uncover. Second, fiscal oversight was assigned to the Appropriations Committees of each chamber, which were to scrutinize agency spending. Finally, the act assigned wide-ranging investigative responsibility to the House Committee on Government Operations and the Senate Committee on Governmental Affairs to probe for inefficiency, waste, and corruption in the federal government. To some degree, all committees perform each type of oversight.

The House and Senate have always had authority to investigate programs and agencies of the executive branch. The first congressional investigation in American history was into conduct of the wars against the Indians in 1792. One of the broadest investigations was an 1861 effort "to inquire into the conduct of the present [Civil] war." Other notable probes have included investigations into the Credit Mobilier in 1872-1873; the Money Trust in 1912; the Teapot Dome scandal in 1923; the Stock Exchange in 1932-1934; and defense spending during World War II.

The 1946 act stated Congress' intention to exercise its investigative authority primarily through standing committees rather than specially created investigating committees. The act provided for continuous review of programs, instead of sporadic hearings whenever errors, malfeasance, or injustices surfaced. The "continuous watchfulness" precept of the act implied that Congress would henceforth participate actively in administrative decisionmaking, in line with the observation that "administration of a statute is, properly speaking, an extension of the legislative process."[3]

TECHNIQUES OF OVERSIGHT

Congress' decentralized committee system means that oversight is generally done on an ad hoc, unsystematic basis. No single legislative agency or leadership group coordinates the numerous oversight activities of the House and Senate. The objectives of oversight often vary from committee to committee. Some seek administrative efficiency and economy, others to protect and support favored policies and programs, criticize administration actions, publicize member or committee goals, reassert congressional authority, challenge the executive branch, or satisfy the interests of pressure groups. The following sections describe the most common means by which Congress exercises its oversight responsibility.

Hearings and Investigations

The most traditional method of exercising the oversight function is through committee hearings and investigations into executive branch operations. Legislators need to know how effectively programs are working, how well agency officials are responding to committee directives, and the scope and intensity of public support for government programs.[4]

Although excessive use of hearings and investigations can bog down governmental processes, judicious use of the method helps insure a more responsive bureaucracy, while supplying Congress with information needed to formulate new legislation.[5] Committee members and committee staffs may travel, to watch public programs in operation, and may request testimony from citizens and local officials.

Legislative and Committee Veto

Numerous statutes contain provisions that, while giving authority to the executive branch, reserve to Congress the right to approve or disapprove executive actions based on that authority. This power is generally referred to as the "legislative veto."

Typically, one or both houses is authorized to veto executive branch initiatives and decisions. The device irks presidents, who see it as a violation of the constitutional principle of separation of powers and a challenge to presidential authority. Presidents argue that the legislative veto reverses normal lawmaking. The executive branch proposes an action, but Congress can block it without the president having a chance to veto Congress' action. President Ford vetoed several measures containing the veto provision. In a June 22, 1978, message to Congress, President Carter called its use of the legislative veto power "excessive" and "unwarranted"; he suggested further that the legislative veto raised serious constitutional questions.

Table 9-1 Public Laws Containing Legislative and Committee Veto Provisions

Year	Number of Public Laws
1967	4
1968	4
1969	6
1970	11
1971	7
1972	11
1973	14
1974	25
1975	21
1976	19
1977	28

Source: Compiled by Clark F. Norton, Congressional Research Service.

In addition to the veto power of one or both houses, a few statutes also require "that decisions of executive departments and subordinate agencies be reviewed by a congressional committee prior to their execution."[6] Under terms of such legislation, commonly termed the "committee veto," executive agencies and congressional committees are expected to "come into agreement" before delegated authority can be exercised.

Table 9-1 indicates that the trend since 1970 is toward greater use of legislative and committee veto provisions in public laws. This development reflects, in part, Congress' assertiveness in the wake of Vietnam and Watergate.

Statutory Controls

Congressional funding of executive agencies is a two-fold process. The first step is the *authorization* of the programs and funding ceilings initiated by the various standing, legislative committees; the second is *appropriation* of actual monies initiated by the appropriations committee in each house. Authorizations may be annual, multiyear, or perma-

nent. Recently, there has been a trend toward annual authorizations to permit more frequent congressional review of
agency performance. The 1971 Foreign Assistance Act, for
example, placed both the Department of State and the United States Information Agency under annual authorization,
where before both agencies had permanent authorizations. A
Senate report explaining the change stated that annual authorization "for both will enable [the Senate Foreign Relations and House International Relations Committees] to carry out oversight functions more effectively. It would also
make both State and the USIA more responsive to the
Committees and Congress."[7]

Congress probably exercises its most effective oversight
of agencies and programs through the appropriations process.
By cutting off or reducing funds, Congress can abolish agencies or curtail programs; by increasing funds, it can build up
neglected program areas. In either case, it has formidable
power to shape ongoing public policies. The power is exercised mainly by the House and Senate Appropriations
Committees, particularly their subcommittees, whose budgetary recommendations are only infrequently changed by
the full House and Senate. The appropriations committees
define the precise purposes for which money may be spent,
adjust funding levels, and often attach provisos prohibiting
expenditures for certain purposes.

Nonstatutory, Informal Controls

There are various informal ways for Congress to influence federal administrators. Executive officials, conscious of
Congress' power over the purse strings, are atuned to the
nuances of congressional language in hearings, floor debate,
committee, and conference reports. For example, in committee reports the verbs "expects," "urges," "recommends,"
"desires," and "feels" display in roughly descending order
how obligatory a committee comment is intended to be.[8] If
federal administrators believe congressional directives to be
unwise, they are more likely to ask for informal consultation
with members and committee staff than to seek new laws or
resolutions. In fact, executive officials are in frequent contact

with members and staff of committees. Discussing the House Committee on Appropriations, one scholar wrote:

> . . .[there] is a continuing and sometimes almost daily pattern of contacts between the Committee on Appropriations and the executive branch. When Congress is not in session, communication continues by telephone or even, on occasion, by visits to the homes of members of the committee. If the full story were ever known, the record probably would disclose a complex network of relationships between members of the Committee on Appropriations and its staff and officials, particularly budget officers, in the executive branch.[9]

Such informal contacts enable committees to exercise policy influence in areas where statutory methods might be inappropriate or ineffective.

GAO Audits

The General Accounting Office (GAO), an arm of Congress, was created by the Budget and Accounting Act of 1921. Under the direction of the Comptroller General, the GAO conducts audits of executive agencies and programs at the request of committees and members of Congress to insure that public funds are properly spent. The Legislative Reorganization Act of 1970 and the Congressional Budget and Impoundment Control Act of 1974 expanded GAO's investigative authority.[10]

Reporting Requirements

Numerous laws require executive agencies to submit periodic reports to Congress and its committees. More than 1,000 such reports were sent to Capitol Hill during the 94th Congress.[11] Some reports are of minimal value because they are couched in broad language that reveals little about program implementation. Others may be more specific, but the report requirement generally promotes self-evaluation by the executive branch and encourages legislative-executive cooperation.

Ad Hoc Groups

There are numerous informal groups of Senate and House members that focus on specific issues and programs.

There is, for example, a bipartisan organization of representatives and senators called Members of Congress for Peace through Law, which keeps its members informed about defense and foreign policy legislation, undertakes research, conducts discussion groups, and provides liaison with citizens' groups.[12]

Organizations outside Congress also provide information on issues and exert pressure for more ambitious oversight. In recent years, there has been a proliferation of special interest groups, ranging from the Children's Defense Fund, on the one hand, to committees against steel imports or trading with Cuba, on the other. "Think tanks" such as the Brookings Institution and the American Enterprise Institute conduct frequent studies of public policy issues and advise members of Congress and others on how well federal agencies and programs are working.

Senate Confirmation Process

High-ranking public officials are chosen by the president "by and with the Advice and Consent of the Senate," in accord with the Constitution. In general, the Senate gives presidents wide latitude in selecting cabinet members but closely scrutinizes judicial appointments and nominees to regulatory boards and commissions. More and more, Senate committees are probing the qualifications, independence, and policy predilections of presidential nominees, seeking information on physical health and financial assets as well.

Nomination hearings establish a public record on the policy views of nominees, on which appointed officials can be called to account at a later time. To insure that nominees will appear later when asked, the Senate Democratic Conference in 1973 instructed all committees to extract such a pledge prior to sending the appointee's name to the full Senate for action.

Program Evaluation

Program evaluation is a comparatively new approach to oversight that uses social science and management methodology, such as surveys, cost-benefit analyses, and efficiency studies, to assess the effectiveness of ongoing programs. It is a special type of oversight that has been specifically provided for in many agency appropriations measures since the late 1960s and in the Congressional Budget and Impoundment Control Act of 1974. The studies are carried out by the General Accounting Office and by the executive agencies themselves.[13]

Casework

Each senator and representative's office handles thousands of requests each year from constituents seeking help in dealing with executive agencies. The requests range from inquiries about lost Social Security checks or delayed pension payments to disaster relief assistance and complicated tax appeals to the Internal Revenue Service. Most congressional offices employ specialists, called "case workers," to process these petitions. Depending on the importance or complexity of a case, a member himself may contact federal officials, bring up the matter in committee or even discuss the case on the floor. Casework has the positive effect of bringing quirks in the administrative machinery to members' attention, and solutions to individual constituent's problems can suggest legislative remedies on a broader scale.

Studies by Congressional Support Agencies

There are three other support agencies in addition to the General Accounting Office: the Congressional Research Service, the Office of Technology Assessment, and the Congressional Budget Office. Each prepares, or contracts for, reports or studies to assist committees and members in reviewing agency activities and performance. Their analyses frequently spur legislation to correct administrative problems.

OVERSIGHT IN THE 1970s

While some legislators and scholars complain that legislative oversight is still irregular and shallow, the 1970s have seen a surge of legislative interest in the process.[14] The Watergate investigations take their place beside the well publicized reviews of the Central Intelligence Agency, the Federal Bureau of Investigation, and the Internal Revenue Service. Between 1974 and 1975, several House committees more than tripled their oversight hearings. The following year, Speaker Carl Albert noted that congressional review over executive branch activities apparently achieved an all-time high during the first session of the 94th Congress.[15] There are several reasons for the quickening interest.

First, in the early 1970s, it seemed to many members of Congress that Presidents Johnson and Nixon had overstepped their prerogatives at the expense of Congress in several different areas, such as impoundment (refusal to spend appropriated funds), executive privilege, war powers, and the dismantling of federal programs without congressional consent. Members began to call for greater oversight to redress what they saw as an imbalance of power.

Another less tangible, but important, factor is the increasing awareness that the abundance of energy and natural resources Americans have enjoyed may be at an end. This attitude carries over into politics, making legislators more apt to hold administrators "accountable" and to terminate or reduce funding of programs that are not operating effectively.

Finally, as federal programs have proliferated over the last four decades, especially in the 1960s, more and more citizens are directly affected by national government activity. If particular problems persist in such programs as Medicare, welfare, business regulations, or public transportation, there are innumerable constituents ready to alert their congressmen. "We have seen," Representative Philip Sharp, D-Ind., noted, that "more and more of our people feel frustration about dealing with the government — whether they're old people dealing with the Social Security System or taxpayers dealing with Internal Revenue or businessmen dealing with OSHA [Occupational Safety and Health Administration] — and we think we have to do something about this."[16]

Responses to the Need for Oversight

The "post-Watergate" political climate in Washington has strengthened receptivity for new ideas and efforts in legislative oversight. Two examples of fresh ideas in this area are "sunset" legislation and zero-base budgeting (ZBB). Sunset legislation, which has been proposed and supported by more than half the Senate and a quarter of the House, would require a systematic review at set periods of federal programs in specific areas, such as health, welfare, or transportation. The aim of the review would be to determine whether such programs were serving their original purpose, or indeed, any purpose at all. Outmoded or ineffective programs would lose their funding: The sun would set on them, an almost revolutionary concept in the federal bureaucracy, where programs sometimes assume a life of their own and live on when all memory of their initial objectives has faded.

ZBB involves comprehensive justification of funding for federal programs. Typically, executive budget makers and legislators have tended to concentrate on requests for new expenditures and for additional funding for ongoing programs. ZBB would require a top-to-bottom assessment of all programs to insure their cost-effectiveness. The key difference between the two concepts is that sunset is legislatively oriented, while ZBB is primarily an executive budgeting technique.[17]

New Tools and Techniques

Senators and representatives interested in pursuing legislative oversight have at their disposal a broad array of new legislation, most passed since 1970:

● The Legislative Reorganization Act of 1970 strengthened the research, study and investigative capabilities of the Congressional Research Service and the General Accounting Office;

● A 1972 law required Congress to review all executive branch advisory committees;

● Title VII of the 1974 Congressional Budget and Impoundment Control Act provided new program evaluation authority for congressional committees and the GAO;

● The House Committee Reform Amendments of 1974 enhanced the oversight role of standing committees in general, and the Government Operations Committee in particular.

While there are still numerous obstacles to effective oversight, Congress is in a better position than before to assess existing programs, evaluate new proposals, and relate the governmental process to the nation's fiscal capabilities.

LIMITATIONS ON OVERSIGHT

Despite Congress' general interest in oversight, there are factors that limit effective performance. Legislators still have too little time to devote to their myriad tasks, including oversight. The Congress is quite decentralized into the fiefdoms of committees; oversight is too often a "guerrilla foray," rather than the continuous review contemplated in the 1946 Legislative Reorganization Act.

The review process is sometimes inhibited by the alliances that develop between committees, agencies and clientele groups. Examples of these "subgovernments" or "iron triangles," as the alliances are called, are the Merchant Marine Committees-Federal Maritime Commission-Maritime unions axis and the Education Committees-HEW-National Education Association combine.[18] Each component of the alliance is supportive of the other. In such cases, committees are less likely to review agency programs critically.

Another factor limiting oversight is the frequent lack of clarity regarding legislative intent. Public laws are the product of conflict and compromises, and when those compromises are translated into legislative language, it can be difficult to determine with any precision what was intended for program administration. On controversial measures, there may have been no clear consensus on goals or objectives.

The size of government inhibits oversight. To many members of Congress, as to the rest of us, federal agencies often seem impenetrable mazes. Huge investments of time, energy, and staff are required to ferret out administrative inadequacies. Moreover, some members are reluctant to support massive investigations that may only reveal that a program is working fairly well, not a result that attracts much constituent attention.

Most committee members favor oversight and feel that the process is needed to help reveal and correct problems before they reach serious proportions. But a handful may agree with the one chairman who declared, "I am ready to do [oversight] whenever there is evidence, but I want an indictment first."[19]

SUMMARY

To some extent, Congress' interest in oversight has been a cyclical phenomenon. Historically, oversight has often been more intense when the executive and legislative branch of government have been controlled by different parties. Recent changes, which have strengthened the tools of oversight, may have evened out the cyclical curve somewhat by encouraging regular monitoring of federal programs. The changes, combined with the influx of activist legislators, probably mean that in the short and medium term, the legislative branch will actively assert policy and oversight initiatives, regardless of who is in the White House.

The important issue is how to balance Congress' oversight responsibilities with the executive's need for reasonable discretion in program administration. Too much congressional interference can wreak havoc with agency routine. On the other hand, ignoring oversight is tantamount to abandoning implementation to the whims of nonelected officials.

NOTES

1. U.S., Congress, Senate, *Congressional Record,* 93rd Cong., 2d sess., March 28, 1974, 120, 4611.
2. For several studies on oversight, see Morris S. Ogul, *Congress Oversees the Bureaucracy* (Pittsburgh: University of Pittsburgh Press, 1976). Professor Ogul's book contains a lengthy bibliography on oversight. In addition, Joseph Harris, *Congressional Control of Administration* (Washington: The Brookings Institution, 1964); Seymour Scher, "Congressional Committee Members as Independent Agency Overseers: A Case Study," *American Political Science Review,* (December 1960), pp. 911-920; and "Fiscal Oversight of the Central Intelligence Agency: Can Accountability and Confidentiality Coexist?" *New York Journal of International Law and Politics* (Winter 1974), pp. 493-544.

3. David B. Truman, *The Governmental Process* (New York: Alfred Knopf, 1953), p. 439. The continuous watchfulness provision was retitled legislative "review" by the Legislation Reorganization Act of 1970. That act also directed House and Senate committees to submit biennial reports on their oversight activities.

4. Richard F. Fenno, "The Impact of PPBS on the Congressional Appropriations Process." In *Information Support, Program Budgeting, and the Congress*, ed. Robert L. Chartrand, Kenneth Janda, and Michael Hugo (New York: Spartan Books, 1968), pp. 181-182.

5. Congressional claims for agency information may be blocked by executive privilege. See, for example, Bernard Schwartz, "Executive Privilege and Congressional Investigatory Power," *California Law Review* (March 1959), pp. 3-50; Raoul Berger, *Executive Privilege: A Constitutional Myth* (Cambridge, Mass.: Harvard University Press, 1974); *U.S. v. Nixon,* 418 U.S. 683 (1974); and "Symposium: United States v. Nixon," *UCLA Law Review* (October 1974), pp. 1-40.

6. William Rhode, *Committee Clearance of Administrative Decisions* (East Lansing, Mich.: Michigan State Press, 1959), p. 4. On the constitutionality of the legislative veto, see Geoffrey S. Stewart, "Constitutionality of the Legislative Veto," *Harvard Journal on Legislation* (April 1976), pp. 593-619 and "Congressional Veto of Administrative Action: The Probable Response to a Constitutional Challenge," *Duke Law Journal* (May 1976), pp. 285-300.

7. U.S., Congress, Senate, Senate Report No. 92-404, 92nd Congress, 1st session (1971), p. 56.

8. Michael Kirst, *Government Without Passing Laws* (Chapel Hill: University of North Carolina Press, 1969), p. 37.

9. Holbert Carroll, *The House of Representatives and Foreign Affairs,* revised edition (Boston: Little, Brown, 1966), p. 172. A good example of nonstatutory controls involves the reprogramming of funds within executive accounts. Reprogramming refers to the expenditure of funds for purposes not originally intended when Congress approved departmental budgets. Agencies secure approval for reprogramming from appropriate House and Senate committees.

10. For studies of the General Accounting Office, see Thomas D. Morgan, "The General Accounting Office: One Hope for Congress to Regain Parity of Power With the President," *North Carolina Law Review* (October 1973), pp. 1279-1368 and Richard E. Brown, *The GAO, Untapped Source of Congressional Power* (Knoxville: University of Tennessee Press, 1970).

11. *Reports To Be Made To Congress,* Clerk of the U.S. House of Representatives, 94th Congress, 1st session (January 14, 1975).

Also see J. Malcolm Smith and Cornelius P. Cotter, "Administrative Accountability: Reporting to Congress," *Western Political Quarterly* (June 1957), pp. 405-415.

12. Congressional Quarterly *Weekly Report,* July 31, 1970, pp. 1952-1956.

13. See, for example, Joseph Wholey, et al., *Federal Evaluation Policy* (Washington: The Urban Institute, 1970); Joel Havemann, "Congress Tries to Break Ground Zero in Evaluating Federal Programs," *National Journal,* May 22, 1976, pp. 706-713; *Legislative Oversight and Program Evaluation, A Seminar Sponsored by the Congressional Research Service.* Committee Print prepared for the Subcommittee on Oversight Procedures of the Senate Committee on Government Operations, May 1976 (Washington: Government Printing Office, 1976); and "Program Evaluation: A Cautious Perspective," Public Policy Forum, *The Bureaucrat* (April 1976), pp. 3-100.

14. For a critique of comprehensive oversight, see Morris S. Ogul, "Legislative Oversight of Bureaucracy," in *Committee Organization in the House,* Panel discussions before the House Select Committee on Committees, 93rd Congress, 1st session (1973), p. 702.

15. U.S., Congress, House, *Congressional Record,* 94th Cong., 2d sess., January 6, 1976, 122 E6897.

16. *The Wall Street Journal,* March 6, 1975, p. 12.

17. For several analyses of sunset and ZBB, see *Zero-Base Budget Legislation,* Hearings before the Task Force on Budget Process of the House Committee on the Budget, 94th Congress, 2nd session (1976); *Government Economy and Spending Reform Act of 1976, Hearings before the Subcommittee on Intergovernmental Relations of the Senate Committee on Government Operations,* 94th Congress, 2nd session (1976); *The Wall Street Journal,* July 9, 1976, p. 12; and *New York Times,* August 8, 1976, pp. 1, 6.

18. See Theodore J. Lowi, *The End of Liberalism* (New York: Norton, 1969) and J. Leiper Freeman, *The Political Process: Executive Bureau-Legislative Committee Relations,* rev. ed. (New York: Random House, 1965).

19. *Committee Organization in the House,* p. 67.

10

Conclusion

The ideas expressed in this book rest on the assumptions that Congress matters and that its rules and procedures are important.

Congress' policymaking role is firmly grounded in the Constitution. It is true that the preeminent place for Congress envisioned by the writers of the Constitution has been modified by the growth of executive power in the twentieth century. But it is equally true that the constitutional separation of powers has preserved for Congress an independent role that distinguishes it from legislative bodies in most western democracies.

This book has focused on procedures and rules in Congress because their influence permeates the policymaking process. Details of procedure have a policy impact, and it is impossible to understand why certain policies are adopted and others are not without an appreciation of the rules governing the process.

Congressional rules serve many functions — they promote stability, divide responsibilities, minimize conflict in daily decisionmaking, legitimize decisions, and distribute power. Paradoxically, because the rules do distribute power, they create tensions between those whose influential positions are protected by the rules and those who have limited influence. The substantial overhaul of congressional procedures that has taken place in this decade was in large part an effort by junior and newly elected members of Congress to gain more influence. When the two parties dropped seniority as the sole basis for deciding which members would head committees, they were not simply changing a selection procedure; they were creating opportunities for newer members to attain positions of influence.

This change, in turn, greatly affected members' relationships with interest groups and the executive branch. There were now many more points of access for groups trying to influence congressional decisions. Changes in the rules can have broad impact outside Congress.

The effect of rules on policy outcomes has been demonstrated repeatedly in this book. The requirement for an extraordinary majority of the Senate to invoke cloture gives to a well-organized minority the ability to block passage of legislation desired by a simple majority. Civil rights legislation, perhaps the classic case, was repeatedly delayed in the 1950s and 1960s by the use of the filibuster by its opponents.

On the other hand, the rules themselves may change in response to events or policy goals. Some rules are modified or ignored; new ones come out of struggles over a particular problem. Cloture was made somewhat easier in 1975 by changing the majority needed from two-thirds to three-fifths. In 1976, in response, a long-ignored procedure was revived — the post-cloture filibuster. Then this tactic led to the adoption of a new precedent for the presiding officer of the Senate to rule dilatory amendments out of order.

We have also observed cases where an ostensibly procedural goal can be used to mask a policy objective. When members vote to table a piece of legislation, procedurally they are merely postponing consideration of it; nevertheless, this procedure usually kills the legislation and permits members to say they did not take a position on it.

The most significant and enduring feature of the rules is that they require each bill to pass through a labyrinth of decision points before it can become law. It is generally more difficult to pass legislation than to defeat it. These multiple decision points, coupled with weak party discipline, make necessary a constant cycle of coalition building — by means of the various bargaining techniques — to move each measure past potential roadblocks. The shifting coalitions combine, dissolve, and recombine in response to the widely varying issues and the needs of members.

Coalition building is possible for two reasons — first, members of Congress representing diverse constituencies are not equally concerned about the many items on the legislative agenda and, second, members pursue many objectives other than the enactment of legislation. They may seek re-election, election to higher office, appointment to prestigious committees, or simply personal conveniences such as additional staff or office space.

The differential interest in legislation and the nonlegislative goals members pursue create numerous opportunities for coalition building through the three types of bargaining discussed — logrolling, compromise, and the distribution (primarily by the congressional leadership) of nonlegislative favors.

Another factor in determining whether or not a series of majority coalitions can be built is the extent to which members believe that some sort of legislation is required or inevitable on a particular subject. Members may have widely divergent views on the solution to the problem, but they will work hard to compromise their differences when dealing with "must" legislation.

A critical factor influencing the entire congressional process is time. As the two-year cycle of a Congress runs its course, every procedural device employed has a policy consequence if it delays or hastens the processing of legislation. Frequently, as the countdown to final adjournment occurs, the bargaining process shifts into high gear. Bills that have been deadlocked for months are moved along swiftly as logrolling and compromises "save" bills members need. Legislation stalled by opponents, however, dies if not enacted before adjournment.

This book has been written at a time when many congressional rules and procedures have undergone significant revision. Congress, in response to its perception of a growing dominance by the executive, the demands of its junior and reform-minded senior members, negative ratings from the public, and the pressure from interest groups, has revised some of its stronger traditions, such as the selection of committee chairmen by seniority, secrecy of committee proceedings, nonrecorded votes, and the power of the filibuster.

The effect of these changes has been mixed. There is a strong trend toward decentralization, reinforced by the increased importance of subcommittees, the involvement of more and more junior members in policymaking roles, the greater access to members for interest groups and the public, and the more common practice of multiple referral of measures to two or more committees. On the other hand, some changes, such as the new budget process, revitalized party caucuses, and strengthened party leadership, have had a centralizing effect.

In mid-1978 it is difficult to predict the long-term effects of the recent procedural changes. It is certain that from time to time members of Congress will seek additional changes in rules and procedures for a variety of reasons: to remedy specific problems, to become more efficient, to redistribute power, or to affect policy outcomes. In particular, future changes in the rules are likely to focus on revision of the budgetary process, oversight procedures, and use of the post-cloture filibuster. In summer 1978, for example, several members were urging modification of the 1974 budget act to allow more time for committee consideration of authorization legislation.

And so the dynamic interplay between policymaking and the rules continues. Precedents and practices are revised or abandoned and new ones established, often with great difficulty, to respond to changing needs and pressures. Inevitably, enactment of national policies is shaped by congressional rules and procedures.

Glossary

Adjournment sine die — This is used to connote the *final* adjournment of a session of Congress. A session can continue until noon, Jan. 3, of the following year, when a new session usually begins. There is also adjournment to a day certain. By motion or unanimous consent the House or Senate fixes the next time of meeting. Neither house can adjourn for more than three days without the concurrence of the other. A session of Congress is not ended by adjournment to a day certain.

Appeal — A senator's challenge of a ruling or decision made by the presiding officer of the Senate. The senator appeals to members of the chamber to override the decision. If carried by a majority vote, the appeal nullifies the chair's ruling. In the House the decision of the Speaker traditionally has been final. To appeal a ruling would be considered an attack on the Speaker. Rarely are such appeals successful.

Appropriation Bill — Grants the actual monies approved by authorization bills, but not necessarily to the total permissible under the authorization bill. An appropriation bill originates in the House, and normally is not acted on until its authorization measure is enacted. General appropriations bills are supposed to be enacted by the seventh day after Labor Day before the start of the fiscal year to which they apply, but this does not always happen. In addition to general appropriations bills, there are two specialized types. *(See Continuing and Supplemental.)*

Authorization Bill — Authorizes a program, specifies its general aim and conduct, and unless "open-ended," puts a ceiling on monies that can be used to finance it. Usually enacted before an appropriation bill is passed.

Bills — Most legislative proposals before Congress are in the form of bills, and are designated as HR (House of Representatives) or S (Senate) according to the house in which they originate and by a number assigned in the order in which they were introduced, from the beginning of each two-year congressional term. "Public bills" deal with general questions, and become Public Laws if approved by Congress and signed by the president. "Private bills" deal with individual matters such as claims against the government, immigration and naturalization cases, land titles, etc., and become Private Laws if approved and signed.

Calendar — An agenda or list of pending business before committees or either chamber. The House uses five legislative calendars. *(See Consent, Discharge, House, Private and Union Calendars.)*

In the Senate, all legislative matters reported from committee go on a single calendar. They are listed there in order, but may be called up irregularly by the majority leader either by a motion to do so, or by obtaining the unanimous consent of the Senate. Frequently the minority leader is consulted to ensure unanimous consent. Only cloture can limit debate on bills thus called up. *(See Call of the Calendar.)*

The Senate also uses an executive calendar, for treaties, etc.

Calendar Wednesday — In the House on Wednesdays, committees may be called in the order in which they appear in Rule X of the House Manual, for the purpose of bringing up any of their bills from the House or the Union Calendars, except bills which are privileged. General debate is limited to two hours. Bills called up from the Union Calendar are considered in Committee of the Whole. Calendar Wednesday is not observed during the last two weeks of a session, and may be dispensed with at other times — by a two-thirds vote. It usually is dispensed with.

Call of the Calendar — Senate bills which are not brought up for debate by a motion or a unanimous consent agreement are brought before the Senate for action when the calendar listing them in order is "called." Bills considered in this fashion are usually noncontroversial, and debate is limited to five minutes for each senator on a bill or on amendments to it.

Clean Bill — Frequently after a committee has finished a major revision of a bill, one of the committee members, usually the chairman, will assemble the changes plus what is left of the original bill into a new measure and introduce it as a "clean bill." The new measure, which carries a new number, is then sent to the floor for consideration. This often is a timesaver, as committee-recommended changes do not have to be considered one at a time by the chamber.

Clerk of the House — Chief administrative officer of the House of Representatives with duties corresponding to those of the secretary of the Senate. *(See Secretary of the Senate.)*

Cloture — The process by which debate can be limited in the Senate, other than by unanimous consent. A motion for cloture can apply to any measure before the Senate, including a proposal to change the chamber's rules. It is put to a roll-call vote one hour after the Senate meets on the second day following introduction of the motion. If voted, cloture limits each senator to one hour of debate.

Committee of the Whole — The working title of what is formally "The Committee of the Whole House (of Representatives) on the State of the Union." Unlike other committees, it has no fixed membership. It is comprised of any 100 or more House members who participate — on the floor of the chamber — in debating or amending legislation before the body. Such measures, however, must first have passed through the regular committees and be on the calendar.

When the full House resolves itself into the Committee of the Whole, it supplants the Speaker with a "chairman." The measure is debated or amended, with recorded votes as needed. When the committee completes its action on the measure, it dissolves itself by "rising." The Speaker returns, and the full House hears the erstwhile chairman of the committee report that group's recommendations. The full House then acts upon them.

Concurrent Resolution — A concurrent resolution, designated H Con Res or S Con Res, must be passed by both houses but does not require the signature of the president and does not have the force of law. Concurrent resolutions generally are used to make or amend rules applicable to both houses or to express the sentiment of the two houses. A concurrent resolution, for example, is used to fix the time for adjournment of a Congress. It might also be used to convey the congratulations of Congress to another country on the anniversary of its independence.

Conference — A meeting between the representatives of the House and Senate to reconcile differences between the two houses over provisions of a bill. Members of the conference committee are appointed by the Speaker and the president of the Senate and are called "managers" for their respective chambers.

Consent Calendar — Members of the House may place on this calendar any bill on the Union or House Calendar which is considered to be noncontroversial. Bills on the Consent Calendar are normally called on the first and third Mondays of each month. On the first occasion when a bill is called in this manner, consideration may be blocked by the objection of any member. On the second time, if there are three objections, the bill is stricken from the Consent Calendar; if less than three members object, the bill is given immediate consideration.

Continuing Appropriations — When a fiscal year begins and Congress has not yet enacted all the regular appropriation bills for that year, it passes a joint resolution "continuing appropriations" for government agencies at rates generally based on their previous year's appropriations.

Dilatory Motion — A motion, usually made upon a technical point, for the purpose of killing time and preventing action on a bill. The rules outlaw dilatory motions, but enforcement is largely within the discretion of the presiding officer.

Discharge a Committee — Relieve a committee from jurisdiction over a measure before it. This is rarely a successful procedure, attempted more often in the House than in the Senate.

In the House, if a committee does not report a bill within 30 days after the bill was referred to it, any member may file a discharge motion. This motion, treated as a petition, needs the signatures of 218 members (a majority of the House). After the required signatures have been obtained, there is a delay of seven days. Then, on the second and fourth Monday of each month, except during the last six days of a session, any member who has signed the petition may be recognized to move that the committee be discharged. Debate on the motion to discharge is limited to 20 minutes, and, if the motion is carried, consideration of the bill becomes a matter of high privilege.

If a resolution to consider a bill *(See Rule)* is held up in the Rules Committee for more than seven legislative days, any member may enter a motion to discharge the committee. The motion is handled like any other discharge petition in the House.

Occasionally, to expedite noncontroversial legislative business, a committee is discharged upon unanimous consent of the House, and a petition is not required. *(For Senate procedure, see Discharge Motion.)*

Discharge Calendar — The House calendar to which motions to discharge committees are referred when they have the necessary 218 signatures and are awaiting action.

Discharge Motion — In the Senate, a special motion any senator may introduce to relieve a committee from consideration of a bill before it. The motion can be called up for approval or disapproval in the same manner as other matters of Senate business.

Division or Standing Vote — A non-record vote used in both the House and Senate. A division vote, also called a standing vote, is taken as follows: members in favor of a proposal stand and are counted by the presiding officer; then members opposed stand and are counted. There is no record of how individual members voted.

Enacting Clause — Key phrase in bills saying, "Be it enacted by the Senate and House of Representatives. . . ." A successful motion to strike it from legislation kills the measure.

Engrossed Bill — The final copy of a bill as passed by one chamber, with the text as amended by floor action and certified to by the clerk of the House or the secretary of the Senate.

Enrolled Bill — The final copy of a bill which has been passed in identical form by both chambers. It is certified to by an officer of the house of origin (House clerk or Senate secretary) and then sent on for signatures of the House Speaker, the Senate president, and the U.S. president. An enrolled bill is printed on parchment.

Filibuster — A time-delaying tactic used by a minority in an effort to prevent a vote on a bill which probably would pass if brought to a vote. The most common method is to take advantage of the Senate's rules permitting unlimited debate, but other forms of parliamentary maneuvering may be used. The stricter rules in the House make filibusters more difficult, but they are attempted from time to time through devices such as repeated demands for quorum calls.

Floor Manager — A member, usually representing sponsors of a bill, who attempts to steer it through debate and revision to a final vote in the chamber. Floor managers are frequently chairmen or ranking members of the committee that reported the bill. Managers are responsible for apportioning the time granted supporters of the bill for debating it. The ranking minority member of the reporting committee often apportions time for the opposition.

Germane — Pertaining to the subject matter of the measure at hand. All House amendments must be germane to the bill. The Senate requires that amendments be germane only when they are proposed to general appropriation bills, bills being considered under cloture, or often when proceeding under a unanimous consent agreement to limit debate.

Hearings — Committee sessions for hearing witnesses. At hearings on legislation, witnesses usually include specialists, government officials and spokesmen for persons affected by the bills under study. Hearings related to special investigations bring forth a variety of witnesses. Committees sometimes use their subpoena power to summon reluctant witnesses. The public and press may attend "open" hearings, but are barred from "closed" or "executive" hearings.

Hopper — Box on House clerk's desk where bills are deposited on introduction.

House Calendar — Listing for action by the House of Representatives of public bills which do not directly or indirectly appropriate money or raise revenue.

Joint Committee — A committee usually created by law composed of a specified number of members of both House and Senate. Usually a joint committee is investigative in nature. There are a few standing joint committees, such as the Joint Economic Committee or Joint Taxation Committee.

Joint Resolution — A joint resolution, designated H J Res or S J Res, requires the approval of both houses and the signature of the president, just as a bill does, and has the force of law if approved. There is no significant difference between a bill and a joint resolution. The latter is generally used in dealing with limited matters, such as a single appropriation for a specific purpose.

Joint resolutions also are used to propose amendments to the Constitution. These do not require presidential signatures, but become a part of the Constitution when three-fourths of the states have ratified them.

Journal — The official record of the proceedings of the House and Senate. The Journal records the actions taken in each chamber, but unlike the *Congressional Record*, it does not include the verbatim report of speeches, debate, etc.

Law — An act of Congress which has been signed by the president, or passed over his veto by the Congress. Laws are listed numerically by Congress; for example, the Civil Rights Act of 1964 (HR 7152) became Public Law 88-352 during the 88th Congress.

Legislative Day — The "day" extending from the time either house meets after an adjournment until the time it next adjourns. Because the House normally adjourns from day to day, legislative days and calendar days usually coincide. But in the Senate, a legislative day may, and frequently does, extend over several calendar days. *(See Recess.)*

Majority Leader — Chief strategist and floor spokesman for the party in nominal control in either chamber. He is elected by his party colleagues and is virtually program director for his chamber, since he usually speaks for its majority.

Majority Whip — In effect, the assistant majority leader in the House or Senate. His job is to help marshal majority forces in support of party strategy.

Marking Up a Bill — Going through a measure, usually in committee, taking it section by section, revising language, penciling in new phrases, etc. If the bill is extensively revised, the new version may be introduced as a separate bill, with a new number. *(See Clean Bill.)*

Minority Leader — Floor leader for the minority party.

Minority Whip — Performs duties of whip for the minority party, particularly keeping party members informed of floor business and insuring their presence on the floor to support party positions.

Morning Hour — The time set aside at the beginning of each legislative day in the Senate for the consideration of regular routine business. In the Senate it is the first two hours of a session following an adjournment, as distinguished from a recess. The morning hour can be terminated earlier if the morning business has been completed. This business includes such matters as messages from the president, communications from the heads of departments, messages from the House, the presentation of petitions and memorials, reports of standing and select committees, and the introduction of bills and resolutions.

During the first hour of the morning hour in the Senate, no motion to proceed to the consideration of any bill on the calendar is in order except by unanimous consent. During the second hour, motions can be made but must be decided without debate. Senate committees may meet while the Senate is in the morning hour.

Motion — Request by a member of Congress for any one of a wide array of parliamentary actions. He "moves" for a certain procedure, or the consideration of a measure or a vote, etc. The precedence of motions, and whether they are debatable, is set forth in the House and Senate Manuals.

One Minute Speeches — Addresses by House members at the beginning of a legislative day. The speeches may cover any subject, but are limited strictly to one minute's duration.

Override a Veto — If the president disapproves a bill and sends it back to Congress with his objections, Congress may override his veto by a two-thirds vote in each chamber. The Constitution requires a yea-and-nay roll call. The question put to each house is: "Shall the bill pass, the objections of the president to the contrary notwithstanding?" *(See Veto.)*

Pair — A "gentlemen's agreement" between two lawmakers on opposite sides to withhold their votes on roll calls so their absence from Congress will not affect the outcome of record voting. If passage of the measure requires a two-thirds majority, a pair would require two members favoring the action to one opposed to it.

Point of Order — An objection raised by a member that the chamber is departing from rules governing its conduct of business. The objector cites the rule violated, the chair sustaining his objection if correctly made. Order is restored by the chair's suspending proceedings of the chamber until it conforms to the prescribed "order of business." Members sometimes raise a "point of no order" when there is noise and disorderly conduct in the chamber.

President of the Senate — Presiding officer of the Senate, normally the vice president of the United States. In his absence, a president pro tempore (president for the time being) may preside or other senators may occupy the chair.

President pro tempore — The chief officer of the Senate in the absence of the vice president. He is elected by his fellow senators. The recent practice has been to elect to the office the senator of the majority party with longest continuous service.

Previous Question — A motion for the previous question, when carried, has the effect of cutting off all debate and forcing a vote on the subject originally at hand. The previous question is sometimes moved in order to prevent amendments. The motion for the previous question is a debate-limiting device and is not in order in the Senate.

Private Calendar — Private House bills dealing with individual matters such as claims against the government, immigration, land titles, etc., are put on this calendar. The Private Calendar can be called on the first and third Tuesdays of each month.

Privilege — Privilege relates to the rights of congressmen and to the relative priority of the motions and actions they may make in their respective chambers. The two are distinct. "Privileged questions" concern legislative business. "Questions of privilege" concern legislators themselves.

Privileged Questions — The order in which bills, motions and other legislative measures may be considered by Congress is governed by strict priorities. A motion to table, for instance, is more privileged than a motion to recommit. Thus, a motion to recommit can be superseded by a motion to table, and a vote would be forced on the latter motion only. A motion to adjourn, however, would take precedence over this one, and is thus considered of the "highest privilege."

Pro Forma Amendment — *(See Strike Out the Last Word.)*

Questions of Privilege — These are matters affecting members of Congress individually or collectively.

Questions affecting the rights, safety, dignity and integrity of proceedings of the House or Senate as a whole are questions of privilege of the House or Senate, as the case may be.

Congressmen singly involve questions of "personal privilege." A member's rising to a question of personal privilege is given precedence over almost all other proceedings. An annotation in the House rules points out that the privilege of the member rests primarily on the Constitution, which gives him a conditional immunity from arrest and an unconditional freedom to speak in the House.

Quorum — The number of members whose presence is necessary for the transaction of business. In the Senate and House, it is a majority of the membership (when there are no vacancies, this is 51 in the Senate and 218 in the House). A quorum is 100 in the Committee of the Whole House.

Readings of Bills — Traditional parliamentary law required bills to be read three times before they were passed. This custom is of little modern significance except in rare instances. Normally the bill is considered to have its first reading when it is introduced and printed, by title, in the *Congressional Record*. Its second reading comes when floor consideration begins. (This is the most likely point at which there is an actual reading of the bill, if there is any.) The third reading (usually by title) takes place when action has been completed on amendments.

Recess — Distinguished from adjournment in that a recess does not end a legislative day and therefore does not interfere with unfinished business. The rules in each house set forth certain matters to be taken up and disposed of at the beginning of each legislative day. The House, which operates under much stricter rules than the Senate, usually adjourns from day to day. The Senate often recesses.

Recommit to Committee — A simple motion, made on the floor after deliberation on a bill, to return it to the committee which reported it. If approved, recommittal usually is considered a death blow to the bill. In the House a motion to recommit can be made only by a member opposed to the bill, and in recognizing a member to make the motion, the Speaker gives the minority party preference over the majority.

A motion to recommit may include instructions to the committee to report the bill again with specific amendments or by a certain date. Or the instructions may be to make a particular study, with no definite deadline for final action.

Reconsider a Vote — A motion to reconsider the vote by which an action was taken has, until it is disposed of, the effect of suspending the action. In the Senate the motion can be made only by a member who voted on the prevailing side of the original question, or by a member who did not vote at all. In the House it can be made only by a member on the prevailing side. A common practice after close votes in the House and Senate is a motion to reconsider, followed by a motion to table the motion to reconsider. On this motion to table, members vote as they voted on the original question, to enable the motion to table to prevail. The matter is then finally closed and further motions to reconsider are not entertained.

Report — Both a verb and a noun, as a congressional term. A committee which has been examining a bill referred to it by the parent chamber "reports" its finding and recommendations to the chamber when the committee returns the measure. The process is called "reporting" a bill.

A "report" is the document setting forth the committee's explanation of its action. House and Senate reports are numbered separately and are designated S Rept or H Rept. Conference reports are numbered and designated in the same way as committee reports.

Resolution — A simple resolution, designated H Res or S Res, deals with matters entirely within the prerogatives of one house or the other. It requires neither passage by the other chamber nor approval by the president, and does not have the force of law. Most resolutions deal with the rules of one house. They also are used to express the sentiments of a single house, as condolences to the family of a deceased member, or to give "advice" on foreign policy or other executive business. *(See also Concurrent and Joint Resolutions.)*

Rider — A provision, usually not germane, tacked on to a bill which its sponsor hopes to get through more easily by including in other legislation. Riders become law if the bills embodying them do. Riders providing for legislation in appropriations bills are outstanding examples, though technically they are banned.

Rule — The term has two specific congressional meanings. A rule may be a standing order governing the conduct of House or Senate business and listed in the chamber's book of rules. The rules deal with duties of officers, order of business, admission to the floor, voting procedures, etc.

In the House, a rule also may be a decision made by its Rules Committee about the handling of a particular bill on the floor. If the rule is adopted by the House, the temporary rule becomes as valid as any standing rule, and lapses only after action has been completed on the measure to which it pertains.

Secretary of the Senate — Chief administrative officer of the Senate, responsible for direction of duties of Senate employees, education of pages, administration of oaths, receipt of registration of lobbyists and other activities necessary for the continuing operation of the Senate.

Select or Special Committee — A committee set up for a special purpose and a limited time by resolution of either House or Senate. Most special committees are investigative in nature.

Senatorial Courtesy — Sometimes referred to as "the courtesy of the Senate," it is a general practice without written rule applied to consideration of executive nominations. In practice, generally it means nominations from a state are not to be confirmed unless they have been approved by the senators of the president's party of that state, with other senators following their lead in the attitude they take toward such nominations.

Speaker — The presiding officer of the House of Representatives, elected by its members.

Special Session — A session of Congress after it has adjourned sine die, completing its regular session. Special sessions are convened by the president of the United States under his constitutional powers.

Standing Committee — A panel permanently provided for by House or Senate rules, which broadly defines its respective jurisdiction.

Standing Vote — *(See Division Vote.)*

Statutes-at-Large — A chronological arrangement of the laws enacted in each session of Congress. Though indexed, the laws are not arranged by subject matter nor is there an indication of how they affect previous law. *(See U.S. Code.)*

Strike Out the Last Word — A move whereby House members are entitled to speak for a fixed time on a measure then being debated by the chamber. A member gains recognition from the chair by moving to strike out the last word of the amendment or section of the bill then under consideration. The motion is pro forma and customarily requires no vote.

Substitute — A motion, an amendment, or an entire bill introduced in place of pending business. Passage of a substitute measure kills the original measure by supplanting it. A substitute may be amended.

Supplemental Appropriations — Normally are passed after the regular appropriation to meet unanticipated expenses.

Suspend the Rules — Often a timesaving procedure for passing bills in the House. The wording of the motion, which may be made by any member recognized by the Speaker, is: "I move to suspend the rules and pass the bill. . . ." A favorable vote by two-thirds of those present is required for passage. Debate is limited to 40 minutes and no amendments from the floor are permitted. If a two-thirds favorable vote is not attained, the bill may be considered later under regular procedures.

Table a Bill — The motion to "lay on the table" is not debatable in either house, and is usually a method of making a final, adverse disposition of a matter.

Teller Vote — In the House, members file past tellers and are counted as for or against a measure, but they are not recorded individually. The teller vote is not used in the Senate. In the House, the Legislative Reorganization Act of 1970 provided for *recorded* teller votes in Committee of the Whole.

Unanimous Consent Agreement — A Senate accord agreed to by members on the floor. Formulated by party leaders and other senators, it regulates when important bills will be taken up and limits debate on amendments, debatable motions or appeals, points of order, and final passage. Also called a "time-limitation" agreement.

Union Calendar — Bills which directly or indirectly appropriate money or raise revenue are placed on this House calendar according to the date reported from committee.

U.S. Code — A consolidation and codification of the general and permanent laws of the United States arranged by subject under 50 titles, the first six dealing with general or political subjects, and the other 44 alphabetically arranged from agriculture to war and national defense. The Code is now revised every six years and a supplement is published after each session of Congress.

Veto — Disapproval by the president of a bill or joint resolution, other than one proposing an amendment to the Constitution. When Congress is in session, the president must veto a bill within 10 days, excluding Sundays, after he has received it; otherwise it becomes law with or without his signature. When the president vetoes a bill, he returns it to the house of its origin with a message stating his objections. The veto then becomes a question of high privilege. *(See Override a Veto.)*

Voice Vote — In either House or Senate, members answer "aye" or "no" in chorus and the presiding officer decides the result. The term also is used loosely to indicate action by unanimous consent or without objection.

Selected Bibliography

1. Congress and Lawmaking

Berman, Daniel M. *In Congress Assembled.* New York: Macmillan, 1964.

Bibby, John, and Davidson, Roger H. *On Capitol Hill.* 2d ed. Hinsdale, Ill.: The Dryden Press, 1972.

Burnham, James. *Congress and the American Tradition.* Chicago: Henry Regnery, 1959.

Choper, Jesse H. "The Supreme Court and the Political Branches: Democratic Theory and Practice." *University of Pennsylvania Law Review,* April 1974, pp. 810-858.

DeGrazia, Alfred, ed. *Congress: The First Branch of Government.* Washington: The American Enterprise Institute for Public Policy Research, 1966.

Galloway, George B. *The Legislative Process in Congress.* New York: Thomas Y. Crowell, 1953.

Griffith, Ernest S., and Valeo, Francis R. *Congress: Its Contemporary Role.* 5th ed. New York: New York University Press, 1975.

Gross, Bertram M. *The Legislative Struggle.* New York: McGraw-Hill, 1953.

Jewell, Malcolm E., and Patterson, Samuel C. *The Legislative Process in the United States.* 2d ed. New York: Random House, 1973.

Keefe, William J., and Ogul, Morris S. *The American Legislative Process: Congress and the States.* 4th ed. Englewood Cliffs, N.J.: Prentice-Hall, Inc., 1977.

Kornberg, Allan, ed. *Comparative Legislative Systems.* New York: The Free Press, 1971.

Luce, Robert. *Legislative Procedures* Boston: Houghton Mifflin, 1922.

———. *Legislative Assemblies.* Boston: Houghton Mifflin, 1924.

———. *Legislative Principles.* Boston: Houghton Mifflin, 1930.

————. *Legislative Problems.* Boston: Houghton Mifflin, 1935.

Orfield, Gary. *Congressional Power.* New York: Harcourt, Brace, Jovanovich, 1975.

Polsby, Nelson W., ed. *Congressional Behavior.* New York: Random House, 1971.

Rieselbach, Leroy N. *Congressional Politics.* New York: McGraw-Hill, 1973.

Ripley, Randall B. *Congress, Process and Policy.* New York: W. W. Norton, 1975.

Saloma, John S. *Congress and the New Politics.* Boston: Little, Brown, 1969.

Vogler, David. *The Politics of Congress.* 2d ed. Boston: Allyn and Bacon, 1977.

Young, Roland. *The American Congress.* New York: Harper and Bros., 1958.

2. The Congressional Environment

Bauer, Raymond, et. al. *American Business and Public Policy: The Politics of Foreign Trade.* New York: Atherton Press, 1963.

Berry, Jeffrey M. *Lobbying for the People: The Political Behavior of Public Interest Groups.* Princeton, N.J.: Princeton University Press, 1977.

Blanchard, Robert O., ed. *Congress and the News Media.* New York: Hastings House, 1974.

Bolling, Richard. *House Out Of Order.* New York: E.P. Dutton and Co., 1965.

————. *Power in the House.* New York: E.P. Dutton and Co., 1968.

Chamberlain, Lawrence H. *The President, Congress and Legislation.* New York: Columbia University Press, 1946.

Clark, Joseph S. *Congress, The Sapless Branch.* New York: Harper & Row, 1964.

Davidson, Roger H., et. al. *Congress in Crisis: Politics and Congressional Reform.* Belmont, Calif.: Wadsworth Publishing Co., 1966.

Dodd, Lawrence, and Oppenheimer, Bruce, eds. *Congress Reconsidered.* New York: Praeger, 1977.

Fenno, Richard F., Jr. *Home Style.* Boston: Little, Brown, 1978.

Fisher, Louis. "Congressional Budget Reform: The First Two Years." *Harvard Journal on Legislation,* April 1977, pp. 413-458.

Hasbrouck, Paul. *Party Government in the House of Representatives.* New York: Macmillan, 1927.

Hechler, Kenneth W. *Insurgency.* New York: Columbia University Press, 1940.

Holtzman, Abraham. *Legislative Liaison: Executive Leadership in Congress.* Chicago: Rand McNally, 1970.

Hopkins, Bruce R. "Congressional Reform: Towards A Modern Congress." *Notre Dame Lawyer,* February 1972, pp. 442-513.

Huitt, Ralph K. "Democratic Party Leadership in the Senate." *American Political Science Review,* June 1961, pp. 333-344.

Johannes, John. "Congress and the Initiation of Legislation." *Public Policy,* Spring 1972, pp. 281-309.

Jones, Charles O. *The Minority Party in Congress.* Boston: Little, Brown, 1970.

Kernell, Sam. "Is the Senate More Liberal Than the House?" *Journal of Politics,* May 1973, pp. 332-366.

Kravitz, Walter. "Relations Between the Senate and House of Representatives: The Party Leaderships." In *Policymaking Role of Leadership in the Senate.* A Compilation of Papers Prepared for the Commission on the Operation of the Senate, 94th Congress, 2d Session (1976), pp. 121-138.

Moe, Ronald, and Teel, Stephen. "Congress as Policy-Maker: A Necessary Reappraisal." *Political Science Quarterly,* September 1970, pp. 443-470.

Ornstein, Norman, ed. *Congress in Change.* New York: Praeger, 1975.

————. "The Democrats Reform Power in the House of Representatives, 1969-75." In *America in the Seventies,* edited by Allan P. Sinder, pp. 1-48 Boston: Little, Brown, 1977.

Peabody, Robert L. *Leadership in Congress.* Boston: Little, Brown, 1976.

————, et. al. "The United States Senate as a Presidential Incubator: Many Are Called but Few Are Chosen." *Political Science Quarterly,* Summer 1976, pp. 236-258.

Polsby, Nelson W. "Strengthening Congress in National Policymaking." In *Congressional Behavior,* edited by Nelson W. Polsby, pp. 3-13. New York: Random House, 1971.

Price, David. *Who Makes the Laws?* Cambridge, Mass.: Schenkman, 1972.

Ripley, Randall B. *Majority Party Leadership in Congress.* Boston: Little, Brown, 1969.

Schick, Allen. "Budget Reform Legislation: Reorganizing Congressional Centers of Fiscal Power." *Harvard Journal on Legislation,* February 1974, pp. 303-350.

Stewart, John G. "Two Strategies of Leadership: Johnson and Mansfield." In *Congressional Behavior,* edited by Nelson W. Polsby, pp. 61-92. New York: Random House, 1971,

Sundquist, James. *Politics and Policy.* Washington: The Brookings Institution, 1968.

Wayne, Stephen. *The Legislative Presidency.* New York: Harper & Row, 1978.

3. Preliminary Action in the House and Senate

Abram, Michael, and Cooper, Joseph. "The Rise of Seniority in the House of Representatives." *Polity,* Fall 1968, pp. 35-51.

Asher, Herbert B. "Committees and the Norm of Specialization." *The Annals,* January 1974, pp. 63-74.

Beckman, Norman. "Congressional Information Processes for National Policy." *The Annals,* March 1971, pp. 84-99.

Bowsher, Prentice. "The Speaker's Man: Lewis Deschler, House Parliamentarian." *The Washington Monthly,* April 1970, pp. 22-27.

Bullock, Charles S. III. "The Influence of State Party Delegations on House Committee Assignments." *Midwest Journal of Political Science,* August 1971, pp. 525-546.

Cohen, Julius. "Hearing on a Bill: Legislative Folklore?" *Minnesota Law Review,* December 1952, pp. 34-45.

Cooper, Joseph. "The Study of Congressional Committees, Current Research and Future Trends." *Polity,* Fall 1971, pp. 123-133.

———. *The Origins of the Standing Committees and the Development of the Modern House.* Rice University Monograph in Political Science, vol. 56, no. 3, Summer 1970.

Cummings, Frank. *Capitol Hill Manual.* Washington: The Bureau of National Affairs, Inc., 1977.)

Davidson, Roger H. "Representation and Congressional Committees." *The Annals,* January 1974, pp. 48-62.

Dickerson, Reed. *Legislative Drafting.* Boston: Little, Brown, 1954.

Eckhardt, Bob. "The Presumption of Committee Openness Under House Rules." *Harvard Journal on Legislation,* February 1974, pp. 279-302.

Fenno, Richard F. *Congressmen in Committees.* Boston: Little, Brown, 1973.

Fox, Harrison W. Jr., and Hammond, Susan Webb. *Congressional Staffs.* New York: The Free Press, 1977.

Goodwin, George. *The Little Legislatures.* Amherst: University of Massachusetts Press, 1970.

Kofmehl, Kenneth. *Professional Staffs of Congress.* 3d ed. West Lafayette: Purdue University Press, 1977.

Kravitz, Walter. "Evolution of the Senate's Committee System." *The Annals,* January 1974, pp. 27-38.

Manley, John F. "Congressional Staff and Public Policy-Making: The Joint Committee on Internal Revenue Taxation." *Journal of Politics,* November 1968, pp. 1046-1067.

Morrow, William L. *Congressional Committees.* New York: Charles Scribner's Sons, 1969.

Price, David E. "Professionals and 'Entrepreneurs': Staff Orientations and Policy Making on Three Senate Committees." *Journal of Politics,* May 1971, pp. 313-336.

"Private Bills in Congress." *Harvard Law Review* 79 (1966): 1684-1706.

Rules Adopted by the Committees of the House of Representatives. Compiled by the Select Committee on Congressional Operations, 95th Congress, 1st Session (May 1977).

Rules Adopted By Committees of the United States Senate. Compiled by the Senate Committee on Rules and Administration and House Select Committee on Congressional Operations, 95th Congress, 1st Session (November 1977).

Van Der Slik, Jack R., and Stenger, Thomas C. "Citizen Witnesses before Congressional Committees." *Political Science Quarterly,* Fall 1977, pp. 465-485

4. Scheduling Legislation in the House

Albert, Carl. *The Office and Duties of the Speaker of the House of Representatives.* House Document No. 94-582, 94th Congress, 2d Session, 1976.

"Calendar Wednesday." Congressional Quarterly *Weekly Report,* June 16, 1973, p. 1561.

Chiu, Chang Wei. *The Speaker of the House of Representatives Since 1896.* New York: Columbia University Press, 1928.

Cooper, Ann. "Massing the Troops: House Democratic Whips: Counting, Coaxing, Cajoling." Congressional Quarterly *Weekly Report,* May 27, 1978, pp. 1301-1306.

Cummings, Milton C. Jr., and Peabody, Robert L. "The Decision to Enlarge the Rules Committee." In *New Perspectives on the House of Representatives.* 2d. ed., edited by Robert L. Peabody and Nelson W. Polsby, pp. 253-282. Chicago: Rand McNally, 1969.

"Discharge Petition Filed on Elk Hills Oil Reserves Bill." Congressional Quarterly *Weekly Report,* March 16, 1974, p. 702.

Drew, Elizabeth. "A Tendency to Legislate." *The New Yorker,* June 26, 1978, pp. 80-89.

Eisen, Jack. "House District Panel Is Bill-less for This Year." *The Washington Post,* July 26, 1977, p. Cl.

"Explanation of the Private Calendar," *Congressional Record* 123 (April 28, 1977): H3715-H3716.

Froman, Lewis A., and Ripley, Randall B. "Conditions for Party Leadership: The Case of the House Democrats." *American Political Science Review,* March 1965, pp. 52-63.

Houston, Paul. "Regular Recesses Help Congress to Do More Work." *Los Angeles Times,* October 26, 1975, p. 1.

Jones, Charles O. "Joseph G. Cannon and Howard W. Smith: An Essay on the Limits of Leadership in the House of Representatives." *Journal of Politics,* September 1968, pp. 617-646.

Matsunaga, Spark M., and Chen, Ping. *Rulemakers of the House.* Urbana: University of Illinois Press, 1976.

"New Policies and Procedures of Consent Calendar Committee." *Congressional Record* 123 (April 28, 1977): H3782-H3783.

Oppenheimer, Bruce I. "The Rules Committee: New Arm of Leadership in a Decentralized House." In *Congress Reconsidered,* edited by Lawrence C. Dodd and Bruce I. Oppenheimer, pp. 96-116. New York: Praeger Publishers, 1977.

Reid, T. R. "A House Flurry: On Gin, Raisins, Governments." *The Washington Post,* November 1, 1977, p. A2.

Ripley, Randall B. "Party Whip Organizations in the United States House of Representatives." *American Political Science Review,* September 1964, pp. 561-576.

Roberts, Steven V. "House Leaders Hold Up Ethics Bill So They Can Seek More Support." *The New York Times,* April 14, 1978, p. A12.

Robinson, James A. *The House Rules Committee.* Indianapolis: Bobbs-Merrill, 1963.

Scheduling the Work of the House. House Document No. 95-23, 95th Congress, 1st Session (January 4, 1977).

Smith, Howard. "In Defense of the Rules Committee." In *Congressional Reform: Problems and Prospects,* edited by Joseph S. Clark, pp. 138-166. New York: Thomas Y. Crowell, 1965.

5. House Floor Procedure

Alexander, DeAlva Stanwood. *History and Procedure of the House of Representatives.* Boston: Houghton Mifflin Co., 1916.

Baker, Donald P. "Maryland Conservative Is Watchdog of the House." *The Washington Post,* December 18, 1977, p. B1.

Brown, William Holmes. *Constitution, Jefferson's Manual, and Rules of the House of Representatives of the United States, Ninety-Fifth Congress.* House Document No. 94-663, 94th Congress, 2d Session. Washington: U.S. Government Printing Office, 1977.

Cannon, Clarence M. *Cannon's Procedure in the House of Representatives.* House Document No. 122, 86th Congress, 1st Session. Washington: U.S. Government Printing Office, 1959.

Clausen, Aage R. *How Congressmen Decide.* New York: St. Martin's Press, 1973.

Damon, Richard E. *The Standing Rules of the U.S. House of Representatives.* Ph. D. dissertation, Columbia University, 1971.

Deschler, Lewis. *Deschler's Procedure in the United States House of Representatives.* 2d. ed., Washington: U.S. Government Printing Office, 1977.

―――. *Deschler's Precedents of the United States House of Representatives.* House Document No. 94-661, 94th Congress, 2d Session. Washington: U.S. Government Printing Office, 1977.

Froman, Lewis A. *The Congressional Process: Strategies, Rules and Procedures.* Boston: Little, Brown, 1967.

Harlow, Ralph V. *The History of Legislative Methods in the Period Before 1825.* New Haven, Conn.: Yale University Press, 1917.

Hinds, Asher, and Cannon, Clarence M. *Hinds' and Cannon's Precedents of the House of Representatives* (Washington: U.S. Government Printing Office, vols. 1-5 by Hinds in 1907; vols 6-11 by Cannon in 1936).

House, Albert V., Jr. "The Contributions of Samuel J. Randall to the Rules of the National House of Representatives." *American Political Science Review,* October 1935, pp. 837-841.

Kingdon, John W. *Congressmen's Voting Decisions.* New York: Harper & Row, 1973.

MacNeil, Neil. *Forge of Democracy: The House of Representatives.* New York: David McKay, 1963.

Morrison, Geoffrey. "Champ Clark and the Rules Revolution of 1910." *Capitol Studies,* Winter 1974, pp. 43-56.

Polsby, Nelson W. "The Institutionalization of the House of Representatives." *American Political Science Review,* March 1968, pp. 144-168.

Rhodes, John J. "Floor Procedure in the House of Representatives." In *We Propose: A Modern Congress,* edited by Mary McInnes, pp. 201-206. New York: McGraw-Hill, 1966.

Riddick, Floyd M. *The Organization and Procedure of the United States Congress.* Manassas: National Capitol Pblshrs, 1949.

Robinson, William A. *Thomas B. Reed, Parliamentarian.* New York: Dodd, Mead and Co., 1930.

Siff, Todd, and Weil, Alan. *Ruling Congress: A Study on How the House and Senate Rules Govern the Legislative Process.* New York: Grossman, 1975.

6. Scheduling Legislation in the Senate

Berlow, Alan. "Criminal Law Codification Bill." Congressional Quarterly *Weekly Report,* January 21, 1978, pp. 142-147.

Bone, Hugh A. "An Introduction to the Senate Policy Committees." *American Political Science Review,* June 1956, pp. 339-359.

Clark, Joseph S. *The Senate Establishment.* New York: Hill and Wang, 1963.

Gannon, James P. "The Senate's Chief Engineer." *The Wall Street Journal,* June 16, 1977, p. 20.

———. "The Democrats' Whip, Senator Cranston, Emerges As Key Asset for Carter." *The Wall Street Journal,* March 15, 1977.

Glass, Andrew J. "Mansfield Reforms Spark 'Quiet Revolution' in Senate." *National Journal,* March 6, 1971, pp. 499-512.

Huitt, Ralph K. "The Internal Distribution of Influence: the Senate." In *The Congress and America's Future,* edited by David B. Truman, pp. 91-117. Englewood Cliffs, N.J.: Prentice-Hall, 1965.

Jasper, Herb, "Scheduling of Senate Business." In *Committees and Senate Procedures.* A Compilation of Papers Prepared for the Commission on the Operation of the Senate, 94th Congress, 2d Session (1977), pp. 131-139.

Jewell, Malcolm. "The Senate Republican Policy Committee and Foreign Policy." *Western Political Quarterly,* December 1959, pp. 966-980.

Kaiser, Robert G. "Senate Sets Final Canal Treaty Vote." *The Washington Post,* April 6, 1978, p. A4.

Lyons, Richard L. "Senate, House Trying to Mesh Agendas." *The Washington Post,* April 20, 1978, p. A2.

O'Leary, Jeremiah. "Byrd Orders Speedup on Pact Debate." *The Washington Star,* March 4, 1978, p. A-3.

Oleszek, Walter J. "Party Whips in the United States Senate." *Journal of Politics,* November 1971, pp. 955-979.

Polsby, Nelson W. "Goodbye to the Inner Club." *The Washington Monthly,* August 1969, pp. 30-34.

Riddick, Floyd M. *Majority and Minority Leaders of the Senate.* Senate Document No. 95-24, 95th Congress, 1st Session. Washington: U.S. Government Printing Office, 1977.

Robinson, Donald Allen. "If the Senate Democrats Want Leadership: An Analysis of the History and Prospects of the Majority Policy Committee." In *Policymaking Role of Leadership in the Senate.* A Compilation of Papers Prepared for the Commission on the Operation of the Senate, 94th Congress, 2d Session (1976), pp. 40-57.

Stewart, John G. "Central Policy Organs in Congress." In *Congress Against the President,* edited by Harvey C. Mansfield, Sr., pp. 21-33. New York: Praeger, 1975.

Walker, Jack L. "Setting the Agenda in the U.S. Senate." In *Policymaking Role of Leadership in the Senate.* A Compilation of Papers Prepared for the Commission on the Operation of the Senate, 94th Congress, 2d Session (1976), pp. 96-120.

7. Senate Floor Procedure

Angle, Martha. "The Senate's One-Man Wrecking Crew," *The Washington Star,* January 23, 1975, p. A-1.

Beeman, Richard R. "Unlimited Debate in the Senate: The First Phase." *Political Science Quarterly,* September 1968, pp. 419-434.

Bernstein, Robert A., and Anthony, William W. "The ABM Issue in the Senate, 1968-1970: The Importance of Ideology." *American Political Science Review,* September 1974, pp. 1198-1206.

Burdette, Franklin L. *Filibustering in the Senate.* Princeton, N.J.; Princeton University Press, 1940.

Clymer, Adam. "The Great Panama Debate, and How It Grew." *The New York Times,* April 16, 1978, p. E2.

Cohen, Richard E. "Marking an End to the Senate's Mansfield Era." *National Journal,* December 25, 1976, pp. 1802-1809.

Evans, Rowland, and Novak, Robert. *Lyndon B. Johnson: The Exercise of Power.* New York: New American Library, 1966.

Finney, John W. "Senate's Leaders Approve Reforms." *The New York Times,* January 20, 1971, p. 15.

Froman, Lewis A. *The Congressional Process: Strategies, Rules and Procedures.* Boston: Little, Brown, 1967.

Gilfry, Henry H. *Precedents: Decisions on Points of Order With Phraseology in the United States Senate.* Senate Document No. 129, 61st Congress, 1st Session. Washington: U.S. Government Printing Office, 1909.

Harris, Joseph P. *The Advice and Consent of the Senate.* Berkeley, Calif.: University of California Press, 1953.

Huitt, Ralph K. "The Outsider in the Senate: Alternative Role." *American Political Science Review,* Sept. 1961, pp. 566-575.

Jackson, John E. *Constituencies and Leaders in Congress, Their Effects on Senate Voting Behavior.* Cambridge, Mass.: Harvard University Press, 1974.

Keith, Robert. "The Use of Unanimous Consent in the Senate." In *Committees and Senate Procedures.* A Compilation of Papers Prepared for the Commission on the Operation of the Senate, 94th Congress, 2d Session (1977), pp. 140-168.

Keynes, Edward. "The Senate Rules and the Dirksen Amendment: A Study in Legislative Strategy and Tactics." In *The Legislative Process in the U.S. Senate,* edited by Lawrence K. Pettit and Edward Keynes, pp. 104-149. Chicago: Rand McNally, 1969.

Large, Arlen J. "The Man at the Senate's Back Door." *The Wall Street Journal,* September 17, 1973, p. 10.

Lehnen, Robert G. "Behavior on the Senate Floor: An Analysis of Debate in the U.S. Senate." *Midwest Journal of Political Science,* November 1967, pp. 505-521.

Malbin, Michael J. "Compromise By Senate Eases Anti-Filibuster Rule." *National Journal Reports,* March 15, 1975, pp. 397-400.

Matthews, Donald. *U.S. Senators And Their World.* Chapel Hill, N.C.: University of North Carolina Press, 1960.

Peffer, William A. "The Senate's Powers and Functions: Its Rules and Methods of Doing Business." *The North American Review,* August 1898, pp. 176-190.

Rich, Spencer. "Allen a Master of New-Style Filibuster." *The Washington Post,* July 1, 1974, p. A2.

Riddick, Floyd M. *Senate Procedure, Precedents and Practices.* Senate Document No. 93-21. 93d Congress, 1st Session. Washington: U.S. Government Printing Office, 1974.

Ripley, Randall B. *Power in the Senate.* New York: St. Martin's Press, 1969.

Shuman, Howard E. "Senate Rules and the Civil Rights Bill: A Case Study." *American Political Science Review,* December 1957, pp. 955-975.

Senate Cloture Rule. 95th Congress, 1st Session. Printed each Congress at the request of the Senate Committee on Rules and Administration by the U.S. Government Printing Office.

Senate Manual Containing the Standing Rules, Orders, Laws, and Resolutions Affecting the Business of the United States Senate. Senate Document No. 95-1, 95th Congress, 1st Session. Washington: U.S. Government Printing Office, 1977.

Senate Rules and the Senate as a Continuing Body. Senate Document No. 4, 83rd Congress, 1st Session. Washington: U.S. Government Printing Office, 1953.

Siff, Todd, and Weil, Alan. *Ruling Congress: A Study of How the House and Senate Rules Govern the Legislative Process.* New York: Grossman, 1975.

Wolfinger, Raymond E. "Filibusters: Majority Rule, Presidential Leadership, and Senate Norms." In *Readings on Congress,* edited by Raymond E. Wolfinger, pp. 296-305. Englewood Cliffs, N.J.: Prentice-Hall, 1971.

Zweben, Murray. *Enactment of a Law.* Senate Document No. 94-152, 94th Congress, 2d Session. Washington: U.S. Government Printing Office, 1976.

8. Resolving House-Senate Differences

Fenno, Richard F., Jr. *The Power of the Purse: Appropriations Politics in Congress.* Chapter 12. Boston: Little, Brown, 1966.

Ferejohn, John. "Who Wins in Conference Committee?" *Journal of Politics,* November 1975, pp. 1033-1046.

Gore, Albert. "The Conference Committee: Congress' Final Filter." *The Washington Monthly,* June 1971, pp. 43-48.

Horn, Stephen. *Unused Power: The Work of the Senate Committee on Appropriations.* Washington: The Brookings Institution, 1970, pp. 154-173.

Manley, John F. *The Politics of Finance: The House Committee on Ways and Means.* Chapter 6. Boston: Little, Brown, 1970.

McCall, Samuel W. *The Business of Congress.* Chapter 9. New York: Columbia University Press, 1911.

McCown, Ada C. *The Congressional Conference Committee.* New York: Columbia University Press, 1927.

Oleszek, Walter J. "House-Senate Relationships: Comity and Conflict." *The Annals,* January 1974, pp. 75-86.

Paletz, David L. *Influence in Congress: An Analysis of the Nature and Effects of Conference Committees Utilizing Case Studies of Poverty, Traffic Safety, and Congressional Redistricting Legislation.* Ph. D. dissertation, University of California, Los Angeles, 1970.

Pressman, Jeffrey L. *House vs. Senate: Conflict in the Appropriations Process.* New Haven: Yale University Press, 1966.

"Reform Penetrates Conference Committees." Congressional Quarterly *Weekly Report,* February 8, 1975, pp. 290-294.

Riggs, Richard. "Separation of Powers: Congressional Riders and the Veto Powers." *University of Michigan Journal of Law Reform,* Spring 1973, pp. 735-759.

Rogers, Lindsay. "Conference Committee Legislation." *North American Review,* March 1922, pp. 300-307.

Steiner, Gilbert. *The Congressional Conference Committee, Seventieth to Eightieth Congresses.* Urbana, Ill.: University of Illinois Press, 1951.

Strom, Gerald S., and Rundquist, Barry S. "A Revised Theory of Winning in House-Senate Conferences." *American Political Science Review,* June 1977, pp. 448-453.

Vogler, David J. *The Third House: Conference Committees in the U.S. Congress.* Evanston, Ill.: Northwestern University Press, 1971.

9. Legislative Oversight

Aberbach, Joel D. "The Development of Oversight in the U.S. Congress." In *Techniques and Procedures for Analysis and Evaluation.* A Compilation of Papers Prepared for the Commission on the Operation of the Senate, 94th Congress, 2d Session (1977), pp. 53-69.

Adams, Bruce. "Sunset: A Proposal for Accountability in Government." *Administrative Law Review,* Summer 1976, pp. 511-542.

Behn, Robert. "The False Dawn of the Sunset Laws." *The Public Interest,* Fall 1977, pp. 103-118.

Bibby, John F. "Committee Characteristics and Legislative Oversight of Administration." *Midwest Journal of Political Science,* February 1966, pp. 78-98.

"1976 Bicentennial Institute-Oversight and Review of Agency Decisionmaking." *Administrative Law Review,* Fall 1976.

Bolton, John R. *The Legislative Veto: Unseparating the Powers.* Washington: American Enterprise Institute for Public Policy Research, 1977.

Brown, Richard E. *The GAO: Untapped Source of Congressional Power.* Knoxville, Tennessee: University Press, 1970.

Dixon, Robert G. "The Congressional Veto and Separation of Powers: The Executive on a Leash?" *North Carolina Law Review,* April 1978, pp. 423-494.

Fitzgerald, John L. "Congressional Oversight or Congressional Foresight: Guidelines from the Founding Fathers." *Administrative Law Review,* Summer 1976, pp. 429-445.

Freeman, J. Leiper. *The Political Process: Executive Bureau-Legislative Committee Relations.* rev. ed. Garden City, N.Y.: Doubleday and Co., 1965.

Gray, Kenneth E. "Congressional Interference in Administration." In *Cooperation and Conflict,* edited by Daniel J. Elazar et al., pp. 521-542. Itasca, Ill.: F. E. Peacock Publishers Inc., 1969.

Hammond, Susan Webb; Fox, Harrison W. Jr.; Moraski, Richard; and Nicholson, Jeanne B. "Senate Oversight Activities." In *Techniques and Procedures for Analysis and Evaluation.* A Compilation of Papers Prepared for the Commission on the Operation of the Senate, 94th Congress, 2d Session (1977), pp. 70-105.

Harris, Joseph P. *Congressional Control of Administration.* Washington: The Brookings Institution, 1964.

Havemann, Joel. "Congress Tries to Break Ground Zero in Evaluating Federal Programs." *National Journal,* May 22, 1976, pp. 706-713.

Henderson, Thomas A. *Congressional Oversight of Executive Agencies.* Gainesville, Fla.: University of Florida Press, 1970.

Johannes, John R. "Study and Recommend: Statutory Reporting Requirements As A Technique of Legislative Initiative in Congress — A Research Note." *Western Political Quarterly,* December 1976, pp. 589-596.

Kaiser, Fred. "Oversight of Foreign Policy: The U.S. House International Relations Committee." *Legisltive Studies Quarterly,* August 1977, pp. 255-280.

Kaufman, Herbert. *Are Government Organizations Immortal?* Washington: The Brookings Institution, 1976.

Krasnow, Erwin G., and Shoosan III, Harry M. "Congressional Oversight: The Ninety-Second Congress and the Federal Communications Commission." *Harvard Journal on Legislation,* February 1973, pp. 297-329.

Lees, John D. "Legislatures and Oversight: A Review Article on a Neglected Area of Research." *Legislative Studies Quarterly,* May 1977, pp. 193-208.

Ogul, Morris S. *Congress Oversees the Bureaucracy.* Pittsburgh, Pa.: University of Pittsburgh Press, 1976.

Pearson, James B. "Oversight: A Vital Yet Neglected Congressional Function." *Kansas Law Review,* Winter 1975, pp. 277-288.

Scher, Seymour. "Conditions for Legislative Control." *Journal of Politics,* August 1963, pp. 526-551.

Schick, Allen. "Congress and the 'Details' of Administration." *Public Administration Review,* September/October 1976, pp. 516-527.

Taylor, Telford. *Grand Inquest: The Story of Congressional Investigations.* New York: Simon and Schuster, 1955.

Wholey, Joseph, et. al. *Federal Evaluation Policy.* Washington: The Urban Institute, 1970.

10. Conclusion

Bailey, Stephen K. *Congress Makes a Law.* New York: Columbia University Press, 1950.

Berman, Daniel M. *How A Bill Becomes A Law: Congress Enacts Civil Rights Legislation.* 2d ed. New York: Macmillan, 1966.

Cleveland, Frederic N. *Congress and Urban Problems: A Casebook on the Legislative Process.* Washington: The Brookings Institution, 1969.

Eidenberg, Eugene, and Morey, Roy D. *An Act of Congress.* New York: W. W. Norton and Co., 1969.

Ferejohn, John A. *Pork Barrel Politics.* Stanford, Calif.: Stanford University Press, 1974.

Maslow, Will. "FEPC: A Case History in Parliamentary Maneuver." *The University of Chicago Law Review,* June 1946, pp. 407-444.

Peabody, Robert L., et. al. *To Enact A Law.* New York: Praeger, 1972.

Redman, Eric. *The Dance of Legislation.* New York: Simon and Schuster, 1973.

Robinson, James A. *Congress and Foreign Policy-Making.* Homewood, Ill.: The Dorsey Press, 1962.

Schlesinger, Arthur, Jr. "Congress and the Making of American Foreign Policy." *Foreign Affairs,* October 1972, pp. 78-113.

Stennis, John, and Fulbright, J. William. *The Role of Congress in Foreign Policy.* Washington: American Enterprise Institute for Public Policy Research, 1970.

Index

A

Abourezk, James (D S.D.) - 171-173
Abzug, Bella (D N.Y.) - 111
Ad hoc Agreements - 173
Ad hoc Committees - 58, 59
Adjournment - 17, 154, 219
Adoption of the Rule - 106, 107
Aiken, George (R Vt.) - 169, 185
Albert, Carl (D Okla.) - 83, 98, 209
Allen, James B. (D Ala.) - 183
Amendments
  Amendments in disagreement - 193
  Committee amendments - 117, 159
  Conference committee - 191-193, 197
  Degrees of - 119, 159
  Final House passage - 127
  Germane. *See* Germane Amendments.
  House floor procedure - 114-121
  House-Senate comparison - 141, 142
  Markup strategies - 71, 72
  Nongermane. *See* Nongermane Amendments.
  Policy amendments - 177
  Previously noticed - 118
  Pro forma amendments - 114, 115, 121, 227
  Riders - 117, 118
  Senate floor procedure - 158-164
  Strategic uses, tactics - 119, 120, 159-161
  Types - 116-118
  Voting in House - 41, 127
  Voting in Senate - 159, 161-164
American Enterprise Institute - 207
Anderson, Clinton (D N.M.) - 160
Appeals - 54, 142, 219
Appropriations Bills - 117, 118, 177, 219
Appropriations Committees
  Chairmen, reforms - 64
  Oversight function - 201, 204, 205
  Privileged legislation - 86, 87
  Waivers of points of order - 92
Authorizations - 44, 201, 204, 205, 219

B

Baker, Howard H. Jr. (R Tenn.) - 145, 161, 172
Bayh, Birch (D Ind.) - 72, 146
Bills. *See* Legislation.
Bingham, Jonathan B. (D N.Y.) - 194
Black Caucus - 34
Bolling, Richard (D Mo.) - 90, 93, 120
Brademas, John (D Ind.) - 68, 69
Brookings Institution - 207
Buckley, James (Cons-R N.Y.) - 163
Budget, Federal. *See also* Congressional Budget and Impoundment Control Act of 1974.

C

D

T